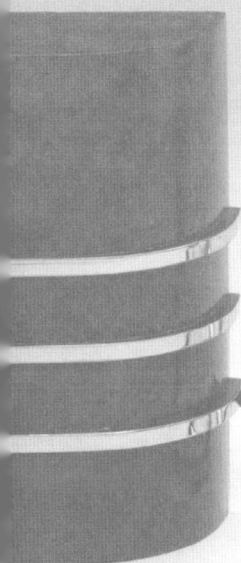
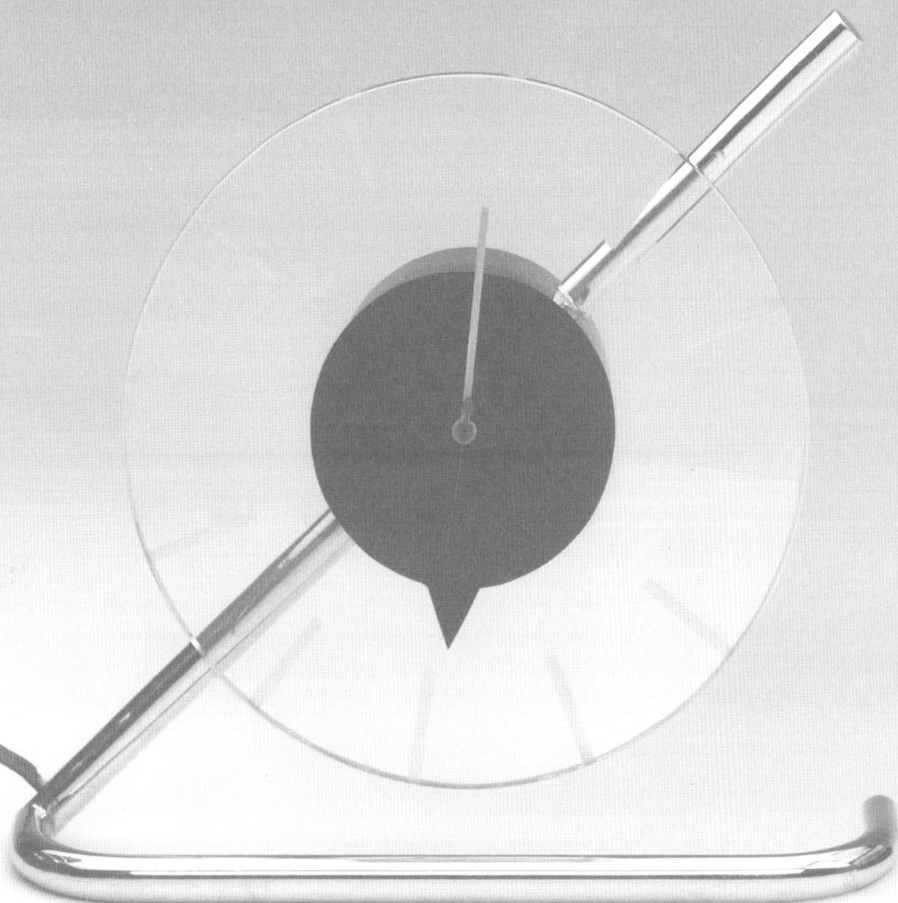
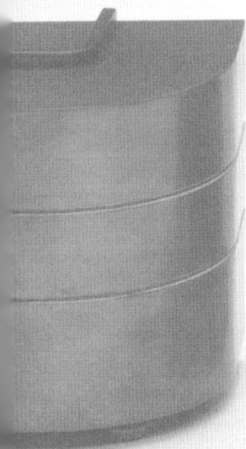

AMERICA GOES
MODERN

Nonie Gadsden
with Kate Lanford Joy

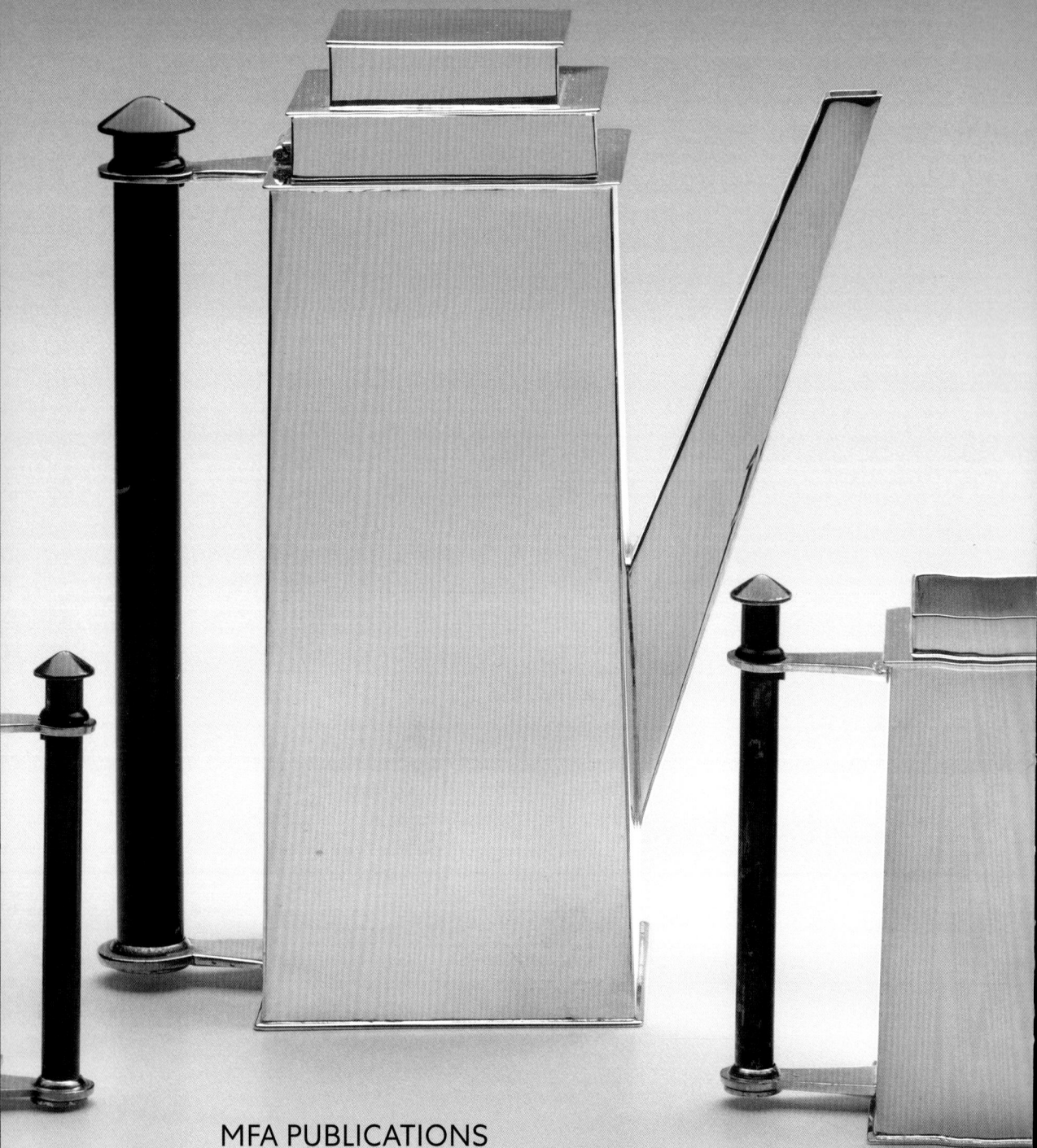

MFA PUBLICATIONS
MUSEUM OF FINE ARTS, BOSTON

AMERICA GOES
MODERN

THE RISE OF THE
INDUSTRIAL DESIGNER

Contents

Collector's Foreword

Forty years ago, when I started collecting American modern design from between the wars, nobody was interested. I bought it because I loved it, not because anyone else was doing it. Yet, I felt like I always had to explain and justify my interests to others. I was amazed that they did not see the beauty and excitement in the machine age that I did. Then I met Fred Sharf. And, finally, someone else got it.

Fred and I shared an interest in design from the 1920s and 1930s. He collected architectural drawings of skyscrapers and objects that showed the evolution of transportation in the twentieth century—cars, trains, and airplanes. His widow, Jean, explained that "Fred was collecting architectural drawings, then got intrigued by the cars depicted in front of the buildings." Fred was like that—passionate and impulsive, but generous with his knowledge and advice. My collection focused on objects inside the home—furniture, tableware, radios, and so forth. We both were attracted to the history of the objects and the rapidly changing culture that produced them. This book, which uses objects to learn more about cultural trends of the 1920s and 1930s and their impact on American lives, stems from those shared interests.

Fred not only encouraged my collecting but inspired me as well. He followed his passions. He loved what he bought. He studied it. He wrote essays on it. He stood up for it. And then he gave it to the Museum to share with the public and educate others. He was a great mentor. But for Fred's influence on me, I never would have given my collection to the MFA.

I hope that my gifts, along with Fred's and those of others who have contributed to the MFA's outstanding collection of American modern design, will delight and inspire others, just as Fred did for me.

John P. Axelrod

MODERN
BY DESIGN

In the 1928 article "Going Modern," New York advertising executive Abbott Kimball strove "to give certain practical ideas for *applying the modern movement to every-day business*." He contended that "the question is not whether to 'go modern' or 'not to go modern,' but how far? How fast? And how?" Kimball firmly believed that modern styling, which he described as "geometric, simplified, arresting new beauty," had taken hold in the United States. "Substantial, stable business, which has watched from afar the style frenzy of the so-called fashion and luxury trades, now finds itself caught up in the new tide—without chance of escape. Main Street wants not only smart hats, but smart ice-boxes—style not only in bracelets, but also in plumbing fixtures." According to Kimball, business leaders needed to invest in both "style-influenced merchandise" and a coordinated advertising campaign (the latter of which he was happy to provide) or risk decreased customer interest and flagging sales. But to "go modern" in 1928 meant so much more than styling.[1]

Throughout the 1920s and 1930s, Americans, like citizens of every industrialized society, grappled with what it meant to be modern. The speed of modern life, constantly accelerated by advances in transportation, communication, advertising, mass production, and more, led to a fundamental shift in how people lived their lives and what many chose to live with. These tumultuous decades introduced new modes of city living, the advent of car culture, widespread access to electricity, adventurous new nightlife behavior, the proliferation of plastics, and so much more that directly influenced everyday life. While many of the innovations fueling these new trends date to the turn of the century or earlier, their impact on American lives exploded in the 1920s, culminating in widespread and lasting changes that endure to this day. In the 1920s and 1930s, "going modern" was not just a style—it was a lifestyle, a mindset, a way of living that embraced change, fostered optimism, and propelled the never-ending quest for "progress" and "better living."

To help American manufacturers and consumers navigate the overwhelming and often intimidating transitions of the era, a new profession arose to offer guidance: the industrial designer.[2] Through the power of design—form, color, ornament, and materials—industrial designers strove to both reflect *and* shape the impact of the era's cultural innovations on American modern life. In the process, they established not just a modern American style but a modern American way of living. Paul T. Frankl. Donald Deskey. Viktor Schreckengost. Harley J. Earl. Belle Kogan. Each of these designers created a work of art that embodies a transformative cultural innovation of the interwar years. The stories behind these objects, dating from 1927 to 1934, represent the earliest years of industrial design in the United States and explore the challenges industrial designers faced as well as some of their solutions. The designers chosen for this book include some who were well known in their day, some who are better known today, and others who have still not received the recognition they deserve. It was these multital-ented industrial designers that showed America how to "go modern."

Today, the Industrial Designers Society of America (IDSA) defines the profession as the "practice of designing products, devices, objects and services used by millions of people around the world every day. Industrial designers typically focus on the physical appearance, func-tionality and manufacturability of a product, though they are often involved in far more during a development cycle. All of this ultimately extends to the overall lasting value and experience a product or ser-vice provides for end-users."[3] This comprehensive definition has been refined over nearly a century of shifting practice and education, yet it still centers around the individual industrial designer.

In the 1920s, 1930s, and 1940s, when the field of modern indus-trial design was in its formative years, there were numerous and often conflicting descriptions of the role of the industrial designer—even among the designers themselves. Some drew a sharp distinction between designers who worked in the "art industries" "such as textiles, pottery, furniture [that] have always had the problem of appearance" and those who worked in "industries hitherto artless," as described in the landmark 1934 *Fortune* article, "Both Fish and Fowl," likely written by industrial designer George Nelson.[4] This division between designers working in "traditional craft-based" products (even mass-produced versions of those products) and those working for industry deepened to such a degree over the next decade that two separate professional groups developed: the American Designers' Institute (ADI) and the Society of Industrial Designers (SID). The larger membership of ADI, founded in 1938, included both male and female designers working in all fields. The more exclusive East Coast old boys' club of SID, founded in 1944, restricted membership to those who had "successfully designed a diversity of products for machine and mass production," emphasiz-ing the importance of working in at least three different industries.[5] The infighting and varying definitions still color how industrial design history is seen today.

While the relationship between design and industry began with the nineteenth-century industrial revolution, the professional role of the modern industrial designer emerged when several industrial, economic, and social factors coalesced in the late 1920s. Improvements in manufacturing, such as Henry Ford's pioneering assembly line, the electrification of factories, technological advance-ments in steel and plastics, and the large-scale standardization of parts, dramatically increased manufacturing ability across the United States. Overproduction resulted in a surplus of goods and a saturated market, shifting the nation from a seller's market to one driven by consumer demand. "Consumptionism," as it was termed during the period, simultaneously empowered and encumbered the consumer with the expectation of a higher standard of material living and the constant desire for more, now available on credit. To help sell their

DESKEY

products amid growing competition, manufacturers turned to advertising professionals who spurred on this consumption-oriented society by using images, psychology, and basic human desires to make products more appealing, making the look of the product of equal, if not greater, importance to its functionality. Social factors that supported the rise of the industrial designer included the changing role of women in society. With increased access to education, careers, independence, and voting rights, women—who tended to be more style conscious than men—gained more financial power and market influence. And, a growing curiosity about modernism was stimulated by the 1925 World's Fair, held in Paris (the Exposition Internationale des Arts Décoratifs et Industriels Modernes). The U.S. government, claiming the country had no good modern design to contribute, declined to participate in the fair. Many Americans were outraged and embarrassed that the mighty United States—a nation that now led the world in manufacturing ability, technological innovation, and military strength—would so readily and so publicly admit deficiency and weakness.

While these trends contributed to the emergence of industrial design, one event is often cited as tipping the scales. It was not the stock market crash of 1929 nor the Great Depression that followed— although both certainly hastened the spread of the field and authority of the industrial designer. Instead, it was Henry Ford's decision in 1927 to discontinue the manufacture of his legendary Model T. For nineteen years, Ford's no-frills Model T had dominated the car market, as the company's revolutionary assembly line-production methods allowed for mass production at ever-decreasing prices. Although his factories had built nearly fifteen million Model Ts by the mid-1920s, Henry Ford's sole focus on price and his reluctance to change his product's look ultimately caught up with him. Sales dropped drastically by 1927, forcing Ford to terminate his beloved Model T and shut down his factories for six months to retool for the production of the new, style-conscious Model A.[6]

Some economic historians cite the temporary closure of Ford's factories and the concurrent layoff of sixty thousand workers as the direct cause of the 1927 economic recession, a relatively mild recession that affected large manufacturers more than the average American.[7] Yet, the recession revealed to business leaders the scope of the United States' massive reliance on the automobile (and its related industries) to lead the nation's technological and economic development—and the automobile's impact on society as a whole. As economic historian Thomas Cochran later wrote: "no one has or perhaps can reliably estimate the vast size of capital invested in reshaping society to fit the automobile. Such a figure would have to include expenditures for consolidated schools, suburban and country homes, and changes in business location. . . . This total capital investment was probably the major factor in the boom of the 1920s, and hence in the glorification of American business."[8] Therefore, Ford's concession to "the cult of beauty" served as a wake-up call to many American manufacturers who previously shared his dismissive attitude toward the need for art and style in industrial goods. These men suddenly started paying attention to the words of advertising leaders such as Abbott Kimball or his contemporary Earnest Elmo Calkins, who wrote: "the appeal of efficiency alone is nearly ended . . . beauty is the natural and logical next step" in his influential article "Beauty the New Business Tool," published in *The Atlantic* in August 1927.[9]

That year proved to be pivotal in the formation of modern industrial design. Not only did Ford discontinue the Model T, but his biggest competitor, the General Motors Corporation (GM), led by Alfred P. Sloan, established the first styling department in a major American production car manufacturing company with Harley J. Earl at the helm. Earl is widely credited as the father of automotive design, and he occasionally worked on other GM products, including Frigidaire refrigerators and the 1934 Union Pacific streamliner. He established an independent industrial design firm in 1945, Harley Earl, Inc. (later renamed Harley Earl Associates), that consulted for leading American businesses in the 1940s, 1950s, and 1960s, including the Aluminum Company of America (Alcoa), Paper Mate Pen Company, and the National Biscuit Company. Harley Earl's appointment by GM was a defining moment in the rise of the industrial designer.

Paul T. Frankl also played a vital role in establishing the profession. However, Frankl is best known for his high-end furniture and interiors, such as his Skyscraper Furniture, rather than his work in industrial design. Frankl certainly aspired to design for mass production—a goal instilled in him during his student years in Germany by his mentors Peter Behrens and Bruno Paul—yet American furniture manufacturers were not ready for him, and Frankl had to be resourceful and patient.[10] The Viennese immigrant spent over a decade aggressively trying to educate the American public on the superiority of modern design for modern life. More than any other designer of the era, he helped popularize modern design among the timid American public. Frankl recognized that he had to temper and assimilate modern design's perceived rigidity to American tastes, sometimes forcing him to compromise his own ideals. But this willingness to compromise, to understand the needs and demands of the consumer, and to promote modern design by appealing to the national pride of his customers were all key characteristics of the rising profession of industrial design.

Frankl also served as unofficial dean of the country's growing cohort of modern designers. He mentored those just starting out in the field, including Donald Deskey. Like Frankl, Deskey is best known for his luxury furniture and interiors of the 1930s, such as the widely publicized interiors of Radio City Music Hall (1932). But Deskey also longed to design for mass production, a desire he tried to realize when he founded Deskey-Vollmer, Inc., in 1927. Deskey-Vollmer's modest manufactory created small batches of Deskey's table and lamp designs on

speculation for department stores, galleries, and specialty shops, taking a first step away from custom work and toward quantity production.

At Ohio's Cowan Pottery in 1930–31, Viktor Schreckengost also sought a way to mass-produce his designs, redesigning his well-received *Jazz* bowl twice to try to accommodate larger-scale, standardized production. Both Deskey and Schreckengost failed in these early attempts at industrial manufacturing methods, but their efforts helped to illustrate the need for design and industry to work together. Both men built highly successful industrial design practices in the late 1930s and early 1940s, and Schreckengost established the Industrial Design program at the Cleveland School of Art in 1933, which quickly became known for its training in automotive design.[11] Their early, though unsuccessful, attempts at standardized serial production epitomize the challenges and creative efforts of a wide range of designers in the formation of modern industrial design in the United States.

Belle Kogan faced other challenges. As a woman in a notoriously sexist corporate environment, Kogan had to fight twice as hard as her male contemporaries and have a thicker skin. She managed to build a successful career as an industrial designer working in a range of industries in the 1930s, including silver, pottery, and plastics. She formally established Belle Kogan Design Associates in 1933, boasting an impressive client list in her early years, including Quaker Silver Company, Bakelite Corporation, Celluloid Corporation, Warren Telechron Company, and Samson United. Kogan promoted herself and the field of industrial design in lectures, articles, interviews, and exhibitions, and served as a founding member and early chairperson of the New York chapter of ADI. Her illustrious career continued for over three decades until her retirement in 1970. Kogan was a major figure in the formative years of industrial design. Yet, her contributions to the field have not received the recognition that she so justly deserves.

Each of these designers played a critical role in establishing the new profession of industrial design and in helping America go modern. Their featured designs—a desk and bookcase, a table lamp, a punch bowl, an automobile, and an electric clock—reveal, in their form, function, and attitude, how the process of going modern forever changed American daily life.

SKYSCRAPERS

"The needs of life in the Twentieth Century [are] so entirely different from all earlier times that the surroundings and houses of men must be changed to fit the altered conditions."[1] So wrote architect and interior designer Paul T. Frankl (1886–1958) in 1915, less than a year after the outbreak of World War I prevented him from returning home to Vienna, the heart of European modernism (**FIG. 1**).[2] Stranded in the United States, and struck by the dominance of historically based styles in American homes, the young designer resolved to apply the principles of avant-garde modern design to the specific needs of the modern American lifestyle. By the mid-1920s, Frankl was heartened by the country's embrace of modernism in architecture, declaring that "our main artistic character and our distinctive achievement in the eyes of foreigners is, no doubt, the skyscraper."[3] Yet, the American public's resistance to modern interior design, despite the nation's leadership not only in modern architecture but also in modern business, engineering, and technology, clearly frustrated him: "Modernity and America have in fact come to mean, in the mind of the world almost one and the same thing. Yet we have been rather reluctant in our welcome to the modern movement in the field of decorative arts."[4] Frankl remained committed to creating an American version of modern design that reflected the needs and spirit of his adopted country and also appealed to skeptical American consumers.

Frankl was so dedicated to this vision that he refused an invitation from the U.S. government to attend the Exposition Internationale des Arts Décoratifs et Industriels Modernes, the seminal 1925 Paris Exposition, which introduced modern design to the world. Although the United States had declined participation in the fair, it sent a large delegation of artists, designers, curators, and manufacturers to study

the displays. Claiming that he did not want to be influenced by contemporary European fashions, Frankl instead secluded himself for the summer at his cabin in rural Woodstock, New York. There, surrounded by the glories of the landscape and far from the city, Frankl embraced the modern New York skyscraper as more than an engineering phenomenon, it was artistic inspiration.

According to Frankl, in the process of organizing his workspace he decided to build a bookcase with openings of different heights to accommodate his oversize architecture books. "The result was a corner bookcase with a rather large, bulky lower section and a slender, shallow upper part going straight to the ceiling . . . the top of the lower part formed a table to hold a lamp, flowers, magazines and the like" (**FIG. 2**).[5] As his neighbors in the artists' community of Woodstock noted, his new storage resembled the stepped skyscrapers then being erected in New York and other U.S. cities. And there it was. He had serendipitously and "almost effortlessly . . . accomplished what [he] was striving for, expressing the creative spirit of the time that prompted it."[6]

Frankl immediately developed an entire series of interior furnishings he called "Skyscraper Furniture." Easy to understand and recognize, the distinctive forms of his Skyscraper Furniture captured the attention of a country in the process of being dramatically transformed in scale and speed. The initial line, first sold in the fall of 1925, featured bookcases and desks but expanded in early 1927 to include a wider range of products such as low cabinets, dressing tables, and sofas and chairs, as well as coffee and end tables.

One of these forms, a combination desk and bookcase, perfectly embodies Frankl's goals in both form and function (**FIG. 3**). Its tall height, stepped profile, flat, plain surfaces, and minimal ornament not only evoked the most recent New York skyscrapers but also aligned with his formal criteria for the modern aesthetic, which favored unadorned geometric forms. Additionally, the desk and bookcase's multiple functions, including storage, display, and a hidden work surface—all in a compact, apartment-friendly footprint—suited the evolving needs of modern living.

The vertical orientation of Frankl's combination desk and bookcase immediately calls to mind a skyscraper's defining feature: its unprecedented height. The result of increasing demand for space downtown, skyscrapers were made possible by advances in the mass production of steel and the invention of electric elevators. Steel replaced load-bearing masonry walls, which had been limited to a height of about ten stories as the walls needed to be prohibitively thick at the bottom for additional floors. Steel's strength and durability allowed for slender structural frames that supported thin, exterior curtain walls. This new construction method made it possible to attain previously impossible heights, as seen in New York's fifty-five-story Woolworth Building, designed by Cass Gilbert, which was the tallest skyscraper in the world from 1913 until 1930 (**FIG. 4**). Equally essential

HIGHEST BUILDING IN THE WORLD, 750 FEET ABOVE THE SIDEWALK. 57 STORIES.

FLOOR AREA 27 ACRES, 34 ELEVATORS

APPROXIMATE COST $13,500,000.

70908   WOOLWORTH BUILDING, NEW YORK   COPR. DETROIT PUBLISHING CO.

4 Postcard of the Woolworth Building, New York, about 1913

OPPOSITE: 3 Paul T. Frankl, Skyscraper desk and bookcase, 1927–28

were electric elevators, which, once electricity became available downtown in the mid-1890s, replaced the earlier hydraulic models that were slow, bulky, and limited in range.[7] As soon as electric elevators made upper floors easily accessible and therefore profitable, buildings soared, appearing to reach the sky. Likewise, Frankl's desk and bookcase, which stands just shy of seven feet, would have nearly scraped the ceiling of a standard eight-foot-high room.

The stepped shape of the desk and bookcase mimics the distinctive setbacks required by New York's 1916 Zoning Resolution. Designed to keep skyscrapers from darkening city streets, the new rules required buildings to progressively step back from their property lines upon reaching certain heights, which were determined by each site's location and the width of its adjacent streets. The result was, according to Frankl, "a happy accident, for our building ordinance in New York City was not originally introduced from artistic motives," but it successfully had "broken the solid cube of the old type building into terraced units" that provided "a good deal of interest and decorative value to the mass of the building."[8] In particular, Frankl noted that the setbacks, like those of Ralph Walker's New York Telephone Building (1926), created dramatic contrasts of light and shade on their buildings' otherwise minimally adorned facades (**FIG. 5**). In his desk and bookcase, Frankl highlighted these contrasts of light and shade, solid and void with irregular steps receding in multiple directions. Combined with the assorted open and closed storage compartments facing to the front and side, the piece evokes a syncopated rhythm suggestive of the modern buildings—themselves filled with interior compartments of varying shape and size—and the modern city as a whole.

The flat, plain surfaces of Frankl's desk and bookcase are consistent with the new pared-down simplicity of modern New York skyscrapers in the 1920s. These skyscrapers' predecessors, while innovative in construction, had exteriors ornamented with historical decoration, from the Gothic pinnacles of the Woolworth Building (1913) to the neoclassical pilasters of the Equitable Building (1915). Frankl recalled his disappointment in the elaborate historical ornament on early skyscrapers upon first arriving in New York in 1914. But by the 1920s, American architects began to adopt modernism's preference for unembellished surfaces, and Frankl much preferred the "new setback form void of meaningless trimmings."[9]

Accordingly, the desk and bookcase's ornament is limited to its dynamic arrangement of steps, shelves, cabinets, and drawers, along with a few architecture-inspired elements. Crisp, stepped molding crowns each step, with the molding's upper edges highlighted in black paint to heighten the effect of light and shadow. Reeded decoration, evoking fluted classical columns, adorns its two front feet—taller on the right to counterbalance the piece's overall asymmetry. Simple hardware, a mix of square and rectangular silver-coated brass pulls, attached at perpendicular angles and framed by black paint, echoes the desk and bookcase's many different rectilinear openings. And multiple coats of glossy, light green paint distinguish the interiors of the shelves, cabinets, and drawers from the desk and bookcase's darker walnut exterior.[10] Shades of light green were common on building exteriors in the early twentieth century, from Louis Sullivan's iconic National Farmer's Bank of Owatonna in Minnesota (1908) to Raymond Hood's McGraw-Hill skyscraper in New York (1931)—its use an attempt, possibly, to naturalize the urban landscape in a modern way.[11] According to Walter Rendell Storey in a 1927 *New York Times* article, "the use of pure color," as seen on the desk and bookcase, characterized "furniture made in the modern mode."[12] For Frankl, light green was a cool color well suited to modern backgrounds that afforded a "feeling of greater space," useful in urban apartments.[13]

The presence of these few adornments, although minimal in comparison to historical revival furniture also popular at the time, exemplifies Frankl's attempt to balance the modern and the familiar for American consumers. Throughout his career, but especially during the 1920s, Frankl often contradicted his own writing by tempering his stark modern forms with decorative embellishments derived from traditional designs. For example, the reeded decoration on the feet of the desk and bookcase not only references classical architecture of the past but also disrupts the "continuity of line" that Frankl endorsed. It is the reeded decoration, along with the desk and bookcase's monumentality, that helps to date the object likely to the peak of Frankl's Skyscraper period in 1927 or 1928, as he was transitioning away from classically inspired ornaments to a more refined and simplified modern aesthetic that emphasized pure lines.[14] Frankl chose his limited ornament with care, selecting details that bear a link to architecture in general, or skyscrapers in particular.

Frankl was hardly the first artist to recognize the potential of the skyscraper. Alfred Stieglitz's photograph *The City of Ambition* (1910) depicts the city as a hive of enterprise, crowded with structures spewing smoke (**FIG. 6**). Taking his vantage from the harbor, Stieglitz aimed his camera at New York's dark mass of buildings, capturing how the new skyscrapers altered the city's skyline, shadowed its streets, and "destroyed our sense of scale," as historian Lewis Mumford complained in 1924.[15] In contrast, Max Weber's painting *New York* (1912) provides a bird's-eye perspective radical for its time (**FIG. 7**). Peering down at the thirty-three-story Liberty Tower from its taller neighbor, the Singer Building, Weber's Cubist-inspired painting reduces the neo-Gothic structure to a tall, thin vertical tower rising high above and apart from, the chaotic city below. In architect Murray Leibowitz's 1928 poster-size charcoal drawing, a modern, stepped skyscraper, monumental in scale and dramatically illuminated by electric lighting, appears to pierce the sky (**FIG. 8**). Likely influenced by the frequent comparison of modern skyscrapers to ancient pyramids, Leibowitz drew his building, a generic representation of the new architecture

rather than any specific example, as a symbol of national achievement with divine-like power.[16]

Others in the United States also recognized the modern high-rise's significance and national impact. Architect Francis Lorne wrote in *Arts & Decoration* (1925) that the American skyscraper was "vibrant with life, the first expression of a great people coming into its own."[17] And *New York Times* journalist H. I. Brock reported in 1929 that the modern New York skyscraper with "its present distinctive form" had become an "American Expression of Urban Greatness" and "to the whole of these United States a symbol, a fashion and a heaven-climbing contest." He further explained how New York-style sky-scrapers were popping up in small cities across the country, even

where land was plentiful and zoning restrictions did not exist, because of the architecture's importance to national pride.[18]

Paul T. Frankl harnessed the familiarity and patriotic connotations of this new architectural phenomenon to persuade reluctant Americans to replace their traditional decor with modern furnishings. In doing so, he offered an alternative to the highly popular colonial revival style which was equally imbued with nationalistic pride. Indeed, as Frankl argued, trends in architecture had long inspired interior decoration, and "it would be a little out of keeping to attempt to live today in an atmosphere of the past."[19] Bringing a skyscraper into your home was also playful, humorous, and fun—essential elements of modern American life.

Despite Frankl's (and others') grandiose claims that his new furniture designs were uniquely American, they were also consistent with key principles of modernism current throughout Europe and the United States. These include Louis Sullivan's oft-quoted axiom "form follows function" and the idea that architecture and design must express the spirit of their time. In addition, Frankl was directly influenced by the spare aesthetic of the Wiener Werkstätte, a collaborative design workshop founded in his home city of Vienna in 1903 during his student years. According to Frankl, the Wiener Werkstätte "held the field" of modern design "under the leadership of Joseph Hofmann [sic] . . . for the last quarter of a century."[20] In Berlin, where Frankl continued his studies, he credited Professor Peter Behrens for offering "absolute freedom from any decoration," as was consistent with German designers' early enthusiasm for simple, mass-producible designs.[21]

Frankl was also deeply influenced by the strong verticals and horizontals seen in the work of American architect Frank Lloyd Wright. He first learned of Wright while living in Europe, where Wright's designs were known through the highly influential German publication the *Wasmuth Portfolio* (1911). Once he arrived in the United States, Frankl developed a close relationship with Wright, who would later author the forward for Frankl's book *New Dimensions* (1928). Like Wright, he greatly admired Japanese art and architecture, which Frankl explored firsthand during a visit to Japan in 1914. While there, Frankl acquired lacquered Sendai chests—case pieces that frequently have stepped forms like his later skyscraper designs—which he subsequently sold in his New York gallery. And he credited Japanese art, particularly woodblock prints, for modern design's embrace of flat blocks of bold color, plain surfaces, and asymmetry, writing that "rhythm has been the main influence from the East."[22] Lastly, while the designer strongly opposed the use of paint on wooden furniture, he embraced the Asian use of glossy lacquer—both clear and colored. It appears that Frankl distinguished between paint and lacquer, not as a material, but as a process. For his furniture, he insisted on multiple layers of paint, each hand-rubbed with powdered pumice and oil, in the manner of lacquer. Thus, although most viewers only saw America's skyscrapers in Frankl's new furniture, his designs also were deeply indebted to global influences and the designers and architects who shaped the international modern movement.[23]

Frankl's desk and bookcase not only *looks* like a skyscraper, it also was designed to *function* well in a small skyscraper apartment. In addition to room for storage and display, it features an expandable work surface complete with integrated light bulb, typewriter cavity, and space to push in a chair (**FIG. 9**). Its mixture of several functions within a single piece of furniture and a small footprint suited the limited square footage and spatial flexibility of modern apartment life.

The history of apartment buildings in New York parallels and is related to that of skyscrapers. While the city's first such residences,

built in the 1870s, were walk-ups with only about five floors, they grew taller as innovations in skyscraper construction were made.[24] Despite initial concern that apartment buildings, which were designed for middle- and upper-class residents, would be confused with tenements or dormitories, they quickly became New York's primary housing stock. As architect Charles H. Israels explained in 1901, while "the population of the city has increased by leaps and bounds, its topography allowed for growth in but one direction": up.[25] For Frankl, the high-rise apartment building was an example of the "compression" of modern life, which impacted everything from electricity, with the light of many candles now available in one bulb, to the "modern automobile [which] compresses the power of seventy or more horses in a motor as small as a lamb," to "food is compressed into cans, drugs into tablets, and buildings are pressed together, and, for want of space, must shoot high into the air."[26]

Skyscraper apartments, which made it possible to live "only twenty stories from Broadway instead of forty-five minutes," offered the epitome of modern living.[27] Because of their central locations and the economic advantages of collectivity, their residents had access to the newest amenities before all but the wealthiest single-family homeowners. With early connection to the electric grid, for example, apartment dwellers enjoyed the convenience of the many new modern appliances available, such as a *Magicoal* electric fireplace (specifically noted in at least one 1929 apartment listing), that eliminated the mess, danger, maintenance, and lugging of fuel required by a traditional coal or wood fireplace (**FIG. 10**).[28] Made of aluminum, a new material only available with the advent of electricity, and rubber "coals" through which the light glows, this *Magicoal* model from the late 1930s combined streamlined style with the modern convenience of an on/off switch, while deliberately perpetuating the symbolism of the traditional hearth. Similarly, for his desk and bookcase which presupposed access to electric wiring, Frankl modernized his light source's design as well as its technology. By integrating the electric bulb into a hatch above the desk, it would be readily available with the flick of a switch but completely hidden when not needed.

In addition to having the most modern conveniences, apartments, which typically had only one floor and limited space, were easier to maintain, required fewer possessions and household staff, and fostered a more casual atmosphere than a multistory house. Numerous adaptations developed to accommodate their "constricted spaces that have come to be the rule, rather than the exception."[29] Compact kitchenette units, based on designs for trains and yachts, saved both cooking time (by minimizing steps across the room) and valuable square footage.[30] Intimate "breakfast sets quite modern and attractive" replaced larger "ten-piece dining room sets."[31] Dining alcoves were built into the sides of living rooms.[32] And a sleek electric refrigerator eliminated the need for an icebox with its bulky, messy ice

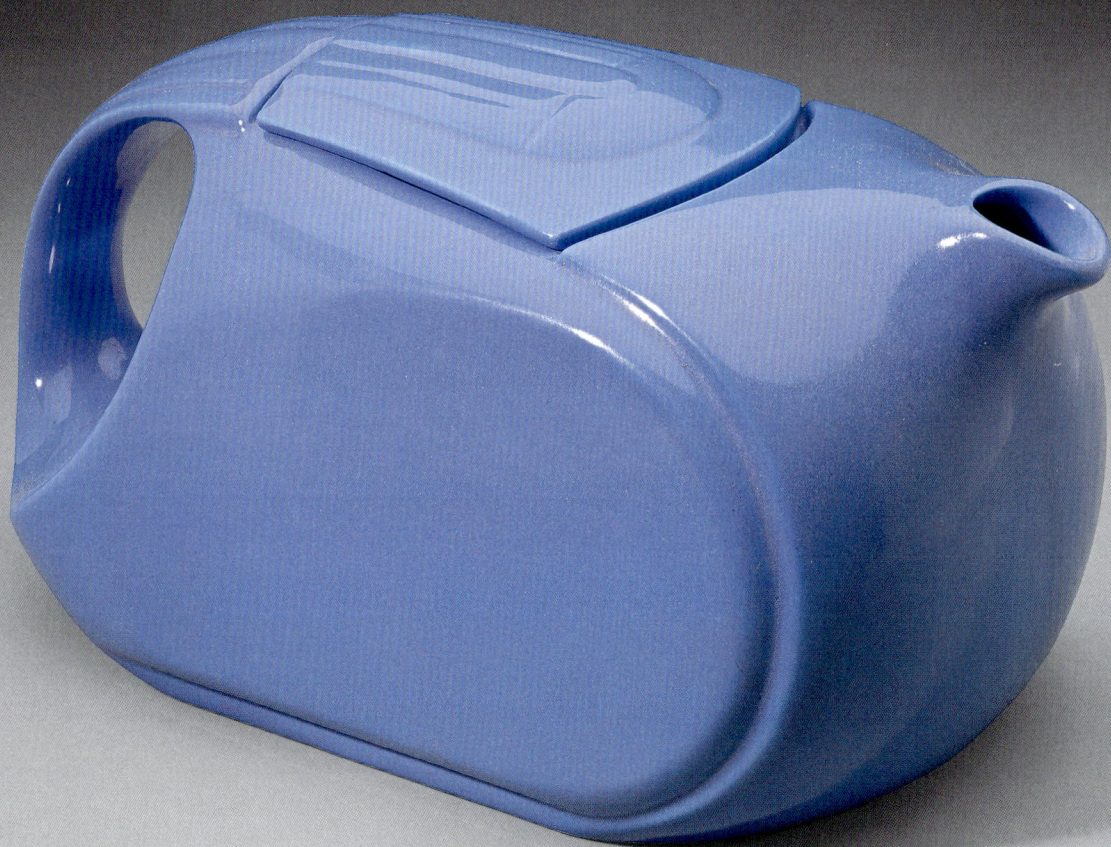

block.[33] To help customers maximize space *inside* their refrigerators, Westinghouse Electric teamed up with the Hall China Company to offer streamlined Refrigerator Ware specially designed to fit into Westinghouse units, including butter dishes, leftover-food containers, and water pitchers. Their stout *Phoenix* pitcher, in rich Delphinium blue, features flat sides for efficient storage and rounded corners for easy cleaning (**FIG. 11**).

To make small apartments feel spacious, furnishings in ornate historical styles were rejected in favor of minimally adorned pieces with a sleek, modern feel. Terraced gardens were created on the set-backs of 1920s buildings.[34] And when entertaining, cocktail parties became more fashionable than sit-down dinners because they required only enough room for guests to stand and a few essential accessories, such as Norman Bel Geddes's chromium-plated *Manhattan* cocktail set. With its slender verticality and stepped tray, the set reflects the New York skyline for which it was named (**FIG. 12**). For Frankl, who marketed his compact Skyscraper Furniture specifically to apartment dwellers, a benefit of smaller residences was that "they have forced us to discard what we do not need."[35] "After all, space is as much at a premium within the home as it is outside of it. Why have a bookcase take up half your floor in squat, rigid formality when your bookcase can rise toward the ceiling in vertical, pyramidic beauty with an inviting informality that should go with books people actually read."[36]

Apartments had to have multifunctional rooms to make the most of their small spaces. To aid in this effort and to coordinate with his Skyscraper Furniture line, Frankl sold movable, stepped, three-part screens with flat geometric designs that he commissioned from fellow New York designer Donald Deskey (**FIG. 13**). According to the *New York Times*, folding screens were "an indispensable help in making one room do the work of two" and could be moved as needed to divide a space.[37] Screens could also shield doorways in order to ensure privacy, a major concern in apartments where private bedchambers or service zones might open off public reception rooms.[38] They could hide modern devices, such as an "obtrusive radiator, radio set," the "ubiquitous telephone," or "a kitchenette in a studio apartment."[39] And they contributed color, decorative interest, and, as in this dynamic example with its curves and triangles in black and aluminum, modern rhythm to an interior.

Other convertible furniture forms used in New York apartments include extension tables that could be expanded for large gatherings and foldaway Murphy beds, patented in 1912, which turned reception rooms into bedrooms. In fact, a pair of pyramidal Skyscraper dresser cabinets by Frankl which share the same history and numerous distinctive characteristics with the desk and bookcase, may have once flanked a Murphy bed (**FIG. 14**). The unfinished inner surface of each dresser shows evidence of having been attached to something else at

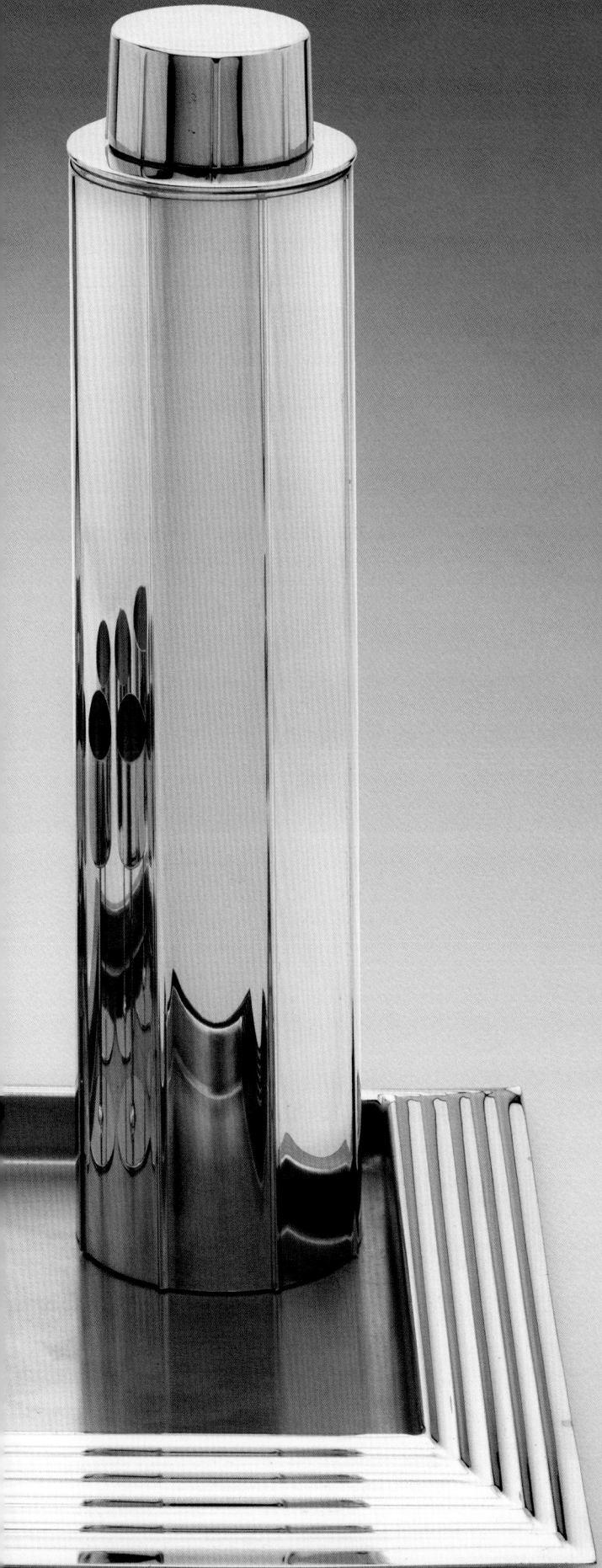

one point, perhaps a cabinet containing a foldaway bed, and the depth of the dressers, twenty inches, corresponds with the depth of a genuine Murphy "In-A-Dor" full or double bed, which, when closed, measured nineteen inches deep.

In the 1920s, foldaway beds were popular not only with those living in small spaces, but their innovation and modern sensibility also attracted high-end hotels and the wealthy (such as Frankl's clients). While the dressers mirror each other on the exterior, offering symmetrical bookends, the interiors of their lower sections reveal separate functions. The doors of one dresser open above the base molding and contain five sliding drawers over an enclosed base. Those of the other dresser extend to the floor (the base molding is secured to the bottom of the doors) and reveal an empty cavity, possibly for a clothes hamper, trash receptacle, or other such object that would need to be dragged out on a regular basis. Surprisingly, given Frankl's extensive advocacy of double-use, space-saving furnishings, the desk and bookcase and dressers are rare examples within Frankl's Skyscraper line to offer such multifunctionality, making them an ideal choice for modern high-rise apartment life.

The connection between Frankl's furniture and the new architecture of New York was immediately celebrated in the press, making Skyscraper Furniture the first modern design widely popular in the United States. "The New Furniture [which] Gives Every One His Own Skyline" was deemed "as American and as New Yorkish as Fifth Avenue itself."[40] It was considered particularly well suited to high-rise buildings where "the traces of steel construction are noticeable in every foot of the wall space in modern apartment-houses."[41] And, as a testament to its widespread popularity, Skyscraper Furniture was the target of a 1928 New Yorker cartoon that humorously questioned the furniture's comfort (FIG. 15). Architect and artist Edwin Avery Park, who thought New York skyscrapers "undoubtedly our most important departure in modern building," praised Frankl's designs for their honest emulation of skyscrapers' form, especially the buildings' flat, undecorated, thin curtain walls. He also claimed that the field of modern design in the United States, at long last, was for Frankl "almost all his."[42]

The compactness of Frankl's designs, making them suitable for small apartments, was also much touted by critics. As Walter Rendell Storey explained, "the new development in the furniture of today . . . is not merely a matter of form. In reality, utility has an even greater claim on its construction . . . We demand convenient furniture today."[43] But, as Good Furniture magazine pointed out, "the people who are interested in Mr. Frankl's not inexpensive art, are those who have all the floor space they require at their command. His patrons come, naturally enough, from circles in which plenty of wealth assures whatever environment they may choose."[44] Yet, Storey countered this apparent contradiction by claiming that the "tendency toward a

"Don't you just love my
skyscraper furniture?"

compact utilization of space is no longer confined to small apartments."[45] In fact, he said "'double-use' rooms are now the fashion,
even where space is not at a premium."[46] Frankl's desk and bookcase,
then, which converts a living space into an office via its expandable
work surface, addressed the current trend for spatial efficiency,
regardless of square footage, that had come to define modern living.

The success of the Skyscraper line compelled Frankl to contract
with multiple small workshops throughout New York City in order to
satisfy demand. Scholars estimate that a few thousand works were
produced between 1926 and 1930.[47] Therefore, there is significant
variation in construction methods, details, and quality among

surviving examples. This may explain the differences between the combination desk and bookcase and pair of dressers discussed above. Both works came out of an estate in the Los Feliz neighborhood of Los Angeles in the late 1970s or early 1980s. Both feature walnut or walnut veneer surfaces with light green accents and black edging, square and rectangular metal hardware framed by black paint, and reeded base moldings. However, there are notable disparities as well. The drawers of the desk and bookcase slide on runners, while those of the dresser are side hung. The veneer on the drawer fronts of the desk and bookcase is significantly thicker than that on the dressers. All edges of the desk and bookcase are sharp, crisp angles, while the dressers feature softer beveled or rounded edges on the top elements. The drawer pulls on both works are identical in design, but close comparison reveals that those on the dressers are slightly larger than on the desk and bookcase. The dressers' exposed top compartments do not have the green lacquer that the desk and bookcase's compartments do. And the black edging differs between the two forms: the edging on the desk and bookcase is confined to the horizontal surfaces of the stepped elements, while that on the dressers covers the step rise as well. Such discrepancies would suggest that these works were not made by the same hand. Yet, each of these features is found in other examples of Frankl's Skyscraper Furniture (with the exception of the central vertical "waterfall" moldings on the dressers that were later additions to unify the two pieces).[48] It may be that Frankl contracted with different workshops to make individual elements of the set to speed production.

The glowing critical praise and commercial popularity of Frankl's Skyscraper Furniture also sparked numerous imitations. Such straightforward, simple forms required only "a straight edge, a square rule, and a compass" for "a likely lad with an eye for artistic proportion . . . to accomplish excellent reproductions."[49] Frankl had designed the furniture with the notion that it would be mass-produced and, while he never achieved that goal, other firms who copied his designs did, including New York's Modernage Furniture Company and Johnson Furniture Company of Grand Rapids. The latter advertised its affordable, skyscraper-inspired *Dynamique* line, designed by David Robertson Smith, as compact, comfortable furniture for modern living. As Frankl later disparaged in his book *Machine-Made Leisure* (1932), "my designs were copied, altered, and vulgarized."[50]

Frankl's furniture leaped to the forefront of a more widespread fad for skyscraper-inspired designs in numerous other media.[51] In 1928, Louis M. Rice designed his silver-plated *Sky-scraper* coffee and tea service for the New York firm of Bernard Rice's Sons, Inc., with squared corners, stepped lids, and patinated "Smoke-Stacks as Handles" (**FIG. 16**).[52] The next year, the Warren Telechron Company released its first alarm clock, the *Electrolarm*, enclosed in a molded plastic case with stepped profile that came in three colors (see **FIG. 94**). Similarly,

the Manning-Bowman Company created a cheerful orange and chrome clock (see **FIG. 84**) in the shape of a skyscraper with spire, designed by Jean George Theobald.[53] An elaborate cigarette lighter, possibly designed by Jules Buoy, honored construction of the Empire State Building, the tallest building in the world upon completion in 1931 (**FIG. 17**).[54] And Harold Van Doren's *Air King Radio* of 1933, with its setback shoulders and vertical reeding, was also based on the skyscraper form, thereby associating the radio's modern communication technology with modern urban architecture (see **FIG. 87**). Other objects referenced skyscrapers more subtly, such as the *Manhattan Group*

vase, designed in the 1930s by the RumRill Art Pottery Company and produced by Minnesota's Red Wing Potteries, and Donald Deskey's stepped screen (**FIG. 18**). What distinguishes Frankl's Skyscraper Furniture from these myriad products is that, for Frankl, skyscrapers were not only a modern style but also a modern way of living for which his desk and bookcase was especially well designed.

In skyscrapers, Frankl found the ideal combination of patriotic and playful appeal, principles of modern design he learned in Europe, and functional utility for high-rise living. With his furniture line, especially the compact, multifunctional desk and bookcase, Frankl had

managed to do the impossible: satisfy both the masses and the modernists. Ultimately, the popularity of skyscraper-inspired interior design was short lived. By the 1930s, streamlined architecture and interior decor was replacing the rectilinearity of earlier products. Frankl, disenchanted with New York, transplanted himself in 1934 to a single-family home in the sprawling city of Los Angeles, where he took on numerous projects, including designing furniture for mass production.[55] His low, organically shaped cocktail table with cork top

(FIG. 19), for example, was produced in the early 1950s by Johnson Furniture Company, one of the firms that had shamelessly copied his earlier Skyscraper designs. Yet, Frankl did more than promote a brief mania for skyscraper-inspired design. His Skyscraper Furniture, designed for multifunctional interiors outfitted with the newest amenities, successfully showed Americans how to live in a modern way.

ELECTRIC LIGHT

Electric light, with its brilliance, accessibility, and flexibility, forever altered how people lived and worked, especially after dark. Though developed decades earlier, it was not until after World War I that electricity impacted the lives of individual Americans on a large scale, first through lighting, then through the countless electrical devices that followed. In the 1920s, as the number of American homes with electricity rose dramatically, the steady glow of electric light became a beacon of modernism, synonymous with America's technological progress and fast-paced urban lifestyle. For American designers and interior decorators, interest in the artistic possibilities of electric light intensified after viewing the 1925 Paris Exposition's innovative and extensive displays featuring the new medium. For Donald Deskey (1894–1989), a young American designer who spent considerable time at the Exposition, electric lighting would soon become an important element of his early career (**FIG. 20**).[1]

Shortly after viewing the Paris Exposition, Deskey moved to New York, where he designed store windows for the Franklin Simon Department Store and then Saks Fifth Avenue. Saks, which had opened in 1924, had a new president by 1926—Adam Long Gimbel— himself recently returned from the Exposition. Gimbel and Deskey had much in common: both were in their early thirties, with roots in the upper Midwest, both had studied architecture, and both were profoundly influenced by what they had seen in Paris.[2] Gimbel was impressed by Deskey's innovative, pared-down approach to store windows, in which he combined a few select wares with abstract backdrops inspired by contemporary artists Pablo Picasso and Georges Braque.[3] In these windows, Deskey experimented with design, materials, and, of course, dramatic lighting. He treated the items for sale as "the characters of a play," illuminated so as to catch the eyes of passersby and to show the goods in the most flattering light.[4]

In 1927–28, Deskey overhauled Gimbel's Park Avenue penthouse in the modern style (**FIG. 21**). It was Deskey's first residential commission. He custom designed a series of furnishings that combined chromium-plated metal with glass in stripped-down geometric forms. In Gimbel's study, Deskey added cork walls, a linoleum floor, and a copper ceiling. One critic, himself a satisfied Deskey client, noted in 1933 that these were "the first rooms done entirely in metal and industrial materials in America; six years later, they are still being photographed as examples of modern design."[5] In this high-profile interior, prominently displayed in the study on a low side table next to a pigskin-upholstered chair, Deskey debuted his first major design for a lighting device: an eye-catching, zigzag-shaped lamp (**FIG. 22**).

Slightly over a foot tall, Deskey's lamp combines a flat rectangular back with three stacked triangular volumes, each concealing an incandescent bulb. Its distinctive shape evokes connections to numerous elements of modern life. The lamp's overall vertical orientation, looming overhangs, and stepped base suggest the skyscrapers then defining the new American city. Its serrated profile references the angularity of Cubism, as well as the teeth of industrial gears. Its upright, tripartite shape is similar to that of recently patented traffic lights that direct the constant stop-and-go of urban space. And its jagged outline calls to mind Mother Nature's powerful lightning bolt, the symbol of modern electricity.

Yet, the most modern aspect of Deskey's lamp is its electrification. The switch on the back permitted it to be turned on and off at will. The flame-free bulbs allowed light to be directed and manipulated in ways that were impossible a generation before. Its cord connected the lamp's user to the rapidly expanding national power grid and, symbolically, to a new and modern way of life. In both form and function, Deskey's lamp utilized modernity to harness the new energy—and light—of modern American life.

In fact, the growth of electric lighting in the United States paralleled the development of Deskey's own career in modern design. During his early years, Deskey regularly encountered the emerging technology, and three experiences likely proved particularly influential in forming his approach to the medium: his childhood in small-town Minnesota, the 1915 Panama-Pacific International Exposition in San Francisco, and the 1925 Paris Exposition.

The earliest electric lights many Americans saw were arc lamps, in which light is created by an electric arc between two separated carbon electrodes. Such lights were displayed at the 1876 Centennial Exposition in Philadelphia (though they were not used to keep the fair open after dark) and were installed in 1878 at Wanamaker's, also in Philadelphia, the first department store to be lit by electricity. In 1880, arc lights illuminated Broadway in New York City, creating the city's famed Great White Way, photographed a few decades later by Alvin Langdon Coburn (FIG. 23). By the early 1900s, Deskey's hometown of Blue Earth, Minnesota (a train stop near the Iowa border), had single arc lamps suspended at intersections along the unpaved Main Street, shared by old-fashioned horse-drawn buggies and newer automobiles. Yet, because they hummed, flickered, and washed out colors with their blindingly bright light, arc lights were limited to outdoor and large indoor spaces and were not used in residential settings.[6] And although Thomas Edison created the first practical incandescent light bulb in 1879 and fired up his Pearl Street Station in New York in 1882, the spread of domestic electric light nationwide was limited by the need for an electricity distribution system, which took several decades to develop. Like most Americans at the turn of the twentieth century, Deskey likely spent his childhood evenings beside a liquid fuel or gas lamp. But he would have experienced pockets of electric light downtown, in the streets and possibly also in stores (like his father's dry goods business) where single incandescent bulbs, often left bare and hanging from the ceiling, were beginning to appear in small towns throughout the country.

As early as 1915, when young Deskey toured the Panama-Pacific International Exposition, San Francisco's city streets and public centers were well illuminated. Even more spectacular lighting could be seen within the fair, the first to integrate electric lighting throughout rather than feature it only in a specific building. The Exposition's "Scintillator" exhibit projected colored rays of light over the city's foggy harbor to "weave in the night sky auroras of ever-changing colors," creating "a world of art that no one had ever imagined before."[7] For Deskey, who was pursuing a career in painting at the time, the notion that electric light was a new medium with which an artist could "paint" might have taken root here.

Ten years later, the 1925 Paris Exposition brought the unadorned geometric forms of modern design to the world's—and Deskey's—attention. Modern electric light was equally featured, with a towering

glass fountain by Lalique, a nightly waterfall spectacle on the Seine, and the Eiffel Tower all dramatically illuminated after dark. Within the exhibits, new lighting fixtures demonstrated both an expanded interest in directing electric light and the new preference for modern design.[8] A precursor of the iconic *PH* lamp series, designed by Poul Henningsen of Denmark and produced by Louis Poulsen & Company, took first prize for its attractive solution to providing multidirectional light without glare. A similar lamp from the next year uses the same shape of shade to provide profuse light (**FIG. 24**). Bauhaus-trained Marcel Breuer's geometric task lamps received accolades for shielding the eyes while brightening a work surface. And, French designer Pierre Chareau's use of lighting drew attention, both in an office beneath an illuminated dome and in a dining room with pendant lamps made of overlapping alabaster rectangles around and through which light penetrated. According to journalist Margot Amory, who selected Chareau for special recognition, "a pleasanter light is obtained by combining diffusion and refraction." Amory continued by praising all the lighting designers at the exhibition for trying "to handle electricity as electricity, and not as a perverted form of a candle."[9]

Deskey brought all of these experiences with him when he moved to New York in 1926. There he found a community already actively engaging with the possibilities of controlling, shaping, and optimizing electric light. One issue of ongoing discussion was glare. Concerns about the unpleasant and potentially harmful effects of bright light arose early on, giving rise to a new profession: the illuminating engineer. At the 1906 inaugural meeting of the Illuminating Engineering Society, a New York organization aimed at educating both the public and professionals on electric light, President L. M. Marks identified discomfort from glare as one of two major issues to be addressed (the other being cost). Over the following two decades, illuminating engineers turned lighting from a functional utility into an art form. As leading lighting designer Walter Kantack jubilantly described in 1931, light is "a tangible something which we can utilize and mould and bend . . . In other words, *light can be made to do things.*"[10]

Along with glare, how to light the exteriors of New York's new skyscrapers also dominated early lighting debates. Illuminating engineer Bassett Jones Jr. complained that improper lighting obscured both the structure and ornament of a building by making its form dissolve at night into a glittering spectacle. Instead, he argued that architectural lighting should be designed to emphasize a building's three-dimensionality and stability. Concealed floodlights aimed up at the building's surface were preferred over visible lamps shining outward, as were simplified, modern building exteriors with limited ornament so as not to cast shadows. According to Jones, with architectural lighting "it is more often a question of quality than quantity," for "in seeing we do not see light—we see its effects, and it is effect for which we must strive."[11] Setback skyscrapers were especially suited

to electric lamps because their steps provided convenient places to hide floodlights. The effect of such lighting can be seen in Murray Leibowitz's 1928 speculative skyscraper drawing, with its upward-facing floodlights and brightly illuminated crown (see **FIG. 8**). Later, as seen in Berenice Abbott's 1933 photograph, architects and illuminating engineers shifted their strategy yet again to employ light from inside a building to illuminate the area outside of it, and New York City's rapidly rising skyline became defined at night by the internal glow of its buildings (**FIG. 25**).[12]

As individual households increasingly gained electric light in the 1920s, debate became centered on how to use light inside the home. *Vogue* explained in 1929, "There are two schools of modern lighting. One chooses to flood the room with light; the other . . . strives to bring certain objects into relief in an atmosphere of soft lighting."[13] Walter von Nessen's chrome floor lamp illustrates the first option by projecting light upward to reflect off the walls and ceiling, thereby filling the space (**FIG. 26**). Other lamps were tailored to specific purposes. For example, those used for reading aimed light downward while shielding the eyes, as in Deskey's lamp with hemispherical shade (**FIG. 27**). A pair of wall brackets might wash confined sections of the wall with gentle light, adding subtle illumination to a space. Lamps with translucent shades, such as the *Counter-balance* lamp designed by William Lescaze, simultaneously provide both ambient and focused light (**FIG. 28**). Similarly, Deskey's distinctive zigzag lamp, with its bold sawtooth profile, projects light downward while also reflecting it throughout the room as light bounces off its shiny surfaces. Most modern interiors combined multiple lighting approaches by mixing a variety of electric lamps within each room.

These lamps, and the flexibility they brought to interior lighting, altered the look and layout of the American home. They also transformed how people lived within it. Freed from the need to cluster around a single flame-based light source that required monitoring, individuals could disperse throughout the home, gaining greater privacy. Children could play safely after dark without direct supervision, reading in bed was no longer hazardous, and previously menacing dark hallways and stairwells could be made bright with the flick of a switch. Yet, some remained wary of the new technology, scared of the wires tangled outside above their heads and reluctant to bury wires in their walls for fear of electrocution or fire. To reassure potential customers of electricity's safety and convenience, the Alabama Power Company introduced the Reddy Kilowatt cartoon character in 1926. With his lightning-bolt body, light-bulb nose, outlet ears, and safety gloves and shoes, Reddy literally put a friendly face on electricity. Over the next fifty years, this popular trademarked figure, seen here in a marketing sign dating from after World War II, was licensed by more than 150 investor-owned electric utilities across the United States (**FIG. 29**).

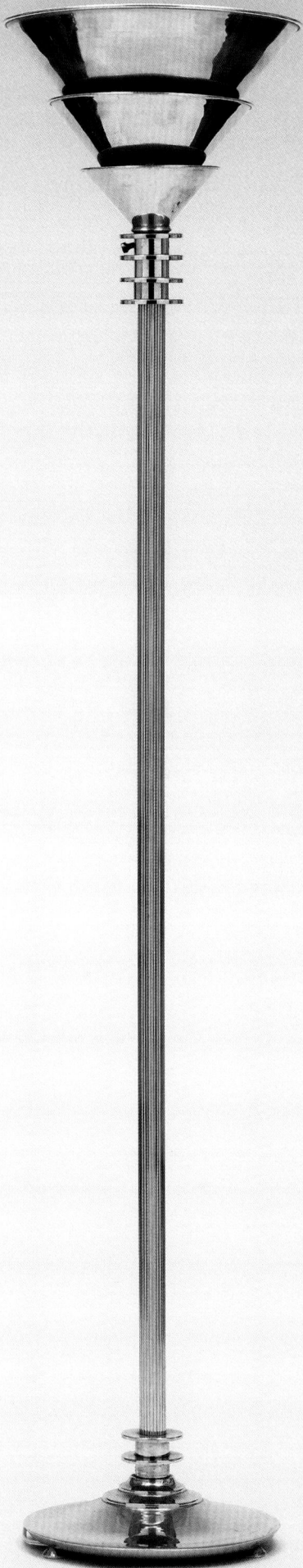

Deskey seized the opportunity to capitalize on the new demand for domestic electric light. In 1927, while continuing his custom work for individual clients such as Paul Frankl (see **FIG. 13**) and designing for companies engaged in mass production, Deskey partnered with salesman Phillip Vollmer to establish an interior furnishings company under the name Deskey-Vollmer, Incorporated. Deskey drew the designs, Vollmer managed the finances, and their small manufactory produced a limited output of lamps, tables, and accessories in small batches on speculation for department stores, galleries, and specialty shops.[14]

Deskey-Vollmer's product line, though small in scope, included a selection of floor lamps along with a wide array of table lamps made of various industrial materials such as chrome, nickel, aluminum, wood, glass, and occasionally plastics, all designed to be easily reproduced through mass production. Although originally a custom design for Adam Gimbel, the zigzag lamp appears to have been put into limited production, as a handful are known today. Deskey-Vollmer also provided tables to hold their lamps that were lower than usual so the lamp would "shield the eyes while at the same time permitting the light to fall upon the book" (according to *Arts & Decoration* magazine in 1927).[15] These low side tables, along with related coffee tables, suited the casual entertaining practices of apartment dwellers in the 1920s and 1930s (FIG. 30). The tables had to be small, strong, and sturdy, with a durable top that offered, according to Deskey, "resistance to cigarette burns and . . . the alcoholic concoctions of that era."[16] To achieve this, Deskey pioneered the use of metal for home furnishings in the United States (as debuted in Gimbel's apartment) and experimented with Vitrolite (structural glass) and Bakelite (plastic) laminate for tabletops. In adopting new materials for its stylish table lamps and side tables, as well as for its ashtrays and other accessories, Deskey-Vollmer modernized the American home interior, yet the company's influence was constrained by its small-batch production.

A vast array of other new electrical devices followed light into the home. Small, relatively affordable household appliances, such as percolators, irons, vacuum cleaners, toasters, and fans, were the first to be adopted by homeowners once their homes were wired. Many of these items were already present in early electrified homes by the 1910s, although initially these wares were modern in their functionality but not in their styling. It was not until the late 1920s, as electricity spread to more households, demand (and thus competition) increased, and the impact of styling was more widely recognized, that the new industrial designers created appliances that embraced modernity in form as well as function. Deskey's zigzag lamp exemplifies this shift, as does the sleek chrome-plated electric percolator with jade Catalin (plastic) handles released by Manning-Bowman Company in 1928 (FIG. 31). The sharply angled handles not only accentuate the tapered body of the percolator but also resemble wings or fins, perhaps modeled after early experiments in the nascent field of modern rocketry widely publicized at the time.

Two other electrical devices that soon gained household popularity—and modern styling—were radios and clocks. Radio brought modern music (especially the newly popular jazz), sports, news, theater, and commercials into the home, connecting individual households to a developing national popular culture.[17] Originally used by the military during World War I as a point-to-point communication tool (a form of wireless telegraphy), radio shifted to a broadcast model with General Electric's formation of the Radio Corporation of

America (RCA) in 1919. A manufacturer of radio receivers as well as founder of the first national broadcast network (NBC, formed in 1926), RCA only produced battery-operated models until 1925, when it released the first commercially successful plug-in radio, the *Radiola 30*—a traditionally styled wooden cabinet model proudly declared by advertising to require "no more care than an electric lamp!"[18]

Other companies also pivoted to enter the burgeoning wired radio market (though batteries remained essential in portable devices

and rural areas). For example, Michigan automobile parts maker Sparks-Withington began manufacturing radios under the Sparton name in 1925. Realizing by the early 1930s that "the point has been passed where just any radio will do," the company emphasized its superior sound quality and hired industrial designer Walter Dorwin Teague to modernize its look.[19] Teague's *Bluebird* tabletop radio, unveiled to the public in 1935, was marketed as "Radio's Richest Voice Now Combined with Radio's Smartest Styling" (**FIG. 32**).[20] Its design features a record-shaped disc of mirrored blue glass accented by chrome speed lines.[21] By contrast, Harold Van Doren and Gordon Rideout's large 1933 radio, made of the new moldable Plaskon (plastic) for Brooklyn's Air-King Products Company (see **FIG. 87**), has a strikingly different yet equally modern smooth, white exterior.

Electrical clocks, on the other hand, did not gain favor until the late 1920s, once utility companies had made substantial improvements in power distribution. A glitchy power supply wreaked havoc on early electric clocks, making them unreliable and burdensome to maintain. Frustrated by electricity's inconsistency, Henry Warren of Massachusetts' Warren Telechron Company, a clock manufacturer, designed a frequency regulator for power stations to prevent an irregular power supply from altering his clocks' time. His "Master Clock" was installed by Boston's dominant electric company in 1916, but it took over a decade for supply regulators to be installed at power stations throughout the grid. In the meantime, Warren tried to help his customers by outfitting his clocks, including the 1928 *Modernique* designed by Paul Frankl (**FIG. 33**), with a "current interruption indicator," a small hole that showed red when a power irregularity required that the clock's time be reset. The growing reliability of electric power in the late 1920s caused demand for electric clocks to skyrocket—sales of clocks in the United States increased from 87,000 in 1927 to nearly 4.3 million in ten years.[22]

Like other electrical appliances such as light fixtures and radios, electric clock designs often referenced new and iconic elements of American modern life. Frankl's *Modernique* assumed a subtle skyscraper-like form, while Gilbert Rohde's small aluminum desk clock, one of several he designed for Michigan's Herman Miller Clock Company (founded in 1927), looks like an automobile gauge (**FIG. 34**; bottom row, third from right). Another Rohde clock has a translucent glass face supported by a dramatically bent metal rod reminiscent of the legs on tubular steel tables and chairs (**FIG. 34**; top row, second from left). Lawson Time Incorporated of Los Angeles (formed in 1933) produced several digital-faced clocks designed by Paul Feher and George F. Adomaitis, including the *Arlington* (**FIG. 34**; bottom row, third from left), advertised as "sensationally different in its method of recording time."[23] Lawson Time's *Zephyr* digital clock (**FIG. 34**; bottom row, second from left) was wrapped in swooping parallel lines suggestive of train tracks and the record-breaking train that shared its name—the Burlington *Zephyr* of 1934 (see **FIG. 62**).

In the same mode, designers also harnessed visual references to electricity itself to emphasize the modernity of their designs. Such references could be made even in objects that themselves were not electrified. Designer Raymond Hood featured stacked, spaced discs that mimic the shape of insulators on utility poles to ornament the legs of a table he designed for Rex Cole's refrigerator showrooms in New York City (**FIG. 35**). The discs also echo the stacked circles of the electric compressors atop the General Electric monitor-top refrigerators

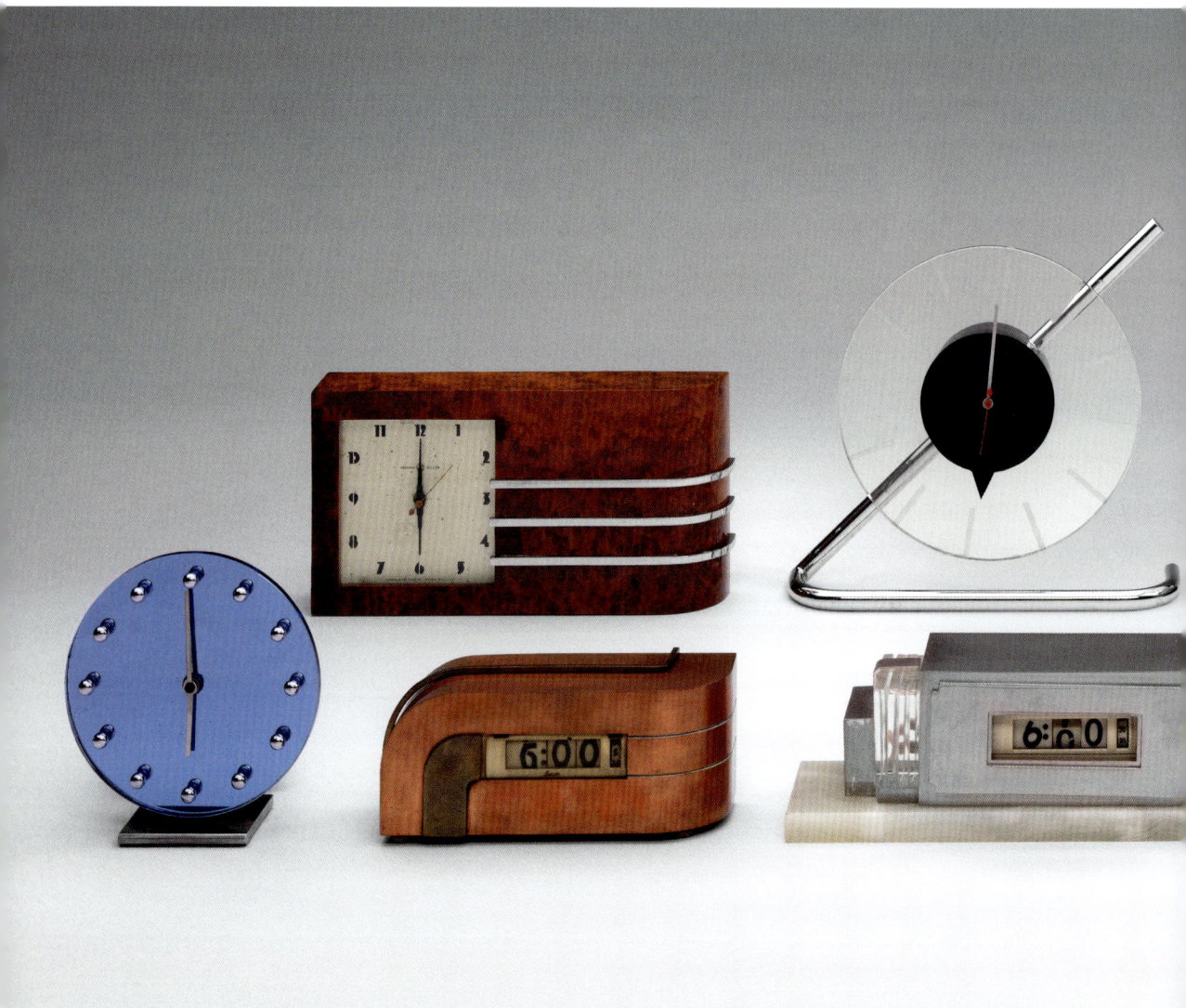

34   Assortment of electric clocks from 1929–38

OPPOSITE: 36   Ruth Reeves, *Electric* coverlet, 1930
35   Raymond Hood, Table, 1931

(first released in 1927) for sale nearby. Similarly, Ruth Reeves titled a textile pattern *Electric* (1930) because of its jagged shapes evocative of lightning (**FIG. 36**).[24] While Reeves's fabric could modernize any space, it was deemed particularly suitable for upholstery in new radio rooms, specially designated spaces devoid of "the noise of passing motors or streetcars . . . the rattling of dishes, or other noises that may interfere with the full enjoyment of your radio."[25] Lightning bolts, a ubiquitous symbol for the new utility at the time, also were employed by General Electric, RCA, and AT&T, among others, on everything from their logos to their buildings.

Whether used as a power source or as a design element, electricity equaled modernity—and Deskey's zigzag lamp did both. The modern look of the zigzag lamp was further enhanced by Deskey's choice of materials. The lamp's frosted glass, though not a new material, diffuses light rays in accordance with the modern era's concern for glare. And its gleaming metal form was electroplated in either silver, as in the example featured here, or chrome.[26] Silver electroplating dates to the mid–nineteenth century (an early use of electricity), but chromium-plating was perfected only in 1924. Both excel at reflecting

74   AMERICA GOES MODERN

light; silver also suited the desire for luxury demanded by some of Deskey's high-end clients. Deskey's later adoption of chrome may have been a step toward mass production of the design, though that never came to fruition. Today five examples of the zigzag lamp design are known to survive: three in silver plate and two in chrome.[27]

The zigzag lamp was featured in several prominent and well-publicized modern interiors in addition to Adam Gimbel's apartment. In 1928, Deskey installed a "Man's Room" at the first exhibition of the American Designers' Gallery, established to promote modern design and the "artist-designer."[28] His room, complete with bar, smoking paraphernalia, gaming table, bookshelves, and upholstered seating, delighted critic C. Adolph Glassgold, who praised Deskey's use of industrial materials and "modern style."[29] The furnishings were largely repurposed from Deskey's earlier design for Gimbel's apartment, including a small desk, side table, and his prized zigzag lamp. Despite the many new lamp designs he was creating, Deskey continued to highlight the zigzag form. And he even complemented the lamp in the exhibition display with a harmonious ashtray in which the lamp's triangles were reconfigured into a pyramid (**FIG. 37**).[30]

Two of the extant silverplate lamps, including the one featured here, share a common history. Their original owner is thought to have been C. Templeton Crocker, a Yale graduate with wide-ranging interests—from writing opera to leading scientific explorations in the Pacific—and extravagant taste.[31] Crocker inherited millions from his grandfather, a railroad tycoon. His penthouse on San Francisco's Russian Hill, with interiors created in 1929 by Jean-Michel Frank of Paris, was a showcase of modern French design, mixing sleek geometric forms with opulent and often unusual materials such as sharkskin, mica, and animal hides. Most spectacular were the lacquer wall panels by French specialist Jean Dunand installed in the dining room, breakfast room, and master bedroom. A sophisticated lighting plan throughout combined concealed lighting devices with table lamps, many of rock crystal. Deskey's silverplate lamps likely stood on low tables flanking Crocker's bed. In fact, a side table Dunand created for the apartment bears a similar three-tiered, angular form and silver-colored glossy finish (FIG. 38). The zigzag lamps were among the few U.S. designs incorporated into this French-dominated interior that privileged expensive luxury materials and Cubist-inspired shapes.[32]

American interior decorator Frances Miller similarly employed a second set of Deskey's zigzag lamps in 1929 in the sprawling Long Island home of her father, James Breese, a civil engineer turned stockbroker/photographer with a passion for sports cars and shortwave radios. The lamps, which were likely chrome, were used in a bedroom filled with modern materials: jute on the walls, cork on the floor, asbestos for the ceiling, and chrome trim around the windows, doors, and bed.[33] For the bedroom, Miller combined a mirrored dressing table that had integrated lighting with Deskey's zigzag lamps on matching two-tier bedside tables by Forzina, Inc. Like the penthouse apartments of Crocker and Gimbel, images of James Breese's interiors were published in widely circulating magazines such as *House & Garden* as models of early modern design, reinforcing the role of Deskey's zigzag electric lamp as the epitome of fashionable modernity.[34]

The early 1930s were a time of transition for Deskey. He separated from Vollmer in 1931 and seemingly abandoned his interest in mass production to focus on high-end custom work, such as his design for Abby Aldrich Rockefeller's Topside Gallery. His work at Topside likely secured his next and most prestigious job at Radio City Music Hall, which opened in December 1932. Deskey's designs for the venue's dozens of lounges and lobbies were part of an immense development project of Abby's husband, John D. Rockefeller Jr., in collaboration with the Radio Corporation of America, whose dominance in the entertainment industry had grown with the rising popularity of radio and cinema. In addition to coordinating the work of several other designers and artists, Deskey himself designed many of the rooms' custom furniture, carpets, wallpaper, ashtrays, and lamps using aluminum, plastic, and other industrial materials to create "some of the

finest modern furniture placed in a public building in this country."[35] Lighting, as always, played a prominent role in his interior compositions. His floor and table lamps bring a sense of human scale to Radio City's many large spaces, a practice advocated years earlier by Bassett Jones Jr.[36] By contrast, the immense cylindrical crystal chandeliers contributed by Edward F. Caldwell & Company enhance the grandeur of the sixty-foot-tall foyer.

The Radio City project marked a change in Deskey's approach to modern design. In a 1933 essay, Deskey criticized the zigzag motif as a design element being stuck, along with triangles and elegant leaping deer, "indiscriminately on anything."[37] Others in the mid-1930s also rejected the zigzag's jaggedness, saying that, while it was emblematic of "the jazz epoch" and "our harsh adjustment to a fast changing world," its time had passed.[38] Instead, designers started to embrace the curves and rounded edges of streamlined design and increasingly replaced table and floor lamps with lighting devices hidden in the furniture or architecture of the room itself.

Although Deskey may have abandoned the angular form of his groundbreaking early lamp design, he continued to experiment with lighting throughout the rest of his career. In the 1960s, over eleven thousand Deskey-designed lampposts flooded New York City, offering safety without glare and creating a modern landscape in stark contrast to Deskey's childhood memories of Minnesota.[39]

NIGHTLIFE

New York City nightlife, characterized by the casual mingling of both genders in public after dark, lubricated by ample alcohol and entertainments, first emerged in the 1920s. Many elements of this modern nightlife developed between 1880 and 1920, including the ongoing electrification of the city, the advent of nightclub-style entertainment and public dancing, the loosening of social restrictions on women, the popularization of cocktails, and "the newest and smartest thing in 'modern' music": jazz.[1] But it was alcohol Prohibition laws enacted in January 1920 that brought these elements together in a new way, and with a new attitude. New York's flagrant defiance of Prohibition was legendary, and its new nightlife scene captured the attention of the nation. "The city that never sleeps," as a 1924 silent film nicknamed the city, fascinated a nation coming to terms with the casualness and spontaneity of modern society. In the 1920s, New York, especially at night, became a nationwide subject of moral and legal debate, a model to follow (or avoid), and a massive tourist draw. For designer Viktor Schreckengost (1906–2008), a frequent visitor, the city's modern nightlife was a source of artistic inspiration (**FIG. 39**).[2]

The son of a kiln loader in a pottery factory town, Schreckengost attended the Cleveland School of Art, where he studied ceramics with Guy Cowan and Arthur Baggs. When the American Federation of Arts' International Exhibition of Ceramic Art came to Cleveland in 1929, Schreckengost was introduced to the work of Viennese ceramic artists Michael Powolny, Valerie Wieselthier, and Susi Singer Schinnerl. Inspired by "how fresh everything was" and the joyfulness of Powolny's pieces—"like all the time he worked on them he was happy and enjoying himself"—he quickly arranged to become the first American to study in Powolny's classroom at Vienna's Kunstgewerbeschule.[3] There he learned to hand-model hollow figures and to capture in clay the immediacy, vitality, and delight of the Viennese work, such as this endearing bear by Powolny with white crackle glaze (**FIG. 40**). Schreckengost was so impacted by his formative year abroad that he permanently changed the spelling of his first name from Victor to Viktor.[4]

Although Schreckengost had spent numerous weekends in New York during his art school days in the late 1920s, perhaps his most influential trip to the city was in 1930, upon his return from Vienna. On August 28, he stepped off the recently launched high-speed ocean liner the SS *Europa* onto Brooklyn's Pier 4, seeing the city with fresh eyes.[5] His experience in Vienna surely gave him new perspective and helped him to recognize the city's unique traits. Traits that symbolized modern America to the rest of the world. The new skyscrapers that dominated the skyline were on top of that list, and the city's Prohibition-era nightlife was close behind. Young Schreckengost, a jazz aficionado, likely stayed in New York City for a night to take in some shows before heading back home to Ohio, where he was engaged to begin work as a designer at his former teacher Guy Cowan's studio, Cowan Pottery.[6]

Once at Cowan Pottery a few weeks later, Schreckengost received a commission for a punch bowl with a New York theme.[7] Drawing upon his recent experiences in the city, the twenty-four-year-old wrapped the vessel with a Cubist-inspired collage of skyscrapers, light-up signs, alcoholic drinks, and instruments of a jazz band (**FIG. 41**). The finished product captured the essence of New York's famed modern nightlife. Originally titled *The New Yorker*, the bowl is now commonly known as the *Jazz* bowl, in reference to the word "JAZZ" in its design as well as the soundtrack of its era (**FIG. 42**).[8]

Stylistically, Schreckengost's *Jazz* bowl reveals his up-to-date knowledge of modern art and design. The bowl's composition of overlapping images and words, derived from Cubism and collage, effectively conveys the crowded and hectic feel of New York, which in 1930 grew busier and taller by the day. From graphic design, Schreckengost got his spare, linear flat style and bold limited color scheme. He specifically credited the reductivist posters of Austrian Joseph Binder, whose work is seen here in a later design for the 1939 World's Fair, with exerting a direct influence upon him (**FIG. 43**).[9]

Imagery on the *Jazz* bowl includes two clusters of skyscrapers that clearly establish the scene as New York. Although they do not resemble any specific buildings, the towers' expanding profiles replicate the sense of looking up from below, with the tops of the looming buildings appearing to reach the stars. Three blank street signs (projecting from streetlights) suggest the endless intersections visitors must pass while traversing the city.[10] The overlapping "Stop" and "Go" circles represent traffic signals and recall both the speed and the abruptness of city travel. And the ocean liner, seen peeking out from behind the soaring skyscrapers, symbolizes New York's importance to both immigration and international travel. In fact, the ship even features the distinctive pair of low funnels belonging to the SS *Europa*, which Schreckengost recently had taken from Europe to New York.

Several images depicted on the *Jazz* bowl reference the city's new nighttime illumination. The trio of glaring streetlights (albeit depicted in the style of old-fashioned gas lamps) evoke the city's bright electric lighting that, starting in the 1880s, turned Broadway into a new center of nighttime entertainment (see **FIG. 23**). The cluster of signs conjures the quintessential American urban landscape upon which this nightlife centered: Times Square. Famous for its visual cacophony of electrified signs, Times Square gained its current name, subway station, and first New Year's Eve party only in 1904, with the opening of the New York Times skyscraper building. By the 1930s over eighty theaters had been built in the area, each with multiple illuminated signs. Flashing, colored, and moving signs competed for the attention of passersby while advertising everything from stars of the stage and late-night refreshments to a range of consumer goods, making the square as much a destination as its theaters (**FIG. 44**).

BELOW: 42 Rollout of *Jazz* bowl

OPPOSITE: 41 Viktor Schreckengost, *Jazz* bowl, designed 1930

43   Joseph Binder, *New York World's Fair*, 1939

OPPOSITE: 44   Walker Evans, *Times Square / Broadway Composition*, 1930

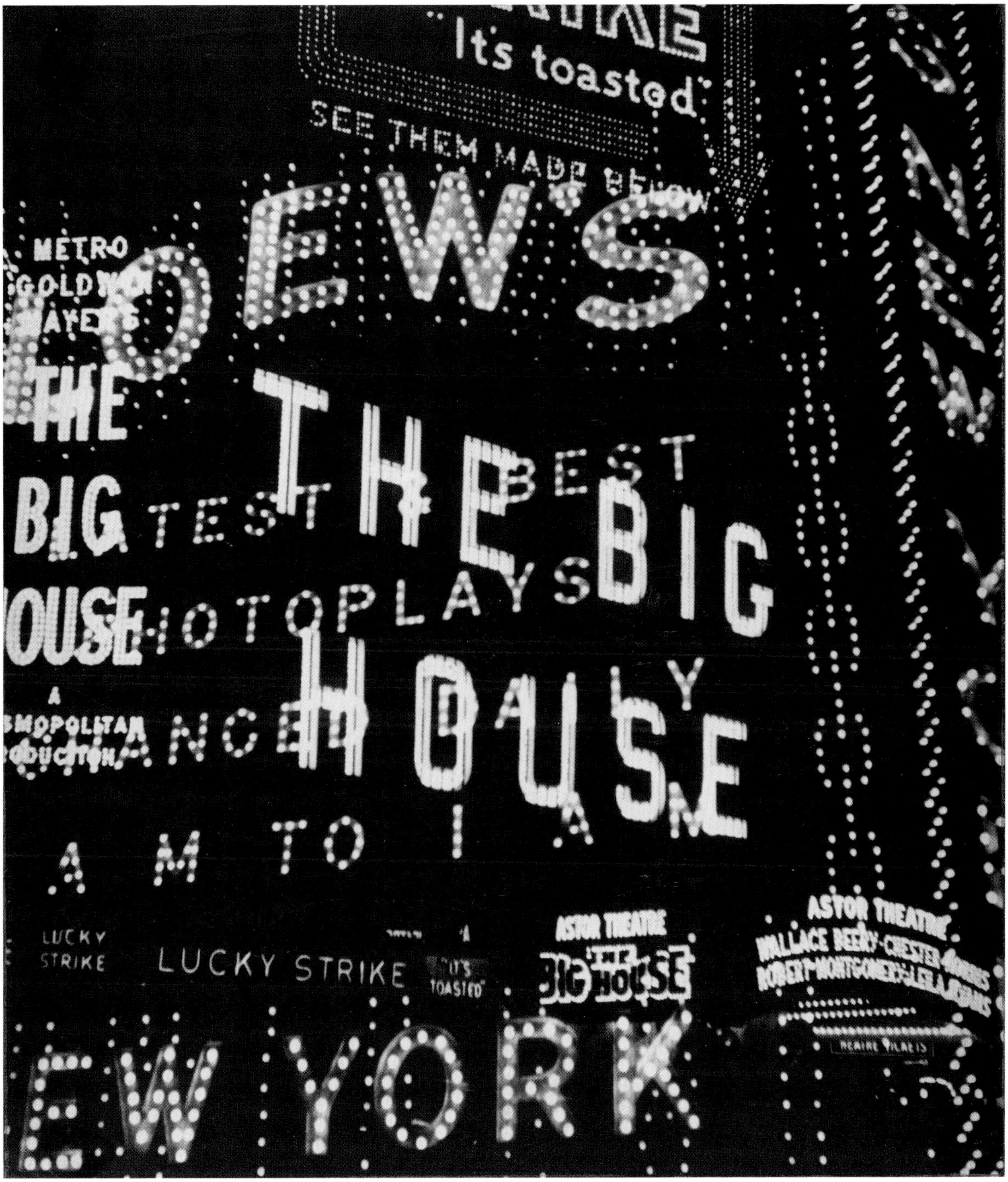

It's toasted
SEE THEM MADE BELOW
METRO
THE
BIG
THE
BEST
BIG
LUCKY
STRIKE
LUCKY STRIKE
ASTOR THEATRE
ASTOR THEATRE
YORK

Four signs depicted on the *Jazz* bowl refer to a selection of Times Square's many entertainments. The foremost reads "Follies," a direct reference to Florenz Ziegfeld's renowned variety shows that first premiered in 1907 and the theater's electrically lit signage—with the letters outlined in bare bulbs on its marquee. Two other signs say "Dance," while a third, off to the side, reads "Café," all likely referring to the new nightclub-style establishments with food, drinks, and dancing that emerged at the turn of the twentieth century as after-party locations for patrons of Broadway's theatrical shows. The bowl's image of a clock face is likely meant to suggest the Paramount Building at 43rd and Broadway, which opened in 1926.[11] Its time reads 3:30, thirty minutes past the city's mandated (as of 1927) but frequently ignored closing time.

Schreckengost depicted five revelers emerging from beneath the "Café" sign. Their various hats reflect the diversity of fashions, and thus people, to be seen in New York at night, from the traditional, formal top hat to trendy fedoras, and from a hip porkpie to a classic bowler. The cartoon-like quality of the carousers' faces speaks to the artist's initial course of study in cartoon illustration at the Cleveland School of Art. Perhaps the men, inebriation indicted on one face by *x*'s for eyes, have recently purchased alcohol, an activity made illegal by the National Prohibition Act, enacted at 12:01 a.m. on January 17, 1920. Under Prohibition, the manufacture, transportation, and sale of alcoholic beverages within the United States was banned, and entrepreneurial bootleggers took over the now outlawed—and unregulated—trade in intoxicating beverages. Much of public nightlife was forced into speakeasies, or establishments illegally serving alcohol. These new enterprises ranged widely in character, from locked doors requiring a password, to longtime restaurants trying desperately to stay in business, to new nightclubs featuring live performances and dancing. One of the most famous nightclubs of the era was Harlem's Cotton Club, run by mobster Owney Madden who used his underground connections to obtain alcohol. The subterfuge, illegality, and potentially poisonous alcohol added a sense of danger (requiring you to "ring up your friend next morning to find out whether he is still alive"), while the ability to navigate the underground world became a badge of sophistication.[12] For Schreckengost, like many Americans, the "wetness" of New York's nightclubs, so vividly featured on the *Jazz* bowl, must have seemed a stark contrast to Sebring, Ohio, his dry hometown in the heartland of American temperance. Yet, Schreckengost was known to have enjoyed alcohol himself—his favorite drink later in life was a gin martini garnished with an onion, called a Gibson.[13] In fact, he even inserted himself into the crowd of revelers depicted on the *Jazz* bowl by signing his name just beneath the faces of the men out on the town.

Alcohol itself figures prominently on the *Jazz* bowl. Two immense corked bottles stand as tall as the skyscrapers, one of wine or champagne and the other, liquor. A serving tray bears drinks: two glasses of wine and a martini with swizzle stick and garnish (perhaps Schreckengost's preferred onion?). During Prohibition, liquor supplanted beer as the nation's most popular source of alcohol because it was easier to smuggle and make in small batches. To extend or disguise expensive and often inferior liquor, many turned to mixers. As a result, cocktails' popularity, which had been rising since the late nineteenth century, soared. Their illicit nature, endless variations, witty or evocative names, and small serving size perfectly suited the individualism and speed of modern urban America. Their brazen promotion in popular novels and movies, including *Gentlemen Prefer Blondes* (1925) and *Our Dancing Daughters* (1928), made them even more exciting and glamorous. And their frequent accompaniment by illegal gambling, denoted on the bowl by the large dice pictured just below the martini glass, added to the speakeasies' risky thrill.[14]

Private cocktail parties combined speakeasies' sophistication—and trendy mixed drinks—with the exclusivity and security of being at home. And, since Prohibition did not outlaw the *consumption* of alcohol or the ability to serve it to guests in your home, such gatherings became widely popular. Voguish hosts could become bartenders, flaunting their drink-mixing skills and showmanship with stylish cocktail shakers, such as Gorham's angular *Modern American* model in silver designed by Erik Magnussen in 1928 (**FIG. 45**). Gorham, despite deliberately avoiding the word "cocktail," shamelessly advertised its "beverage set" as the perfect way to "toast happiness" with friends.[15] Equally modern cocktail sets also were made in less expensive pewter, silverplate, and chrome. Russel Wright's 1930 pewter set, with cups the same shape as one half of its shaker, demonstrates modernism's preference for simplified geometric forms, while Norman Bel Geddes's chrome *Manhattan* design for Revere Copper and Brass celebrates the skyline of the city itself (**FIG. 46**; see **FIG. 12**). Hosts could further evoke the modern atmosphere of urban nightlife through the new technologies of record players and radios, which brought many of New York's nighttime entertainments directly into their living room.

Like alcohol, music is key to the *Jazz* bowl's design. Written in bold stylized letters on a drum head, the word "JAZZ" is encircled by the major elements of a jazz band: wind instruments represented by a pair of saxophones (an instrument Schreckengost himself played), horns including a trumpet beside a larger trombone (seen only as sound holes), and a rhythm section complete with drum, high-hat cymbals, and keyboard (represented here by a theater's organ pipes). The trumpet, trombone, and one saxophone emit sound waves, while the second saxophone "is waiting his turn" according to Schreckengost, as jazz music often requires.[16] Repeated motifs evoke musical sound or notation, such as solid and hollow dots, wavy lines, and zigzags, which taken together suggest a jazz riff. The overlapping of images calls to mind jazz's complicated, offbeat rhythms, and

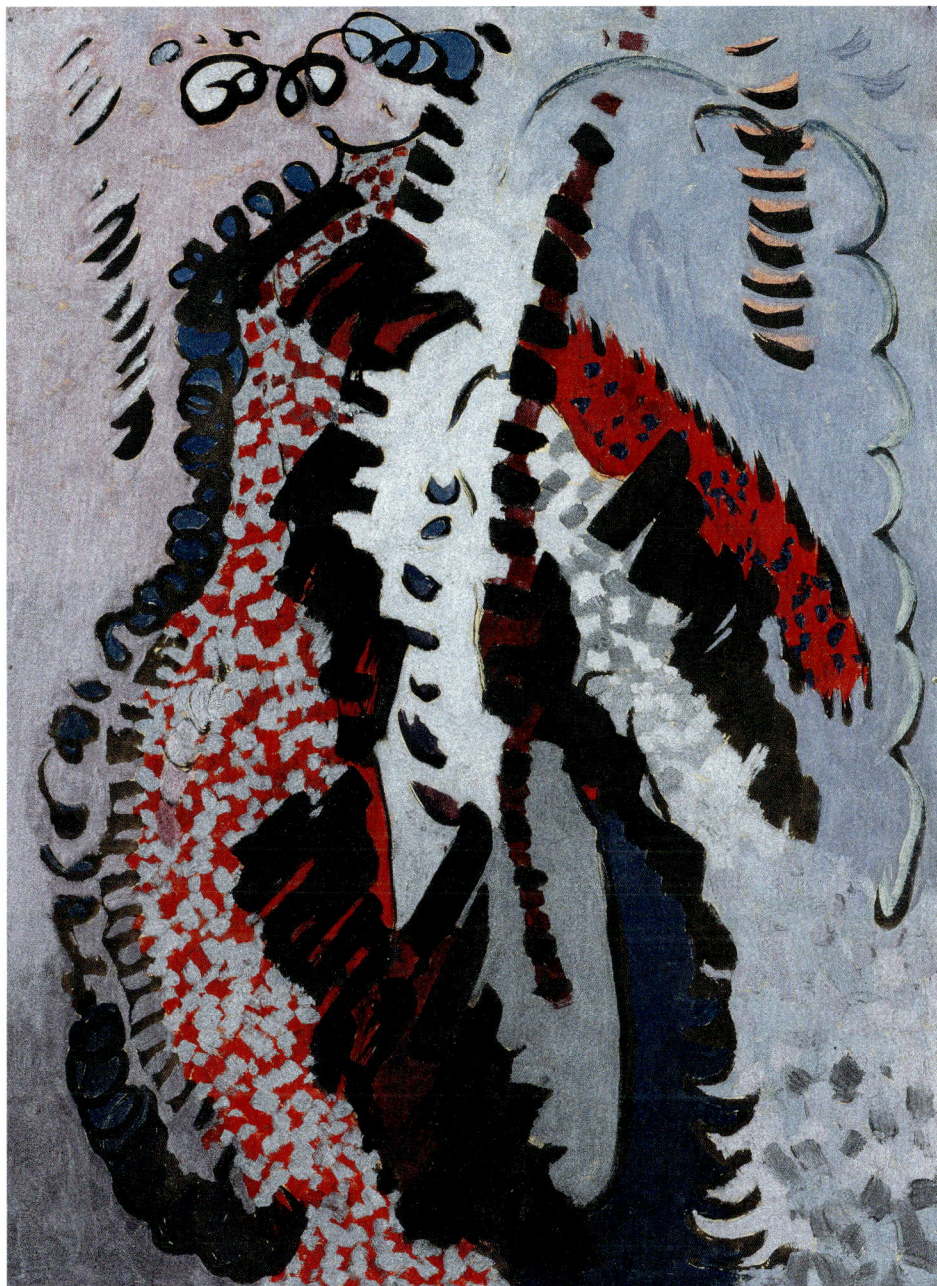

Schreckengost's scratched, sketch-like lines allude to the genre's improvisation. The *Jazz* bowl's composition lacks a clear hierarchy to its individual elements, reflecting a jazz band's egalitarian organization and the genre's convention of giving each instrument its moment to shine.

Schreckengost was not the first modern artist to harness the characteristics of jazz music to visually represent modernity. Some attempted to translate the rhythms and emotions of jazz music into colors and shapes, such as Arthur Dove in his 1927 abstract work, *George Gershwin—I'll Build a Stairway to Paradise* (**FIG. 47**). To create this work, Dove repeatedly listened to an instrumental recording of Gershwin's song by the Paul Whiteman Orchestra to capture the upbeat, joyful spirit of the composer's music in metallic silver, reds, and blues. Other artists depicted scenes from the jazz world, such as Norman Lewis's 1943 *Harlem Jazz Jamboree* (**FIG. 48**). With its jumble of faces, expressions, and textures depicted using dynamic black outlines and accents of bright red and deep blues, Lewis vividly portrayed the vivacious spirit and intimacy of a Harlem jazz club. Like both of these canvases, the imagery on Schreckengost's bowl relies on quick, choppy lines, repeated patterns, and individual style to evoke the modernity of jazz.

Despite its embrace of jazz style and characteristics, the *Jazz* bowl lacks any direct reference to a crucial element of jazz culture: race and racial mixing. Jazz music was first developed by Black musicians in New Orleans and spread throughout the country during the Great Migration, when, in the 1910s alone, it is estimated that nearly half a million Black people fled Jim Crow segregation of the South for cities in the North.[17] These new urban communities sparked a flourishing of Black cultural expression in literature, poetry, theater, visual art, philosophy, and music. Although vibrant Black communities developed in Detroit, Cleveland, Philadelphia, and especially Chicago, among others, New York's Harlem became the mecca of this rising racial consciousness and expression, called the New Negro Movement at the time and now often referred to as the Harlem Renaissance. Perhaps more than any other artistic product of the New Negro Movement, jazz music had the farthest reach and greatest immediate cultural impact throughout the United States and abroad. In addition to touring shows and recorded albums, radio broadcasts of Duke Ellington's Cotton Club shows went nationwide in 1929, turning the jazz great into a household name and the Harlem nightclub into a requisite tourist stop.

Jazz was firmly linked with Black culture in the public mind, despite the pervasive efforts of white musicians to appropriate the new modern sound. For some intellectual leaders of the New Negro Movement, its riotous culture often reinforced racial stereotypes, rather than rise above them.[18] Indeed, some of what drew white patrons to Harlem's jazz clubs such as the Cotton Club was the perceived exoticism (and eroticism) of its all-Black dancers, musicians, and waitstaff. Even venturing into the predominantly Black neighborhood of Harlem to get to the venue could add to the thrill and allure for white patrons. Because of its association with the Black community, jazz was the subject of outcry based in racial prejudice among more conservative circles. A 1921 article—"Does Jazz Put the Sin in Syncopation?"—called "Jazz . . . the accompaniment of the voodoo dancer, stimulating the half-crazed barbarian to the vilest deeds."[19] Prominent white Americans, including Thomas Edison and Henry Ford, denounced jazz as a detrimental foreign influence on traditional

Anglo-American culture, with the anti-Semitic Ford particularly condemning Jewish Americans in New York's music industry (such as George Gershwin) for promoting jazz through their work for the Broadway stage.[20] Such anti-jazz sentiment only augmented the music's rebellious appeal during Prohibition, however, and further enhanced the speakeasies that played jazz music's allure.[21]

Schreckengost first encountered jazz music through his older sister's records and became an accomplished musician himself.[22] He enthusiastically attended live performances in Cleveland, Vienna, and Harlem, and credited Black jazz musicians Duke Ellington and Cab Calloway as strong influences on him. Schreckengost particularly recalled "a magical night" with a friend from Vienna seeing "Calloway at the Cotton Club," a night he has said was an inspiration for the *Jazz* bowl.[23] Calloway, famous for his exuberant dancing and scat singing, brought his band to Harlem's Cotton Club for several weeks in the summer of 1930 before becoming the club's headliner in 1931. In order to have seen Calloway before making the *Jazz* bowl in the fall of 1930, Schreckengost would have had to visit the club on his return from Vienna on August 28, 1930.

Although race is only implied on the *Jazz* bowl, Schreckengost created other pieces in which it was overtly featured. While in Vienna, he made figural sculptures of Black "singers and dancers and jazz musicians playing saxes and drummers and all kinds of stuff."[24] These sculptures depict racial stereotypes rather than actual people, with their exaggerated features calling to mind blackface makeup used to depict harmful caricatures (**FIG. 49**). Upon his return from Europe and after he created the *Jazz* bowl, Schreckengost painted *Blue Revel* (1931), a scene of racially stereotyped Black jazz musicians accompanying scantily

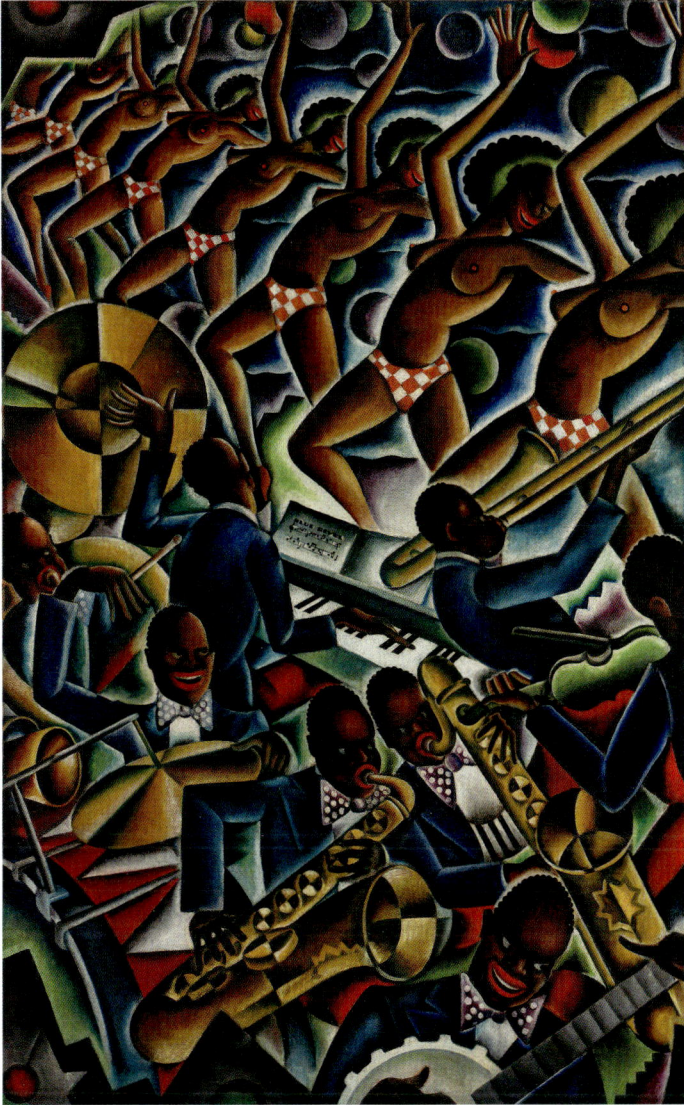

clad dancing girls (**FIG. 50**). It epitomizes the eroticism many deemed embedded in jazz, to which the adjectives "sizzling," "hot," and "torrid" were often applied.[25] While reminiscent of the Cotton Club, the painting also could have been inspired by Cleveland's own Globe Theater or numerous other venues of the day that promoted racial stereotyping.

Alternatives to such work were offered by countless newly empowered artists of the New Negro Movement, including Chicago painter Archibald Motley. Motley's *Cocktails* of about 1926 boldly portrays a social gathering of stylish young Black women brazenly enjoying a variety of alcoholic drinks during Prohibition (**FIG. 51**). His depiction of Black bodies with varying skin tones gives "each one of them character as individuals" in contrast to pervasive caricatures of the time.[26] Although the *Jazz* bowl avoids the offensive depictions of some of Schreckengost's other work, it fails to acknowledge the central role of Black Americans in the creation of jazz culture and modern nightlife.

Similarly, Schreckengost's *Jazz* bowl does not explicitly feature women; rather it only obliquely references them with its advertisement for the Follies, famous for its Ziegfeld girls, and its pair of "DANCE" signs. But on a plate he made in the same style and around the same time, the designer featured the mixed-gender socializing for which modern nightlife is well known (**FIG. 52**). His dancing couple, caught twirling in an alcohol-fueled embrace, nearly fills the plate, seemingly oblivious to the bubbly drinks precariously set on the round café tables that surround them. Jazz music accompanied the modern dances of the 1920s, including the Charleston, Black Bottom, Shimmy, and Lindy Hop, all of which have origins in Black communities.[27] The perceived sexuality of these dances prompted accusations that the music encouraged promiscuity, and several attempts were made to eliminate jazz dances from public dance halls. But, in spite of these conservative efforts, widespread public dancing and drinking, along with unchaperoned mingling with members of the opposite sex, proliferated, reflecting dramatic changes in women's lives in the early years of the twentieth century.

Schreckengost may have left out direct references to Black culture and the changing roles of women in his design for the *Jazz* bowl to avoid potential concerns with his anonymous client. Although these elements were consciously omitted, they were inherently implied and therefore are important to acknowledge in order to understand the full context in which the bowl was made. Schreckengost was commissioned to make the *Jazz* bowl at a transitional time in Cowan Pottery's history. Six months before he joined the firm, it had embarked on an expansion that included a new branch office in New York to facilitate commissions through nearby galleries (such as the Brownell-Lambertson Gallery, which enabled the *Jazz* bowl project).[28] Yet, by the time Schreckengost arrived in the fall of 1930, Cowan Pottery's finances had deteriorated rapidly, along with the national economy, and, after a large order was returned unsold, the company entered receivership, ultimately closing a year later. In the company's final year, essentially free from financial concerns, Guy Cowan fostered a studio atmosphere that supported experimentation, and the Pottery turned out some of its most innovative designs, including Schreckengost's *Jazz* bowl.[29] Although originally created for a commission, Cowan promptly sought to put the *Jazz* bowl into production, ultimately making dozens of bowls in three different versions.

To express the *Jazz* bowl's lively, modern nightlife scenes, Schreckengost employed the ancient ceramic drawing technique of sgraffito, recently revived at Cowan Pottery, where it was called "Dry Point."[30] Schreckengost first covered the undecorated bowl with black engobe (a thick slip) into which he then scratched lines to reveal the white clay underneath. After an initial firing, the entire vessel was sprayed with blue glaze, turning the white lines blue as well as subtly tinting the black, and fired again.[31] The sketch-like, scratched lines vary

53 Arthur E. Baggs, Vase, 1922

in depth and width, evidence of the artist's hand that effectively conveys the frenetic energy of New York at night. The sgraffito technique and Egyptian Blue glaze (inspired by the recent discovery of King Tut's tomb) are believed to have come to Cowan via glazing specialist Arthur Baggs, who was at Cowan from fall 1925 through summer 1928.[32] Baggs employed both in his earlier work at Marblehead Pottery in Massachusetts, such as this vase with delicate tree decoration (FIG. 53). Schreckengost also used the sgraffito technique to create undulating lines representative of ocean waves and seaweed on a series of fish vases (FIG. 54). In contrast to this hand-drawn decoration technique, Schreckengost chose to cast the body of his *Jazz* bowl in a mold, with the foot formed separately and then applied.

Schreckengost's original design featured a parabolic, or U-shaped, bowl, a form chosen because its tall, straight sides suggested the unlimited heights of city skyscrapers.[33] Yet this shape tended to warp in the kiln, forcing it to be revised. The second version, the example discussed here, features a more traditional flared shape, which gave

102   AMERICA GOES MODERN

more strength and stability to the rim.[34] For both of these versions, in order to ensure that each bowl's nightlife imagery was consistent with that of the others, patterns were used for the basic layout but details were done freehand and vary considerably from bowl to bowl. In keeping with Cowan's new studio feel, Schreckengost encouraged improvisation by the artists who executed the details on the bowls, likely Thelma Frazier, Whitney Atchley, Edris Eckhardt, and Charles E. Murphy.[35] Yet, the decorating process, which required scratching the pattern into the glaze by hand, was prohibitively time consuming and therefore too expensive to produce in quantity. Schreckengost had to recalibrate again. For the third version of the *Jazz* bowl, the nightlife scene was formed in relief by the bowl's initial casting. This model was fired prior to being coated with black engobe that could then be scraped off fairly quickly to reveal its raised design before being glazed and fired again.[36] The *Poor Man's Jazz* bowl, as the third version is commonly called, is significantly smaller than Schreckengost's original and lacks its parabolic form and handmade spontaneity. While it is not known exactly how many *Jazz* bowls were created, at least twelve examples of the first version are known today, eight of the second version (including the one shown here), and sixteen of the molded third version.[37] In addition, Schreckengost also created a few individual punch bowls with sgraffito imagery of nightlife less specific to New York—*Cocktails & Cigarettes, Rhythm in Blue, Night Club*—as well as coordinating plates, such as *Danse Moderne*.[38]

Despite its modern imagery and connotations that bring the atmosphere of adventurous New York nightlife into the home, the *Jazz* bowl—meant to serve punch—takes the form of a traditional, old-fashioned vessel. Punch was the original mixed drink and widely popular in early America. Yet, by 1930, cocktails eclipsed punch's popularity. Cowan's 1931 catalog—its final one—optimistically claimed that the company's new designs heralded "the Return of the Punch Bowl" in an effort to defend and justify the significant expenditures of producing a series of outmoded bowl forms. The catalog text also offered potential other uses for the form, suggesting that one of the punch bowls would make "a good trophy or presentation piece for Country Clubs and the like" or "the Punch Bowl filled with leaves or flowers is most effective on a console table."[39] Indeed, if it had not been for the original *Jazz* bowl commission specifically requesting a serving vessel for punch, it seems unlikely Cowan would have produced any such bowls, no matter how modern the imagery.

Schreckengost designed the original *Jazz* bowl without knowing the identity of his client. But "a week after the bowl was shipped, the gallery called to say that the lady who ordered it was so pleased that she wanted to order two more. She said that her husband Franklin loved it, too. One was [for] her house in Hyde Park, New York, and the other . . . the White House in Washington." It was only then that Schreckengost discovered his client was Eleanor Roosevelt, and that her husband, then governor of New York, was running for president in 1932.[40]

Eleanor commissioned the bowl to celebrate Franklin's reelection as governor of New York. By 1930, many former supporters of Prohibition, including Eleanor herself, who did not drink, had changed their mind about the national alcohol ban.[41] Franklin Roosevelt, who had a reputation for mixing unusual gin martinis (with excessive vermouth, a dash of absinthe, and whatever other mixers he had available) at his regularly held cocktail hours, came out vehemently in favor of repeal as the Democratic candidate for the presidency in 1932.[42] He defeated the incumbent, Herbert Hoover, in a landslide, and Congress proposed the 21st Amendment without waiting for his inauguration. On December 5, 1933, upon gaining sufficient states for ratification, FDR immediately announced the end of Prohibition over the radio.

In 1943, ten years after Prohibition's repeal and in the midst of World War II, the military wanted to boost morale of "homesick troops in unfamiliar surroundings" with "a remembrance of something

distinctly American." They chose to stage a New York jazz nightclub in *Life* magazine photographer Gjon Mili's studio. For seven hours, the studio swarmed with jazz leaders gathered for "the greatest jam session ever held in New York," including, among others, Duke Ellington, Eddie Cantor, and Billie Holiday, who got her start as a teenager in Harlem during Prohibition (**FIG. 55**). The performers mixed and mingled with their gathered audience, which included the president of Condé Nast and the editor in chief of *Vogue*, drinking and smoking at a haphazard assemblage of café tables. Audio recordings of the event were sent overseas, and Mili's photographs of the "music indigenous to the U.S." were featured in an October 1943 issue of *Life*. [43] The New York jazz nightclub had become not only a symbol of modernity but also of America itself.

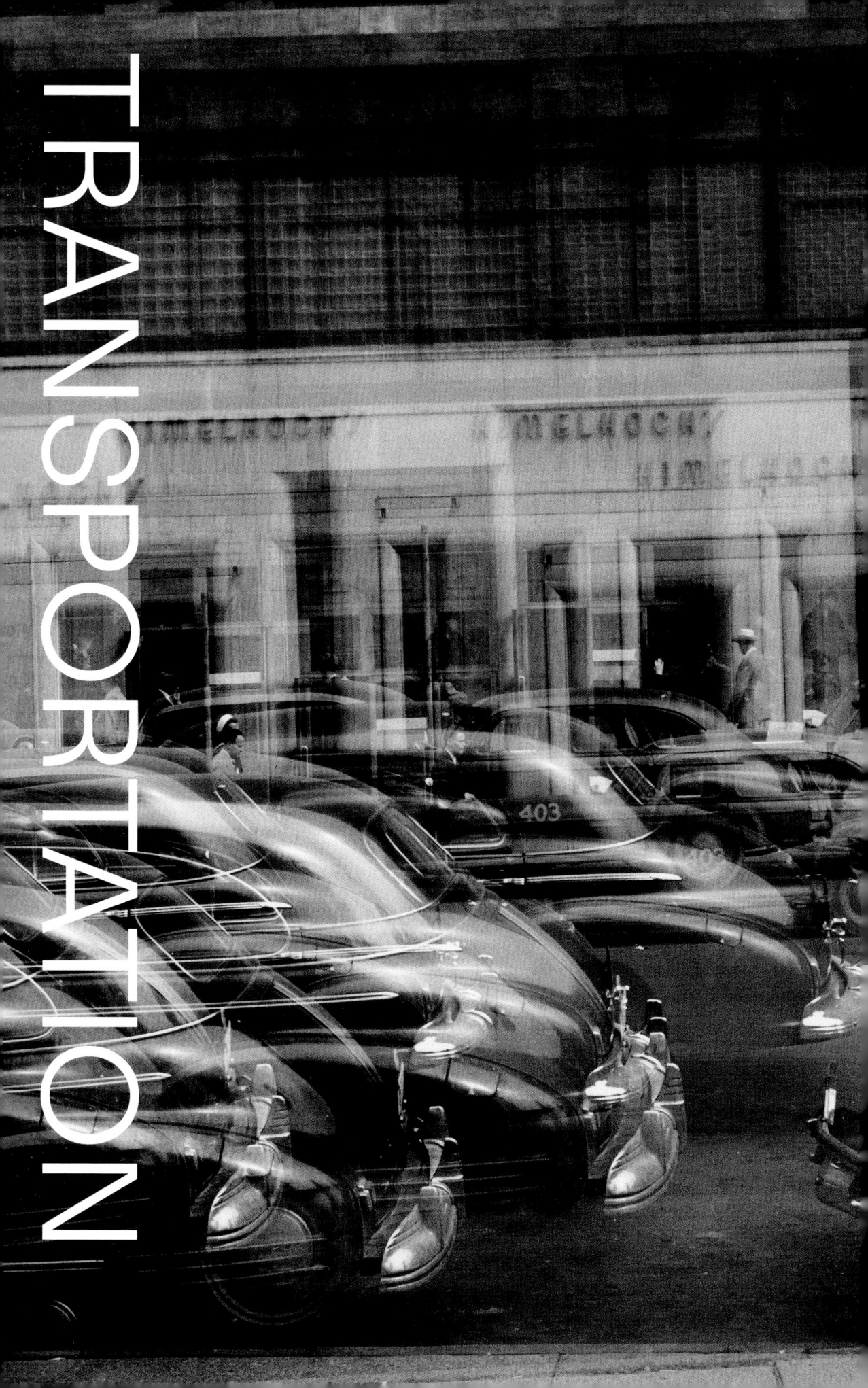

TRANSPORTATION

In 1921, Alfred P. Sloan, recently tapped to run the General Motors Corporation (GM), faced a big challenge. Despite its diversity of makers and models, the GM conglomeration of independent car manufacturers only earned 12.7% of all automobile sales in the United States. Meanwhile, GM's biggest competitor, the Ford Motor Corporation, only offered one product—the Model T—yet claimed an astonishing 56% of market share.[1] Knowing he could not match Ford's production efficiency and volume, or the Model T's low cost, Sloan took another approach and focused on design. He reorganized GM to offer a series of automobile lines that suited the American public's various tastes and budgets—from utilitarian, affordable Chevrolets to glitzy, expensive Cadillacs—all of which were restyled annually to reflect changing fashions and foster a sense of progress. Sloan's strategy worked and GM's sales increased, but he needed to sustain this new style initiative. To do so, he turned not to his engineers but to a flashy and charismatic stylist, Harley J. Earl.[2]

Before coming to GM in 1927, Harley J. Earl (1893–1969) made a name for himself in his hometown of Los Angeles, creating custom car bodies for Hollywood's elite. One-of-a-kind, handcrafted automobile coaches built on separately acquired chassis were an exclusive alternative to production cars in the early twentieth century. Earl had grown up in his father's horse-drawn carriage turned automobile shop, which also made props for early movies.[3] In 1919, shortly after Earl returned home from studying engineering at Stanford University, the family shop was acquired by Cadillac's West Coast distributor, Don Lee, who kept Harley on to run the custom business. As he later joked, Earl got started in the car design business "in a big way" as one of his first specialty commissions was an oversize custom car for silent film comedian and actor Roscoe "Fatty" Arbuckle.[4] Built on an enormous Pierce-Arrow chassis, the completed car cost over $25,000. Ever the showman, Earl capitalized on Arbuckle's soaring popularity by putting the finished car on view in Don Lee's Cadillac showroom, where it drew an estimated ten thousand onlookers in just under a week.[5] Other clients included Mary Pickford, Tom Mix, Douglas Fairbanks, and Cecil B. DeMille.

Standing six feet four inches tall and with a personality to match his size, Earl cultivated a reputation for making "cars for the stars" that attracted attention in the car industry.[6] After bragging to Cadillac's head, Larry Fisher, that he could "make a car . . . , like your Chevrolet, to look like a Cadillac," Earl was summoned from Los Angeles to Detroit to prove his talent as a design consultant for GM's newly conceived LaSalle model.[7] The LaSalle was to be a youthful, stylish, less expensive companion to the Cadillac, filling a gap where the company was losing sales to competitors. Earl based his design on the Hispano Suiza, a super luxury car made in France, and managed to keep production costs within budget. Released in March 1927, Earl's LaSalle was a resounding success (FIG. 56). Critics praised it: "In the design of the

bodies the engineers have struck out boldly in the direction of new effects. The result is a body design that is new, striking and decidedly distinctive. The cars are racy and graceful, well proportioned and beautifully harmonious."[8] And, more importantly, sales were strong. The LaSalle gained attention and fame as the car of Charles Lindbergh, whose record-breaking transatlantic flight took place that May, and as the honorary pace car for the Indianapolis 500, one of the most famous motor car races in the world. The LaSalle's undisputed success in both reviews and sales prompted Sloan to establish GM's Art and Colour Section, the first styling department at a U.S. automobile company. He hired Harley Earl to direct it.

In the process of building his team and launching a unified approach to car design, Earl inaugurated the field of automobile styling and trained the first generation of American car designers.[9] Although his team met some resistance from seasoned engineers and production men who questioned the need for the department's services, Earl persisted, often winning over his detractors or outwitting those who tried to undermine him. For example, when uncooperative engineers told him his ideas were impossible, Earl hired his own engineers in the Art and Colour Section to prove otherwise. But the Great Depression posed new challenges. By 1932, Cadillac's LaSalle—Earl's first success—was slated for cancellation after the following season because sales had dropped by 85% over the past three years.[10] GM had already eliminated Buick's companion line, the Marquette, and Oldsmobile's Viking. To save the LaSalle line, GM's Art and Colour designers needed what Earl would later describe as one of his team's "explosive bursts of spanking-new themes."[11] They seized upon the growing trend of streamlining.

Streamlined design, which emphasized fast-paced motion and efficiency with generous curves, rounded corners, and long lines, stemmed from the science of speed and airflow. In the 1920s, the study of streamlining took on renewed importance with the rise of airplanes and efforts to increase their speed, range, and carrying capacity. Early adaptations of streamlined principles can be seen in the closed cockpit, cantilevered wings, and ribbed metal of a *Ford Trimotor* airplane model (**FIG. 57**). Ford's fleet of Trimotors initiated commercial aviation in the United States when it began operations in 1926. While initially focused on aviation, research on streamlining quickly impacted the design of other modes of transportation, including ocean liners, trains, streetcars, and, of course, automobiles. The first automobiles to embrace streamlining were custom-built race cars that competed in the highly publicized land speed and endurance competitions held at Daytona Beach, Florida, and at Utah's Bonneville salt flats. These cars proved that streamlining made a difference at high speeds.[12] As the *New York Times* explained in 1928, "The designer strives for a form without projections; for it is easier to drive a smooth, correctly designed bulk through the air than to rake it with many excrescences."[13]

Inspired by these race cars and the research behind them, car companies began conducting their own aerodynamic experiments, with Chrysler engaged in wind tunnel tests by 1927 (under consultation with aviation pioneer Orville Wright). At first, however, designers' streamlined proposals were rejected by automobile executives for being too radical. The few exceptions, including the 1931 REO Royale and 1932 Graham Blue Streak, both designed by Amos Northup, only adopted streamlined elements in a tentative way, largely in their fenders. Yet, the November 1932 publication of industrial designer Norman Bel Geddes's book *Horizons* proved a turning point. Geddes had spent years proposing radically aerodynamic concepts for all types of transportation. With his characteristic bravado and flair for drama, Geddes complemented his futuristic visions of a streamlined world with rhetoric imbued with optimism, progress, and imagination. His book was rife with fantastical concepts akin to the design he used for a medal to celebrate GM's twenty-fifth anniversary in 1933. This silver-plated bronze medal features a speeding, teardrop-shaped vehicle with a perpendicular wing rising above it and the motto, "To the Advancement of Motor Transportation" (**FIG. 58**).[14] *Horizons*, and the

57 *Ford Trimotor* airplane model, about 1929

extensive press surrounding it, provided streamlining with a massive promotional push, advocating it as the way of the future. Carl Otto, one of Earl's designers, later recalled that the book "had great impact" on GM's Art and Colour Section.[15]

Earl's team began exploring how rounded curves and fluid shapes would look on their highest-end car bodies. This key moment of transition is captured in a preliminary Cadillac-LaSalle design model that mixes a newly streamlined grille and fenders with an older-style car body (FIG. 59). Models, such as this one-quarter-scale example made of painted mahogany, played a crucial role in Earl's unified design approach. Prior to his arrival at GM, each element of a car was designed and made separately, then assembled. As Earl described, "Fisher Body would draw up the body and the hood, and then they would model the

body . . . And then the divisions would take that drawing, and they would put on their front end and their fenders and wheels, and then they would all go to work and make it and put them together. Well, when I worked on the LaSalle, we didn't do it that way. We made it all one: built it right together as one unit, rather than separate it."[16] Models were essential to this process, as Earl's design team worked out the countless details that made up a car's new look, from overall form to finishes, in a range of body styles, including two-seater coupes and larger sedans. While some models were made of wood, such as this example, others were sculpted in clay over a wood frame-work, a process that allows for rapid adjustments and remains part of the car design process to the present day. In their studio, Earl's team created myriad exploratory drawings and models (in both clay and wood) in a range of scales, from tabletop to full size.

The most distinctive streamlining features of this design model are its skirted fenders, characterized by truncated, tapered backs and bulbous fronts. These fenders expand the body of the car, visually filling the space behind each wheel, instead of being winglike projec-tions. Channels between the fenders and the car's front end were designed for airflow in order to limit drag at high speeds.[17] With these few early streamlined features, the preliminary design model serves as a preview of GM's ultimate embrace of curves in its 1934 LaSalle pro-duction car. On the finished 1934 LaSalle, the car's fenders wrap even more fully over the front wheels to completely hide the chassis (**FIG. 60**). Reviewers compared them to the cowling of airplane landing gear, and they also resemble the teardrop shape deemed most aero-dynamic in wind tunnel experiments.[18] This teardrop shape is echoed by the headlights, the torpedo-shaped hood ornament, and, as exclaimed by the *New York Times*, "even . . . in door handles."[19] Also, in contrast to this preliminary model, the completed LaSalle incorpo-rated curves throughout its entire body, extending from the rounded fenders to the cab's roof, back, and windows. These curves soften the car's angles and protruding parts, both eliminating drag and unifying the design. As GM designer Bill Mitchell later said of his predecessor, Earl "liked round, big rounded surfaces . . . that was new, really."[20] To ensure that the overall unity of the curvaceous design was empha-sized, GM recommended only one body color, as the design had "no logical breaking point for two-tone color application."[21] This monotone approach to car design was already evident in the preliminary wooden model, on which black paint covers its original yellow, possibly part of a color trial. It also features real rubber tires and metal handles, head-lights, hubcaps (including an innovative "knock-off" hubcap on the spare tire), and a removable (and thus exchangeable) grille.[22]

The model's sharply tapered hood, along with its arresting V-shaped radiator grille and angled windshield, evokes a sense of fast, forward motion, much like that of a race car. Such features made Earl's cars "look like they are going like hell just sitting still," a characteristic

that the designer desired.[23] On the finished 1934 LaSalle, this effect was augmented by having the front become even more narrow than shown on the model. In fact, the production car's hood was so tapered that it needed an inline engine rather than the Cadillac-derived V-8 engine that had been previously employed, a notable downgrade in power and performance in order to accommodate the new design. Other distinctive features of the finished 1934 production car not shown by this early model include the five "porthole" hood vents on either side of the front, the "biplane" strip bumpers, a streamlined back with hidden compartment for the spare tire, and the rubberized fabric roof insert that was needed on closed cabs until 1935 when GM's all-steel "Turret Top" was introduced.

The model emphasizes the car body's long, low shape, well suited for pleasure cruising on smoothly paved roads at high speeds. By contrast, the earliest production cars, such as the Kissel (FIG. 61) and Ford's Model T, closely followed the form of the horse-drawn carriages they replaced. And thus, they were vertically oriented, boxy, and tall, with a reputation for slow and steady progress on any terrain. The trend away from carriage-style bodies toward lower, longer cars was an essential precursor to streamlining. Earl later said his "primary purpose for twenty-eight years has been to lengthen and lower the American automobile, at times in reality and always in appearance."[24]

Given the significant time lapse between the conception of a new design and the public release of a production car, the LaSalle model itself likely dates to 1930–33, with certain details, such as the grille and fenders, reworked over the course of those years. The ultimate goal was to strike an ideal balance between modern and marketable, as Earl wished to lead the car industry while acknowledging the public's "resistance to sudden and extreme change."[25]

The origin of the LaSalle design for 1934—most notable for the "pontoon" fenders seen in embryonic stages on the preliminary design model—makes for a dramatic story. Upon returning from Europe's fall car shows in November 1932, Earl encountered a full-size rendering recently drawn by designer Jules Agramonte for a new front-end. According to one of the designers working in the studio, "Earl came in and got terribly excited about it, and they were working on it night and day from then on."[26] With a flair for presentation honed during his time in Hollywood, Earl orchestrated a theatrical reveal the following August to the GM executives who intended to scrap the line. As he raised a curtain unveiling a full-size wooden mockup of a completed 1934 LaSalle design, Earl announced, "This, gentlemen, is the LaSalle we will NOT be building."[27] The GM execs were so taken by the new design that they approved the LaSalle's continuation on the spot.

By carefully incorporating the trend for streamlining without being too radical, Earl prevailed. His LaSalle line was saved. Dubbed "The World's Newest Car" in its promotional advertising, the streamlined LaSalle was introduced to the public at the January 1934 New York Auto Show, but due to its late approval, it was not put into production until March of that year.[28] Demand was high, and, for a second time, a LaSalle was given the honor of setting the pace in Indiana. Unlike Chrysler's more radically streamlined Airflow, also unveiled in 1934, Earl's car struck an ideal balance between the new and the familiar. As GM's marketing explained, "La Salle body styling is advanced, modern and beautiful . . . [without being] gaudy, extreme or freakish."[29] Harley Earl's 1934 LaSalle was the first American production car to *successfully* employ streamlining in a big way.

Despite streamlining's basis in scientific study, by 1934 it had become more about creating the appearance of speed rather than actual efficiency. As a *New York Times* reviewer of the 1934 car show explained, "although streamlining has been of material aid in beautifying the car, the average driver has benefited only slightly in added mileage or gas-saving. Despite all the promotion and ballyhoo about the high percentage of gas-saving, actual tests prove that there is a saving, but it becomes material only at very high speeds. Wind noises, however, have been decreased to a great extent."[30] GM president Sloan acknowledged the same shortly thereafter, saying that while GM's cars were influenced by "the trend toward streamlining—a vogue very much in evidence at this time . . . the contribution of streamlining is definitely limited to the question of styling."[31] But by then, streamlining featured so prominently in America's national culture that its look mattered more than its performance.

Only a few months after the 1934 New York car show, two new "streamliners" were unveiled at the Century of Progress International Exhibition's second season in Chicago. These trains, made for the Chicago, Burlington & Quincy and Union Pacific Railroads (and both driven by power systems developed by GM), became instant icons. As *Business Week* later reported, upon first seeing the sleek, all-metal trains stripped of extraneous details, "something clicked in the mind of Mr. Average Man, and the streamlined era had arrived."[32] Called "wingless airplanes on tracks," the trains offered the railroad industry hope of recapturing customers lost to the automobile.[33] To get to the Exhibition's opening on May 26, 1934, the Burlington Zephyr made its first highly publicized dusk-to-dawn run from Denver to Chicago, cheered on by admirers all along the route and shattering speed records. High-end working models were sold to enthusiastic fans (**FIG. 62**), and the train even starred in its own movie: *The Silver Streak* (1934). For the Union Pacific's version, called the M-10000, Harley Earl was asked to consult on the train's design around the same time that his team was working on the new streamlined LaSalle (**FIG. 63**). Although the M-10000's design, with the engine's hood protruding

110 MILE PER HOUR—UNION PACIFIC STREAMLINED PASSENGER TRAIN

below the windshield, resembled an airplane, Earl claimed they actually "copied an automobile."[34] Not to be outdone by its competitor, the Union Pacific train broke the coast-to-coast record in October 1934, streaking across the nation with its sides adorned by bright yellow stripes. Together with the Zephyr, both created such spectacle that reporters said their coverage "reads like a story of a sporting event."[35]

All this sensational press attention on speedy, streamlined vehicles helped the transportation industry market trips as exciting and glamorous experiences. To further attract customers, vehicle interiors were made as streamlined as exteriors, with modern, luxurious fittings that symbolized the fast pace of modern American life. The observation car in the Burlington Zephyr had plush club chairs, pastel walls, pearl gray carpet and curtains, and an overall airy, sleek feel enhanced by the lack of overhead luggage shelves. When American Airlines' DC-3 Flagship planes entered service in 1936, meals were served with silver-plated flatware with handles shaped like the plane's streamlined prow (FIG. 64). The interior of Earl's 1934 LaSalle—described by GM as "the Youthful Aristocrat of Motordom"—featured a symmetrical dashboard with flush, round gauges, chrome accents, and a sleek steering wheel decorated by steel-wire spokes and the car's *LaS* logo.

The association of streamlining with luxury—given the high price tag of the fastest, most prestigious travel—was enhanced by the style's appearance in numerous 1930s Hollywood movies. For example, the set of *Grand Hotel* (1932) starring Greta Garbo largely takes place in a lavish, streamlined hotel lobby centered on a circular reception desk

63 Postcard of a Union Pacific M-10000, about 1934

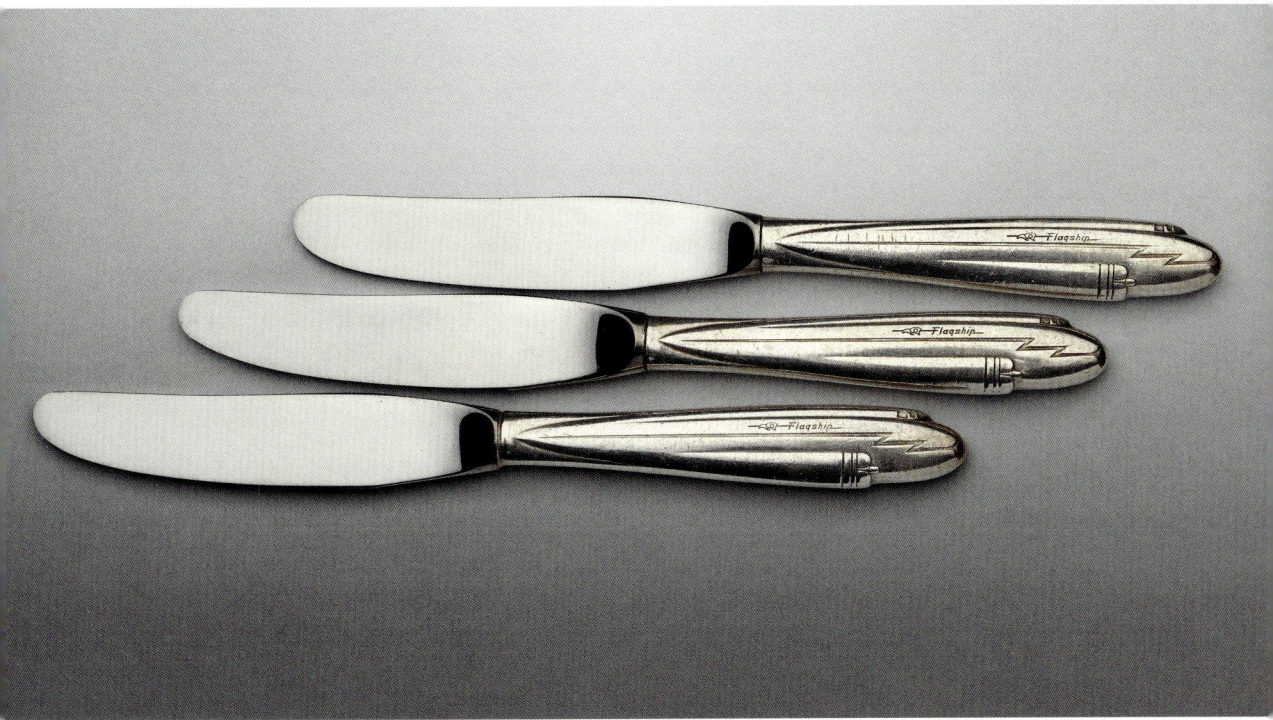

64 *American Airlines DC-3 Flagship flatware, designed 1936*

and bustling with travelers on the move. *Swing Time* (1936) features Fred Astaire and Ginger Rogers's exuberant dancing in a streamlined studio, their speedy tempo matched by the implied motion of the set design. And at the beginning of *Topper* (1937), Cary Grant's character, whose stylish New York penthouse is replete with curves, crashes his futuristic streamlined car with "pontoon" fenders. Hollywood movies and Hollywood stars glamorized and popularized streamlining for the American public.

By merging science with style, streamlining's presence served as a promise of not only speed but also smartness and modern mechanics. Streamlined vehicles hid complex mechanics behind rounded exterior shells, thereby simplifying operation for the consumer and leaving the inner workings to the experts: designers, engineers, manufacturers, and mechanics. In this way—and in an apparent contradiction to the modernist dictate that form should follow function—streamlining reassured the public that they need not concern themselves with such details as how a combustion engine powers a car in order to drive, or how a plane defies gravity in order to fly. The style's connotations of forward motion soon elided with notions of forward progress. This drove industrial designer Egmont Arens to advocate it as a means of economic recovery, writing in a telegram to President Roosevelt that it "has captured American imagination to mean modern, efficient, well-organized, sweet clean and beautiful."[36] And as streamlined design came to symbolize national pride in the country's many technical innovations in transporation, it fostered the sense that the nation was speeding forward out of the Depression into a prosperous, Hollywood-like future in which anything seemed possible.

While the streamlined look gave Americans the impression of luxury, modernity, and progress, the cars themselves delivered on those promises. In 1933, a presidential commission surveying contemporary changes in American life concluded about the automobile "that no invention of such far reaching importance was ever diffused with such rapidity or so quickly exerted influences that ramified through the national culture, transforming even habits of thought and language."[37] The number of cars registered in the United States rose dramatically between 1920 and 1930 from 8.1 to 23 million, and then to 27.5 million over the next ten years.[38] For those who could afford them, automobiles provided freedom from the limitations of rail and trolley lines. Go where you want, when you want; cars offered a new form of independence.

Car infrastructure—roads, parking, services, and destinations—reshaped the landscape. Limited-access parkways, which had no intersections to interrupt traffic flow, were made especially for pleasure cruising, with their paved roads, gentle curves, on- and off-ramps, ample sightlines, and scenic vistas. Though the first such streamlined roadway, the Long Island Motor Parkway (1908), was privately funded, it was followed by government-funded projects, starting with the Bronx River Parkway of 1922. And, while city streets historically had served numerous purposes, from extensions of stores to children's playgrounds, the automobile turned fast, streamlined circulation into their primary function, as emphasized by photographer Harry Callahan's use of overlapping exposures to evoke the swift hustle and bustle of the streets of Detroit (**FIG. 65**). Wherever possible, roads were widened, turns were softened, and a standardized system for traffic control and signage developed. Insufficient parking, especially in high-density, skyscraper-filled cities, resulted in the development of street meters, first introduced in Oklahoma City in 1935, and parking garages, such as the eleven floors for cars included in Detroit's headquarters for GM's Fisher Body division, opened in 1928.

Newly necessary small businesses, such as gas stations and drive-ins, provided service, fuel, and food to those on the road. The Chicago industrial design firm of Iannelli Studios designed a sleek, modern service station sheathed in white terra-cotta tile, steel, and glass with pops of color to indicate the door and pumps (**FIG. 66**). Its horizontally oriented building with protruding central office suggested streamlined traffic flow, and its numerous garage bays and white exterior promised swift, clean, expert service, along with the reassurance that drivers need not be their own mechanics. To animate the rendering, the illustrator depicted a woman driver pulling up to the station in a sleek luxury car similar to models from GM's Cadillac-LaSalle division, the epitome of style at the time. Even a car's fuel could be

DESIGN FOR STANDARD SERVICE STATION

modernized, as a 1934 advertisement claimed, "whether your car is streamlined or not, Blue Sunoco will give you streamlined speed and economy—because its refining process eliminates those undesirable parts of petroleum which retard swift acceleration, high speed and knockless power."[39] Drive-ins similarly supported road travel, with "Quick Service in Your Car" provided by female car hops to customers who remained comfortably ensconced in their vehicles, a new type of private space within the public sphere (FIG. 67).[40]

Cars provided new leisure pursuits, opening the countryside for the increasingly urban-based American public. "The mere possession of a car is the open sesame to a variety of out-of-door delights," said the *New York Times* in 1935.[41] City dwellers could spend a hot summer afternoon at the beach, enjoy a long weekend in the country, or voyage forth on a cross-country camping trek to see the nation's natural beauty at parks recently consolidated under the National Park Service, formed in 1916. They left the city in droves, as one *New York Times*

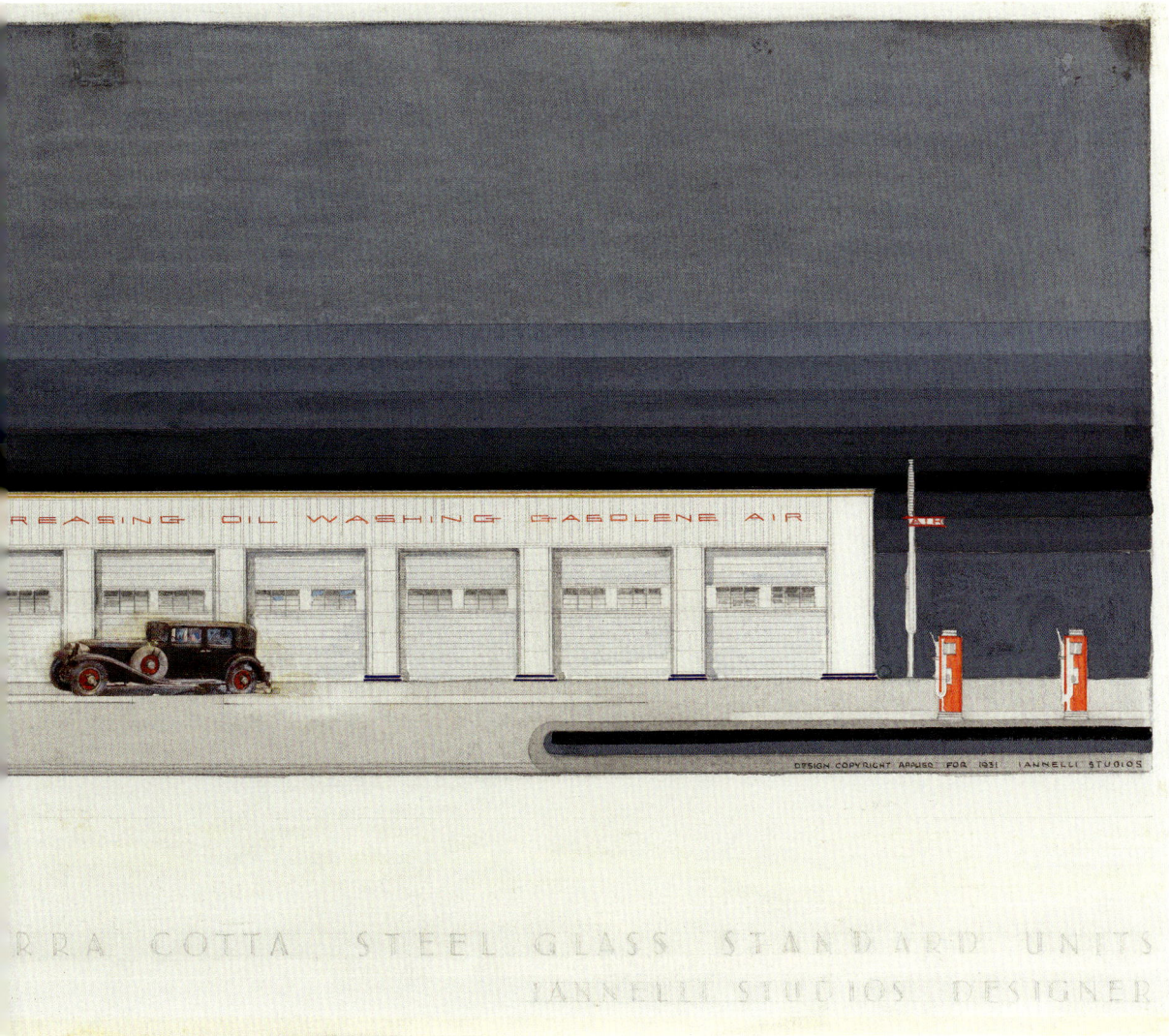

REASING OIL WASHING GASOLENE AIR

TERRA COTTA, STEEL, GLASS STANDARD UNITS
IANNELLI STUDIOS DESIGNER

reporter described in 1935: "Ten years ago the long week-end out of town was the extravagance of the few; now New York takes it for granted."[42]

Numerous new products—often with streamlined styling—aided these driving adventures. Because "vacation time is, before all else, picture-taking time," Eastman Kodak hired industrial designer Walter Dorwin Teague to modernize its personal cameras, which had already spurred a trend for amateur photography in the first decades of the twentieth century.[43] Teague's affordable *Baby Brownie* (1934) and high-end *Bantam Special* (1936) offered customers a range of stylish pocket cameras with which to memorialize their trips. The cameras' streamlined designs, with curved edges and parallel speed lines, evoke the ease and quickness with which they capture their subjects (**FIG. 68**; see **FIG. 88**). Much to the dismay of outdoor purists, music was enjoyed by vacationers who "tune in with the city and civilization from which they pretend to flee" using portable radios and phonographs

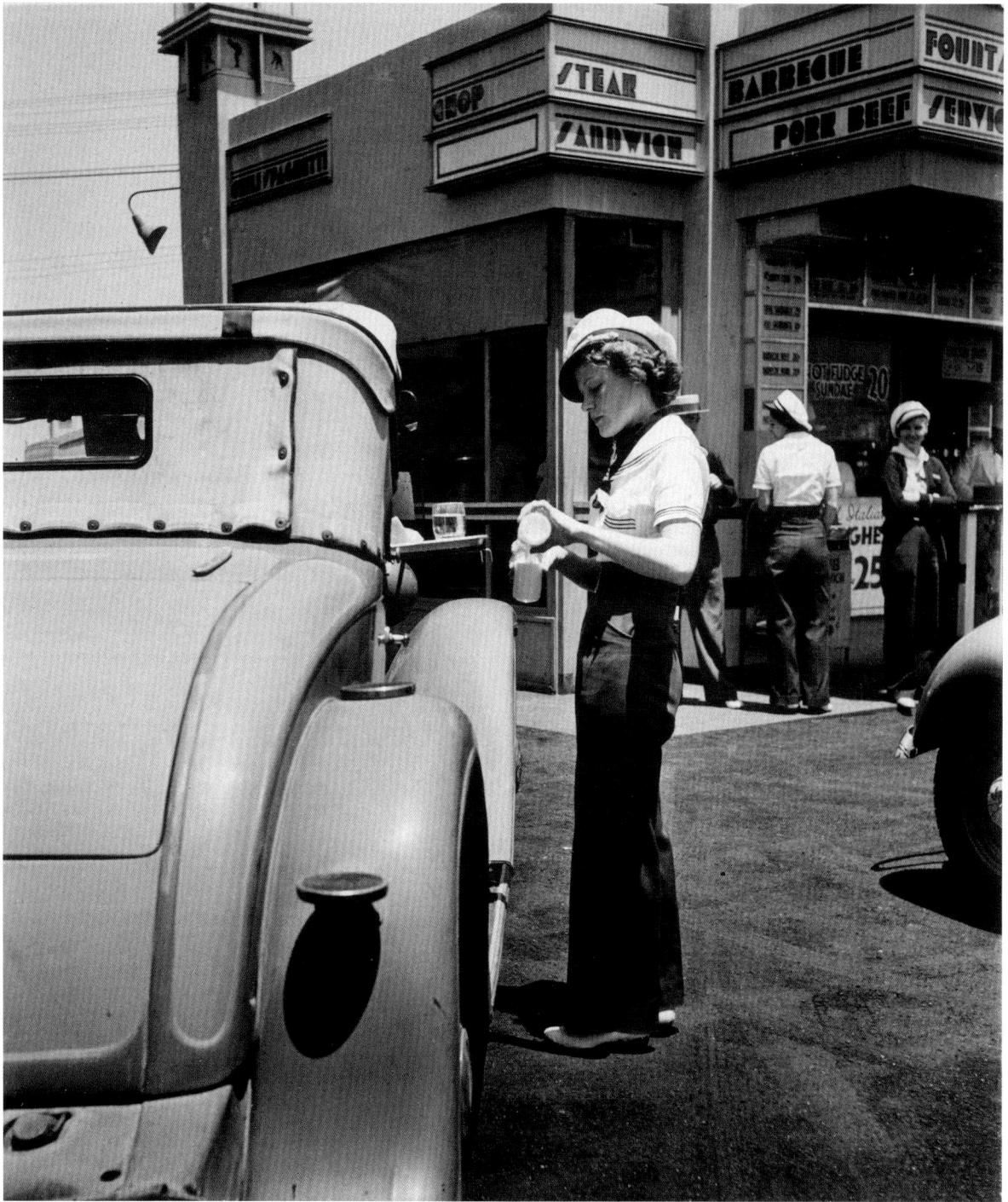

67　John Gutmann, *Car Hops, Early Drive-in Restaurant, Hollywood, California*, 1935

68　Walter Dorwin Teague, *Bantam Special* camera, designed 1936

that could be easily carried in the car, such as the lightweight aluminum example by industrial designer John Vassos for RCA Victor (**FIG. 69**).[44]

At home, automobiles allowed for new residential suburbs with large housing plots that no longer had to be oriented around public transit lines. In these neighborhoods, cars were essential to American family life as well as symbols of prosperity. They brought the family together for vacations and assisted housewives with their domestic duties. Even children could have their own cars. Starting in 1938, Viktor Schreckengost collaborated with Murray Ohio Company, a car parts producer turned toy manufacturer, to create pedal cars. Schreckengost based their streamlined styling on conversations with car designers about upcoming trends (**FIGS. 70, 71**).

Yet, some saw cars as a potential danger to the family unit. Wives, formerly restricted to the home, might drive away from their family, enticed by the thrill of the open road. Young people could travel, unchaperoned, to dances that were "too often followed by the joy ride."[45] And the newly popular Sunday drive cut into church attendance.[46] As Ralph W. Sherman, editor of *Motor* magazine, wrote in 1927 of the societal changes wrought by the automobile, "every time a woman learns to drive—and thousands do every year—it is a threat at yesterday's order of things."[47]

While cars may have encouraged women to be more modern, women, in turn, greatly shaped how those cars looked. Women were understood, as Earl later acknowledged, to "have a lot to say about what they want in the new family car."[48] In the 1920s, women were credited with driving the shift from open to closed automobile cabs, with converting the car "from a clumsy vehicle into a thing of beauty" offered in numerous colors, and with the establishment of the annual automobile restyle. As one reporter chauvinistically claimed, they "have changed the style of their clothes each season for so long, . . . they must have variety in motor car styles."[49] Automobile advertisements featuring stylish women turned the car into a fashion accessory, and new clothing trends for short, straight dresses and snug cloche hats provided the freedom of movement needed for driving. Such clothing, promoted by Hollywood movies, came to symbolize the modern woman's liberation from the home, in part due to the car, and from traditional gender roles. It also provided an opportunity to showcase modern fabrics along with streamlined silhouettes, as seen in a cloche hat and matching scarf made of fabric printed with an abstracted landscape design, that would afford a flash of color and style as one zipped by (**FIG. 72**).[50] General Motors, with its pioneering emphasis on styling, led the industry in focusing on women customers. GM's marketing for the 1934 LaSalle highlighted its fashionable design while also stressing luxury, value, ease of operation, comfort, and fun. For example, the text of a 1934 *Ladies Home Journal* advertisement for the LaSalle opened with "Women of America, *you—above all*

others—know how priceless is *style*. . . . For *nothing* can be *desirable* that is *anyways* out of date." And in the early 1930s, streamlining was the height of fashion.

Although it originated in transportation, streamlining quickly entered the American home as well. The 1932 Philadelphia "Design for the Machine" exhibition contrasted household furnishings with "models of ocean liners, locomotives, airplanes and motor cars . . . [which] suggest the modern background for furnishings and also the sources of some of the forms, structural principles and decorative motifs" on those household goods.[51] The Design for Living House at Chicago's 1933 Century of Progress Exhibition included Gilbert Rohde's clock for Herman Miller, with speed lines of curved, chromium-plated banding wrapping its rounded front corner (**FIG. 73**). And at the National Alliance of Art and Industry's 1934 Exhibition at Rockefeller Center, a critic identified a new "national style" that replaced "sharp edges and corners" with "numerous curved forms . . . in the commercial designs of utilitarian products."[52]

When used on household goods, streamlined design suggested both an enhancement of function and the fast pace of modern life. For example, the curvaceous frame of Kem Weber's *Air Line* chair (1934) offered comfort to the sitter while evoking the cantilevered wings, forward motion, and gravity-defying flight of a plane (**FIG. 74**).[53] Its lightness and ability to break down and pack flat also made it possible to move the chair quickly and easily as needed. The slanted teardrop shape of Peter Müller-Munk's chromium-plated *Normandie* pitcher (1935) implies it pours its contents as neatly and swiftly as the ocean liner of the same name sliced through the water (**FIG. 75**).[54] And the record-shaped disc of Walter Dorwin Teague's *Bluebird* radio (1935) for Sparton, which shares its name and color with the celebrated race car, resembles a vehicle gauge, a reminder of radio's ability to transport listeners instantly through sound (see **FIG. 32**).

Today's streamlined kitchen, with its continuous counters, built-in cupboards, and integrated sink and stove, first developed in the 1930s as the rise of new electrical devices and the decline in domestic hired help prompted a quest for efficiency in food preparation. Appliances,

74   Kem Weber, *Air Line* chair, designed 1934

75   Peter Müller-Munk, *Normandie* pitcher, designed 1935

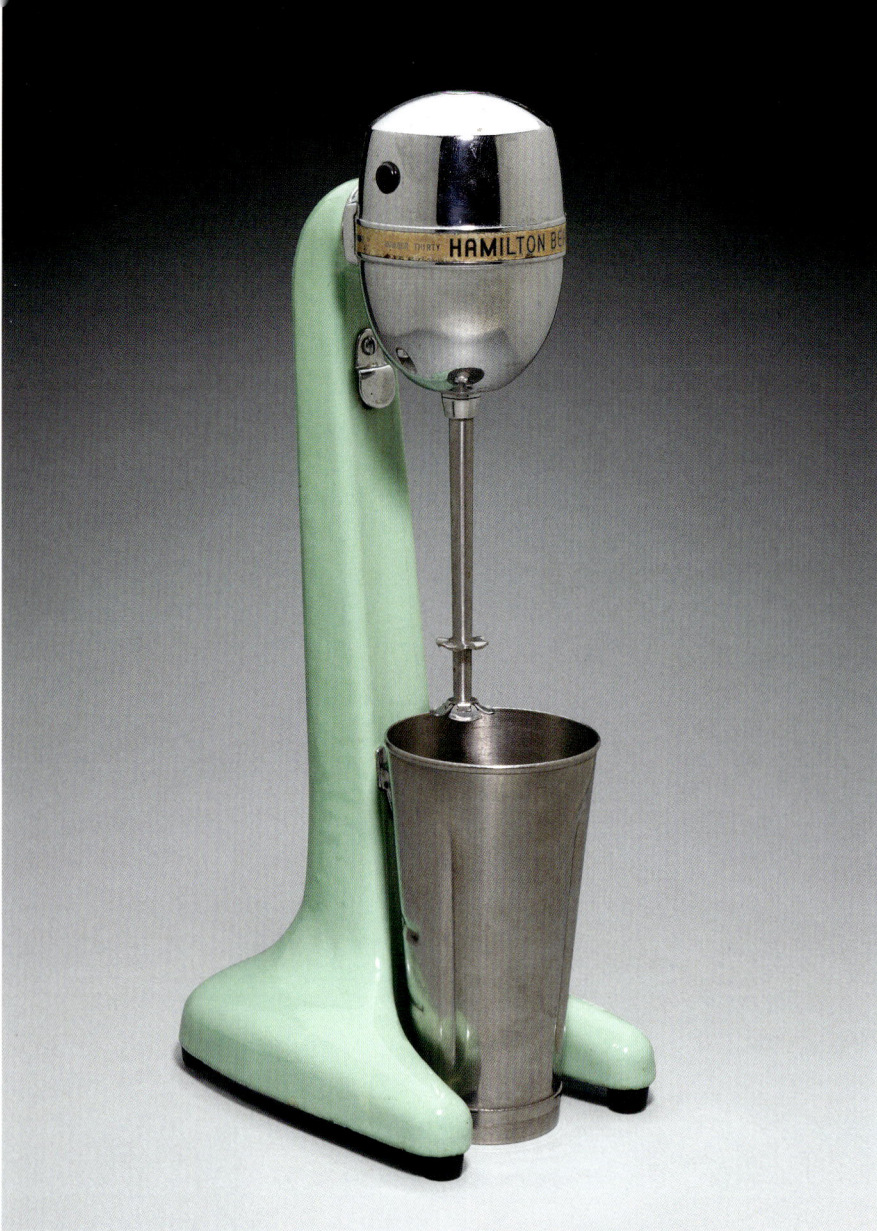

including refrigerators, toasters, and even milkshake mixers were streamlined so that their mechanics were concealed behind rounded exteriors, making the devices look modern but also straightforward to use, quick and easy to clean with no crevices to catch dirt, and void of dangerously protruding sharp corners which could slow cooks down (FIG. 76). Streamlining also extended to tableware, as seen in the brightly colored, curvy, and popular *Fiesta Ware*, designed by Frederick H. Rhead for West Virginia's Homer Laughlin China Company. The straight sides of the *Fiesta Disc* water pitcher (designed 1938) ensured it could be efficiently stored in a cabinet, while its design evoked motion through its wheel-like shape and the expanding concentric circles on its sides (FIG. 77).[55]

The widespread application of streamlining was not without its critics. In reviewing the 1934 Industrial Arts Exposition, Edward Alden Jewell commented on "the present tendency in America to make

'modernism' a fetish," asking, "Is there genuinely a reason why our pencil sharpeners should be 'streamlined'?"[56] Industrial designer Henry Dreyfuss, in *Designing for People*, explained how streamlining first entered the home "in the kitchen, the bathroom, and the laundry, where utility transcended tradition." Yet, he said, it quickly spread so that "hearses and fountain pens and pencil sharpeners were stupidly modeled after the teardrop, which was held up as an ideal form, one which a body free to change its shape would assume, in order to offer a minimum resistance to air. Some critics pointed out that fountain pens and the baby buggies seldom stirred up much of a breeze, and a streamlined pencil sharpener couldn't get away if it tried because it was screwed down, but the critics were readily outshouted."[57]

Indeed, streamlining's promise of speed and efficiency, coupled with luxury and modernity proved a popular, winning combination. While its simulation of speed captured the optimism, freedom, and exhilaration of cars in visual form, its impact extended far beyond things that move. By the late 1930s, streamlining had pervaded the American environment both inside and out, from parkways to water pitchers. Though Harley Earl's embrace of streamlined design for his 1934 LaSalle saved the line for several years, its more enduring legacy was its demonstration of the power of styling—"the Look of Things," as Earl called it—and of the industrial designer in reshaping the entirety of modern American life.[58]

PLASTICS

No material symbolizes modernity more than plastics, yet plastics have long been misunderstood. The confusion over the definition of plastic and the unfamiliarity with the wide range of plastic substances, their properties, and applications are as pervasive today as they were one hundred years ago. Throughout the past century, all plastics were often lumped under the term without differentiation, and trade names, such as Bakelite, were incorrectly applied to all products of the same, or even different, chemical compounds. Plastic has taken on a range of connotations, from miraculous, revolutionary, and modern to shoddy, fake, untrustworthy, and wasteful. Popular understanding of plastic was (and is) as fluid as the material itself.

Although the earliest plastics were developed in the 1800s, the plastics industry truly began to flourish and visibly impact American life in the 1920s and 1930s. It was during those decades that plastics transitioned from being a rare novelty to being an integral part of the modern home. New household appliances such as radios and electric clocks, along with costume jewelry and personal luxury goods, were among the most conspicuous manifestations of the new media in the home. In November 1934, *Modern Plastics* magazine celebrated this proliferation of plastics, reporting that eleven of the Warren Telechron Company's new line of electric clocks "are encased in plastic or part-plastic bases," representing both modern and traditional styles. According to the proselytizing staff writer, the miraculous properties of plastics, including their warmth and texture that harmonize with most other materials, the possibility of a spectrum of colors, and the opportunity to explore new shapes and forms at a reasonable cost, allow Warren Telechron infinite possibilities to satisfy every consumer.[1]

To illustrate this point, the author chose to highlight a humorous little clock fashioned in the shape of a duck (FIG. 78). "Most ingenious of the new models is the 'Quacker' model, designed for a child's room. Here plastics have permitted the designer the fullest sway of his imagination. The clock ceases to be merely a part of the furniture and becomes an educational and entertaining toy—something that parents will willingly buy and children eagerly cherish."[2] The author praises the designer for embracing the possibilities of plastics and transforming the clock from a functional timekeeping instrument into a work of art and a beloved family treasure. But the author got one thing wrong— the *Quacker* is not the result of "the fullest sway of *his* imagination," but the fullest sway of *her* imagination. The design of the *Quacker* (along with its variation without an alarm mechanism, the *Smug*) sprung from the creative mind of Belle Kogan (1902–2000), one of the first women in the United States to establish her name in the field of industrial design (FIG. 79). From being the only girl in her Pennsylvania high school technical drawing class in 1920 to being the recipient of a Personal Recognition Award from the Industrial Designers Society of America in 1994, Kogan worked her way up in a nascent field. Like other early pioneers, she cobbled together a range of training and

78   Belle Kogan, *Smug* clock, designed 1934

OPPOSITE: 79   Belle Kogan, 1947

experiences to inform her practice, including years waiting on customers at her father's jewelry store; intermittent studies at Pratt Institute,
the Art Students League, and Winold Reiss's studio; and employment
as a designer with a silver-plating company. Along the way, she seized
upon the opportunities presented, one of which was the chance to
work with a completely new material: plastics.

When Belle Kogan designed the *Smug* and *Quacker* clocks in
1934, plastics was still an emerging industry, albeit one that was developing rapidly. In the public mind, plastics increasingly symbolized
modernity, technological progress, creativity, and the power of human-
kind to control and manipulate nature. In the years that followed, and
especially when wartime production expanded its development and
use in the 1940s, plastics soared in popularity among manufacturers
and consumers alike, and its possibilities seemed limitless. But even
a decade before the *Smug* clock was made, that was not the case.
Plastics were unfamiliar, confusing in their various properties, costly in
their initial trials, and viewed by many customers simply as inferior
imitations. As Kogan herself stated in 1935: "It is inevitable that in the
near future the world of manufacture will engage in a huge business
of plastics—a business unconceived ten or even five years ago."[3]

Kogan was actively involved in both the development of the
plastics industry and the field of industrial design. Over the course of
her impressive five-decade career, she worked with numerous materials including silver, silverplate, ceramics, glass, and wood. But it was
plastics that offered Kogan some of her earliest opportunities as an
industrial designer, and the *Smug* and *Quacker* clocks were one of her
earliest successes. Although Kogan's activity in plastics touched upon
nearly every major advancement and innovation in the industry prior
to World War II and well into the 1950s, her contributions to both the
plastics industry and industrial design in general have been under-
recognized, likely due to her gender.

Working as a woman in a man's world, Kogan had to overcome
rampant sexism (**FIG. 80**). She later noted that "manufacturers were
quite antagonistic when a woman came around proposing new
ideas—they didn't think a woman knew enough about the mechanical
aspects of the situation. I had to prove I have a practical mind—
I guess it is proof when there are very seldom any corrections in my
designs."[4] More than once, Kogan lost jobs when clients discovered
she was a woman. For instance, a manufacturer of refrigerators and
washing machines who had invited "Mr. Bell Kogan" to Ohio for a
meeting declined her services upon Belle's arrival.[5] Others she felt
"regulated me to all the smaller things" that they deemed more appropriate for a female designer, not giving her the opportunity to work
on trains, cars, large appliances, or even furniture.[6] In response, Kogan
used her gender to her advantage. In the 1935 *Modern Plastics* article,
condescendingly titled "As a woman sees design," she turned the
tables on her male counterparts. She argued that, as a woman, she

knew what women wanted and had special insight into the "feminine buying psychology." "The thing which needs most to be understood by the manufacturer—particularly at this stage of our commercial development—is that the sale of any product is greatly determined by the reaction of the feminine consumer . . . The women of today . . . want attractive things, things which are smart and things which are new . . . Items, to be readily acceptable cannot, however, be too extreme in design. Such items do not fit into the average home, decorated as it is, with objects which are not too modern or severe in color or form."[7]

Kogan is, in fact, one of several women who worked in American industrial design during its early years. Yet, accounts of industrial design in the United States have historically privileged men, such as Walter Dorwin Teague and Norman Bel Geddes, over their female counterparts, including Kogan, Virginia Hamill, Ilonka Karasz, Elsa Tennhardt, Helen Hughes Dulany, and Ruth Reeves, among others. These pioneering women had to contend not only with discrimination from manufacturers, fellow designers, and the general public throughout their careers, but also with the gender biases of historians and those documenting the field for future generations. One of several reasons for such neglect is that female industrial designers were often restricted to working on lower profile products traditionally associated with women, such as textiles, personal accessories, or items geared toward children.

Enclosed in a brightly colored molded plastic case in the shape of a duck, the *Smug* clock may seem like a frivolous novelty or inconsequential child's plaything. However, this clock is a notable example of early modern design in plastic. The *Smug* reveals an in-depth understanding of the diverse and evolving possibilities of early plastics, and, more importantly, the critical limitations of both the material itself, and the public's reception of it. Kogan's familiarity with plastics allowed her the freedom to push the boundaries of traditional clock forms and finishes, and to adopt a more playful tone. By the time she designed the *Smug* and *Quacker* clocks, Kogan had five years of experience with a variety of plastics, including casein, Bakelite, and Catalin. She had learned firsthand the two most important physical properties of plastics that influenced their use in producing consumer goods: their method of manufacture (molded vs. cast) and their ability to take color. More than any other characteristics, these attributes dictated the practical application and public profile of the four dominant plastics manufactured in the United States prior to World War II: celluloid (cellulose nitrate), Bakelite (phenol formaldehyde), Catalin (cast phenolic resin), and Plaskon (urea formaldehyde).

Kogan first encountered the new medium at the very beginning of her design career in 1929 when doing contract work for the Quaker Silver Company, maker of silver-plated novelties based in Attleboro, Massachusetts. James W. Jennings, president of Quaker Silver, asked Kogan to oversee experiments in combining plastics with his company's silver-plated cast metal. He introduced Kogan to a man at the Karolith Company, most likely its founder and director, Alexander S. Zimmerman, who had established the enterprise four years earlier in Long Island City.[8] Karolith was the second firm in the United States to produce casein, a partially synthetic plastic first introduced in Europe in 1900 under the trade name of Galalith. Although casein "had not yet attained perfection," Kogan and Jennings were attracted to the lesser-known plastic by its promise to offer moldable products in a range of colors.[9]

At Karolith, Kogan worked with the chemists to develop a custom set of jewel-tone colors that Included rose quartz, lapis, and amber. She also composed several designs, including a clock design in which she wanted to contrast the casein plastic with metal strips set in by hand.[10] However, her experiments to combine plastics and cast metal failed, and "we came to grief because our material refused to stay where it was put."[11] Kogan discovered that although casein could be molded to shape, it does not produce a stable material for manufacture until it is hardened by soaking for a long period in a solution of formaldehyde and water, which causes significant distortion. Such irregularity likely prevented Kogan's metal strips from adhering properly. As a result, most casein was subsequently cast in sheets and tubes, then manipulated into final shape. Casein ultimately did not fare well with American manufacturers, who were already using celluloid, the first plastic developed in the United States.[12]

Celluloid (cellulose nitrate), which dates to 1869, was initially prized not for being innovative but rather for its ability to imitate

natural materials.[13] This elegant celluloid hair comb, for example, mimics the color and look of tortoiseshell (FIG. 81). In fact, the discovery of celluloid was inspired by a contest to find a suitable replacement for ivory billiard balls. With the incentive of a $10,000 reward from the Phelan & Collender billiards company, John Wesley Hyatt, a printer in Albany, New York, built upon English experiments with nitrocelluous by using camphor, and also created the machines needed to work the new substance into a product.[14] Hyatt patented celluloid in 1870 and established the Celluloid Manufacturing Company the following year. The company quickly expanded its products beyond billiard balls to include dental plates, combs, knife handles, piano keys, and a range of novelties, most of which substituted for increasingly expensive or hard-to-source natural materials.[15] Great pains were taken to mimic the precise look of these natural materials, such as the faux tortoiseshell of the comb featured here. To create its coloring, two batches of celluloid, a lighter transparent brown and darker translucent one, were combined while the material was still in semi-liquid form. Instead of mixing the colors thoroughly, they were manipulated and folded with paddles and knives to achieve the desired mottled effect. Although celluloid provided a convincing imitation of other materials at lower cost, it still required labor-intensive handcraftsmanship to shape the finished product. This reliance on skilled labor, along with celluloid's variability, fragility, and high flammability, significantly hampered its wider industrial use.[16]

The next major advance in plastics technology in the United States came in 1907 when Leo Baekeland invented Bakelite in Yonkers, New York. Bakelite was the first entirely synthetic plastic with no natural ingredients. Bakelite is lightweight, insoluble, hard, durable, unaffected by most chemicals, and an excellent insulator for heat and electricity. Most importantly, it can be molded into any shape. However, Bakelite has its weaknesses as well—to provide the necessary strength to maintain a shape, it requires filler materials, which in turn limit its color palette to dark or mottled pigments to disguise the fillers.[17] In addition, carved steel molds often required both machine and hand labor, greatly increasing the investment costs in the product. Therefore, early use of Bakelite was largely confined to industrial purposes (such as electrical insulation).

In the 1920s, the Bakelite Corporation embarked on a publicity campaign to familiarize manufacturers and the general public with "the Material of a Thousand Uses" and to gain their loyalty before the patents on Bakelite started to expire.[18] But Bakelite's limited range of colors, along with the expense of molds, hindered its expansion into consumer goods. One notable exception was the popular *Automatic Harmonica* released by the Rolmonica Music Company in 1928 (FIG. 82). Like a player piano, the Rolmonica played tunes from paper rolls; the performer simply needed to turn a crank and blow into the instrument. Advertised to both adults and children as a portable musical

instrument, the Rolmonica's Bakelite case perfectly suited its needs. It was lightweight, durable, and shaped precisely to accommodate the performer's mouth, while being warmer and smoother on the user's lips than metal. In keeping with the imitative history of plastics, however, its Bakelite case is still composed of mottled red, brown, and black in a self-conscious imitation of tortoiseshell.

The expiration of Bakelite's patent in December 1927 opened the door for other companies to legally experiment with phenol formaldehyde. In 1928, the American Catalin Corporation introduced cast phenolic resins. Catalin lacked the strength-building fillers of Bakelite, so although it retained all of the other properties of phenol formaldehyde molded resins—including durability and high thermal and electrical resistance—it also had the coveted ability to support a wide range of colors. As a result, the new cast phenolic resins were quickly utilized for household goods—particularly electrical appliances and tablewares. The Manning-Bowman Company wasted no time in adding color to their new machine age–inspired wares, such as their chromium-plated Mixer Set with jade green Catalin handles and knobs, and their skyscraper-shaped electric clock designed by Jean George Theobald, with bright orange inset panels of Catalin (**FIGS. 83, 84**).[19]

Where Catalin made the biggest impact, however, was in costume jewelry. Jewelry made of cast phenolics, such as the multicolored bracelet popularly known as the Philadelphia bracelet, became trendy

83   Manning-Bowman Company, Cocktail set, about 1928

OPPOSITE: 84   Jean George Theobald, Mantel clock K906, 1929–31

in the early 1930s (**FIG. 85**). Not only did the jewelry brighten up a woman's outfit, but its low price point allowed many women to own multiple sets. By 1934, *Modern Plastics* magazine reported that "seventy-five per cent of all costume jewelry sales are cast-phenolics." The same article claimed that "cast-phenolics have seemingly captured the costume jewelry market. In fact, in four short years they have practically *created* a market that hitherto did not exist. . . . Today, a woman may possess more jewelry than Cleopatra could boast of—yet its total cost need not have run over thirty dollars."[20] Plain, uncarved bangles cost as little as twenty cents, though prices increased for more sophisticated designs that involved additional handcraftsmanship for carving and laminating different colors.[21]

The Philadelphia bracelet, which combines five different colors with precise carving, would have cost on the higher end, between $1 and $3. The design (its nickname having come from the record price it set at an antiques show in Philadelphia in the 1980s) is made of cast, carved, and laminated phenolic resin. Yet, the actual manufacturer of the Philadelphia bracelet remains unknown because the Catalin Corporation licensed its new process to numerous material suppliers, including to its competitor the Bakelite Corporation. In a November 1933 issue of *Bakelite Information*, the company announced that it had developed its own cast resins featuring lighter and brighter colors than previously offered.[22] Therefore, despite the Catalin Corporation's formidable attempts to distinguish its brightly hued material through active marketing—calling it "the Gem of Modern Industry"—much of the public, and many manufacturers, continued to call all phenolic resins (and sometimes all plastics) Bakelite, whether it was actually made by the Bakelite Corporation or not.

Kogan designed a pioneering and influential line of cast phenolic jewelry in 1933–34. Notable for its distinctive combinations of two colors, the line was commissioned by jewelry and novelty company Blefeld & Goodfriend, made by Bakelite, and sold at F. W. Woolworth stores nationwide (FIG. 86). The pins, earrings, and rings are carved into simple geometric shapes. The bangles are accented with dots of a lighter color, such as the green version shown here with two elongated yellow dots. Originally created through the time-consuming technique of inlaying, the dots were later formed with injection molding.[23] Kogan's jewelry was appreciated by American women not only for its modern design and brilliant colors but also for its economic value, an especially important consideration during the Depression years.

The last of the four major plastics most commonly used in the United States before 1940 is Plaskon (urea formaldehyde), the material Kogan utilized to create the trailblazing *Smug* and *Quacker* clocks. Plaskon was developed in 1931 to address a specific need for Ohio's Toledo Scale Company. In response to customer feedback, the company wanted to make lighter-weight grocery scales in white, which customers saw as more hygienic. After years of research and experimentation, Plaskon provided the answer as it not only offered an expanded palette of light and bright colors (including white) but also could be molded into form. Its creators quickly recognized the potential of the new plastic for a wide range of consumer goods. They established the Toledo Synthetic Products Company and hired industrial designer Harold Van Doren to assist with promotion and product design.[24] The most ambitious design Van Doren and his partner John Gordon Rideout made for Plaskon was a radio case with a skyscraper-inspired stepped profile. The *Air King* radio, debuted in January 1933, was available in an

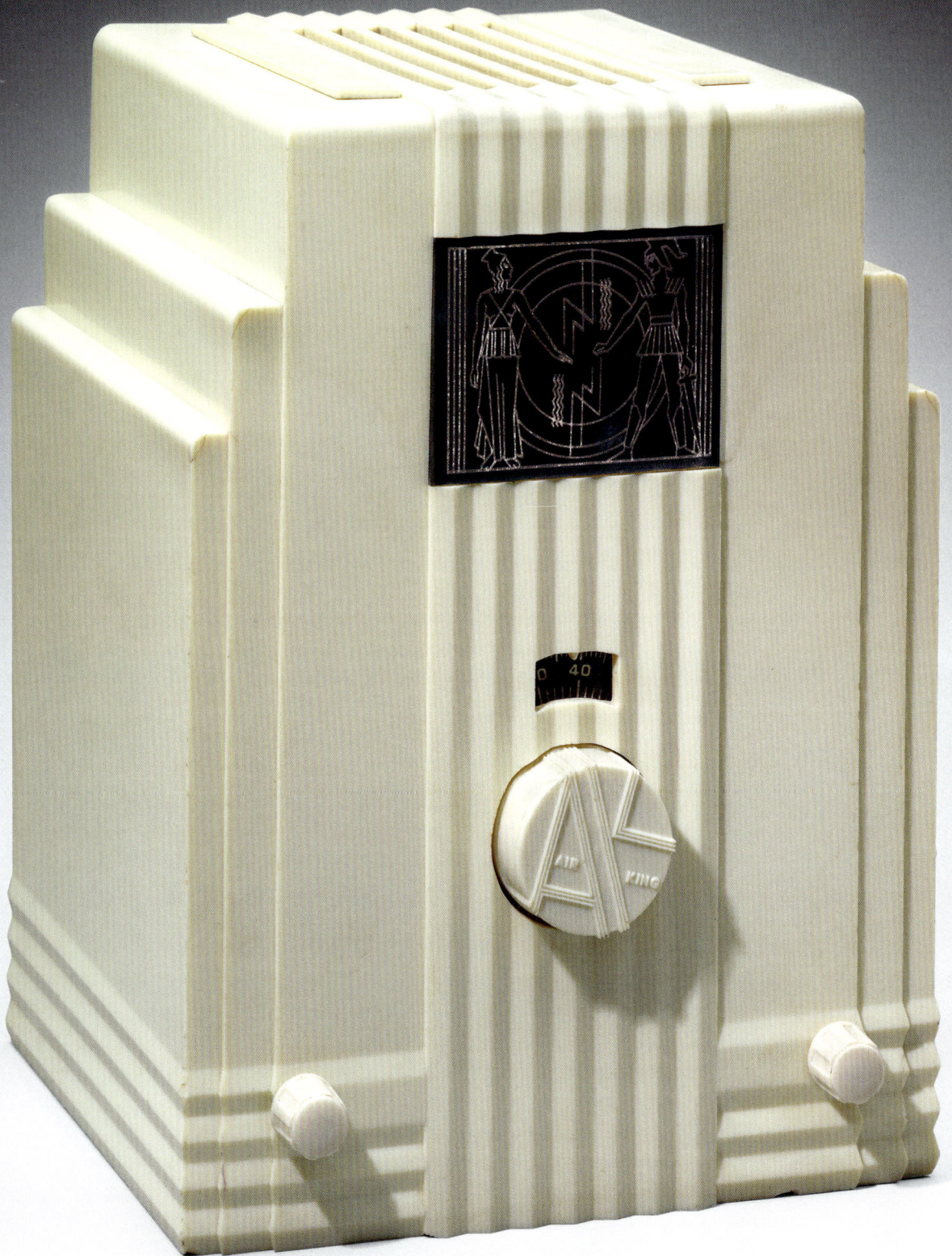

astonishing thirteen colors, including the celebrated white seen in this early example (**FIG. 87**). At twelve inches high, the *Air King* radio's case was touted as the largest plastics molding ever made at that time.

Kogan embraced the potential of Plaskon for her clock designs. The compound's colorfulness and moldability allowed her to break free of the classical and architectural styles that dominated the clock industry, and instead offer something playful, amusing, and undeniably modern: a cartoon-like duck bursting with personality, made of a synthetic compound, and enclosing a clock that runs on electricity.

The design of the *Smug* was not merely playful. The rounded contours of the duck's sculpted body aligned with the latest trend in molded plastics: curves. Facing pressure to reduce the cost of molds, engineers and designers initially moved to more linear designs, such as Van Doren and Rideout's *Air King* radio. Van Doren boasted that his radio case was cheaper to manufacture because "steps, ribs, circles, flutes, etc. . . . could be machined in the mold with the minimum of hand labor."[25] Yet, the sharp edges of Van Doren's design actually still required some hand-finishing. And, manufacturers found it difficult to ensure the even flow of molten plastic material into its corners, which required more pressure in the mold and increased the risk of casting flaws or air pockets.[26] By the time it was released in 1933, Van Doren's skyscraper design may have been in line with the latest developments in mold making, but it was already somewhat out of fashion in the broader, fast-paced world of modern design. Americans were becoming enamored with the curves of streamlining.

"Oddly enough," wrote Franklin E. Brill of General Plastics in 1935, "the streamline shape comes pretty close to the ideal contour which designers have always claimed that plastics should take."[27] Streamlined molds not only were less expensive to create (as they could be cut and polished by machine) but also accommodated the natural properties of molten plastics, used less material, required less pressure, and resulted in stronger products.[28] Curved surfaces enhanced and highlighted the inherent luster of plastics. Together, plastics and streamlined design prospered.

Perhaps the most influential early streamlined design in molded plastic is Walter Dorwin Teague's *Baby Brownie* camera for Eastman Kodak (**FIG. 88**). Composed almost entirely of lightweight molded Bakelite with rounded contours that assisted the user's grip and fluted speed lines wrapping around the case, the affordable, pocket-size camera benefited from the marketing power of both Eastman Kodak and Bakelite. In September 1934, *Modern Plastics* ran a full-page product profile of the new design that stated, "the small size, the clean attractive appearance of the black molded box and the extremely low price made possible by the use of molded parts have, combined, resulted in an instantaneous and nationwide demand for these cameras."[29] With four million sold between 1934 and 1941, the *Baby Brownie* helped to bring streamlined design in plastic to the masses.[30]

Unveiled the same month as Teague's camera, Kogan's *Smug* clock is not as overtly streamlined. The design does not try to capture the appearance of motion or speed, but it certainly privileges curves over sharp edges, revealing an up-to-date knowledge of molding trends. Composed using a two-part mold and seamed along the short ends, the plastic case features a rotund, disk-shaped body (which houses the clock face), topped by a small, round head and a long beak that extends along the curve of the body. A small foot beneath the beak is balanced on the opposite side by a larger, rounded tail. When compared to a second, unrealized design, the version put into production has rounder contours and fewer sharp edges and, therefore, was probably easier and cheaper to make (FIGS. 89, 90).

The interest in plastics from Van Doren, Teague, and Kogan, along with the move toward streamlined contours during the early 1930s, signaled a major shift in the manufacture of plastics: the growing involvement and influence of industrial designers. As competition increased and the range of available plastics grew, understanding their specific advantages and limitations became increasingly essential. Manufacturers needed guidance on which material might best

Oct. 23, 1934.   B. KOGAN   Des. 93,663
CLOCK CASE
Filed July 31, 1934

Fig.1.

Fig.2.

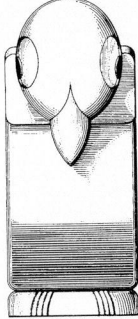

Fig.3.

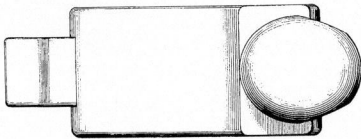

Inventor:
Belle Kogan,
by *Harry E. Dunham*
Her Attorney.

Oct. 23, 1934.   B. KOGAN   Des. 93,662
CLOCK CASE
Filed July 31, 1934

Fig. 2.

Fig. 1.

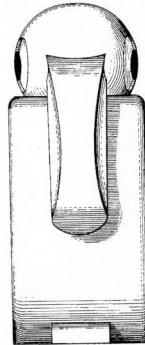

Fig.3.

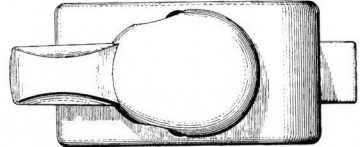

Inventor:
Belle Kogan,
by *Harry E. Dunham*
Her Attorney.

suit their product and on how to style and market it to attract attention. Consumers needed to be convinced that plastics were not cheap imitations but could be valued in their own right. Industrial designers strove to meet the needs of both.

The plastics industry's association with the imitation of natural materials had hindered its growth in consumer goods and limited experimentation in form and style. Timid manufacturers were wary of alienating consumers and therefore clung to the old-fashioned designs deemed more comfortable and familiar. Well into the 1920s and even the 1930s, Bakelite handles imitated mahogany or ebony, and modern appliances made of plastics, such as radio or clock cases, assumed traditional forms like Greek temples or Gothic cathedrals. As the new industrial designers found their voice, they universally denounced the use of plastics to imitate rather than innovate. For Paul Frankl, it was a tragedy that plastics sought to replicate existing materials: "instead of enriching us, they make us poorer being poor substitutes, whereas they might proudly be themselves."[31] For Harold Van Doren, "that strange, almost pathological desire of [plastic] manufacturers to 'imitate' something else was almost the death of a perfectly

good industry."[32] Kogan added, "it is most unfortunate, indeed, that manufacturers fail to take full advantage of plastic materials in creating new designs . . . it should be realized that with new materials which can be so cleverly molded and machined, new forms are not only possible but are to be desired."[33]

Recognizing the influence that the newly high-profile industrial designers wielded on manufacturers and public opinion, the Celluloid Corporation hired Paul Frankl to design two modern vanity sets for its *Arch Amerith* line in 1928 (**FIG. 91**). The company hoped that Frankl's reputation would help boost sales. The results, however, reveal the designer's limited experience working with plastics. Frankl's *Rond* vanity set features the same sleek modern lines that he used for his furniture, with an emphasis on geometry in both form and decoration. The individual pieces are composed of laminated sheets of black, charcoal, and silver celluloid in an irregular striated pattern with circles, dots, and stars inlaid in silver and gold. While there is no denying that Frankl's design is thoroughly modern in form and decoration, he failed to make the most of his material. The set is made of materials Celluloid specifically marketed as high-quality plastics with greater translucence and luster.[34] While the *Rond* styling attempts to capture and emphasize the plastics' luster by complementing it with shimmering metal inlays, the flat surfaces do not fully show off the luster of the plastic itself. Similarly, the laminated dark colors do not highlight the plastic's signature translucence. In addition, Frankl's use of the striated colors in his lamination vaguely suggests wood grain or some other natural material, in direct contradiction with his own written words. Frankl's brash, assertive modernism did not translate well into an intimate vanity set, the epitome of feminine luxury products of the era. To top it off, the set's handles were sharp-edged and uncomfortable. As one reviewer quipped: "Frankl-y, we don't care for them much."[35] Weak sales, combined with high production costs for the intricate decorative inlays, resulted in Celluloid discontinuing the line after only a short time.

Frankl's experience with Celluloid demonstrates that designers needed to collaborate with chemists and engineers to learn the material's properties and limitations, while manufacturers needed to realize that aesthetic changes alone would not serve as a magic bullet to improve sales. Within a few years, designers and manufacturers routinely worked more closely together to develop plastic products. In 1933, H. S. Spencer of General Plastics noted: "industrial design is becoming a very definite factor in industry."[36]

Hoping to capitalize on the growing impact of industrial design, the Bakelite Corporation made a business proposal to some of the biggest names in the field. First, the company organized educational seminars for designers on the possibilities and advantages of Bakelite, and promised ongoing advice from the company's engineers. In return, if a designer convinced a manufacturer to use Bakelite in an actual product, the company offered to feature that designer and their product in an advertising campaign. At least ten designers accepted the proposal, with the advertisements appearing in trade journals in 1933 and 1934. Bakelite's campaign not only was mutually beneficial for promoting the status of the designer, the manufacturer, and the company itself but also further linked plastics and modern design in the public mind.[37]

Professional design input was also increasingly encouraged by the leading trade journal in the plastics industry, *Plastics & Molded Products*. In a front-page article of the June 1932 issue, Frank E. Brill of General Plastics declared, "the sooner we recognize the separate and distinct function of industrial design, the sooner our problems will fade. We must embrace the new machine-age designer."[38] In 1934, the journal itself did just that. A change in management prompted a new name, *Modern Plastics*, a polished new look styled by designer Joseph Sinel, and a shift in mission from an industry trade journal to a promotional tool aimed at wooing manufacturers and the general public with the wonders of plastics.[39] Industrial designers figured prominently within the magazine's new focus. The first restyled issue, released in September 1934, included an impassioned plea authored by Harold Van Doren for manufacturers to invest in good design, along with an interview about plastics with Walter Dorwin Teague. Teague remarked that plastics "have potentialities possessed by no other materials and beauty peculiar to themselves."[40] As evidence, the feature article on Teague's *Baby Brownie* appeared in this issue as well.

Over the course of the next year and a half, *Modern Plastics* ran a series that profiled established designers and interviewed them about the present state and future of plastics. These articles offered designers the opportunity to educate manufacturers and the public on the value that a professional industrial designer brings to a product. In turn, the designers lent both a gravitas and glamour to plastics. Plastics historian Jeffrey Meikle asserts that these articles "promoted the status of industrial design as much as that of the plastic industry," and that, as a result of the journal's commitment to promoting design, it "served for several years as the nation's most important journal of industrial design."[41] In addition to Teague and Van Doren, many of the most celebrated designers of the era appeared in the pages of *Modern Plastics*, including Donald Deskey, Raymond Loewy, Lurelle Guild, Ely Jacques Kahn, and Gilbert Rohde. In December 1935, the journal featured thirty-three-year-old Kogan, whose firm, Belle Kogan Design Associates, had been established in New York City just two years earlier.

That same year, Kogan designed two vanity sets for the Celluloid Corporation that offer a marked difference from Frankl's similar commission of seven years earlier (**FIG. 92**). Both of Kogan's designs, the straight-lined *Capri* and the curvy *Continental*, feature smooth, sleek lines and simplified forms in soft colors accented with rhodium-plated handles.[42] Journalist Marcy Babbitt noted that Kogan's designs are "particularly interesting for their treatment and are indicative of her

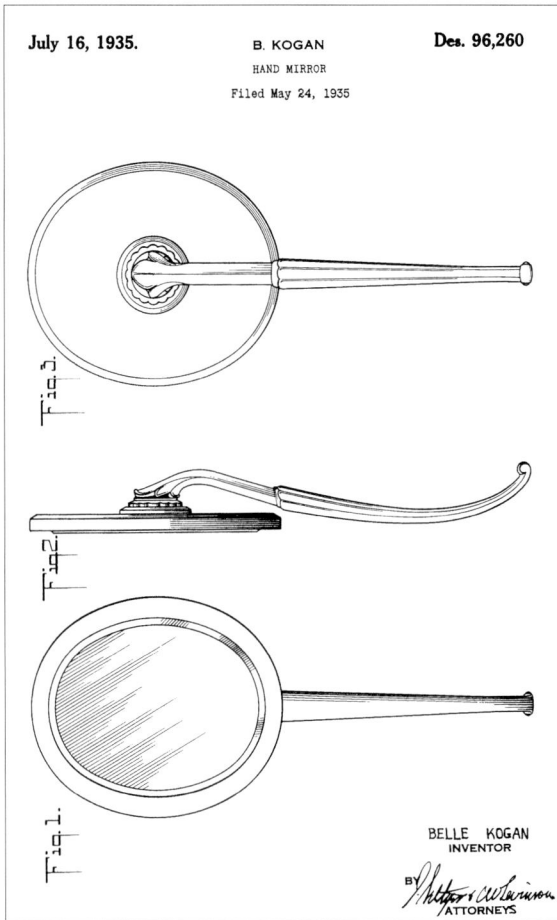

Fig.3

Fig.2

Fig.1

BELLE KOGAN
INVENTOR

BY

ATTORNEYS

psychology when designing in plastics. . . . the plastic surfaces were left entirely unadorned, so that the beauty of the material would not be hidden beneath any superfluous decorations." Her elegant, more tempered approach to modernism prompted the writer to claim "these sets can fit as gracefully into the home decorated along strictly modern lines as they can into the home which finds greatest enjoyment and comfort in period styles."[43] Kogan considered not only the look of the product but also where it would be used and by whom.

With the *Smug* and *Quacker* clocks, meant for a child's bedroom, Kogan embraced the designs' intended audience. Kogan's charming duck, with its rounded features, large doleful eyes, and bright colors, shares many attributes with prominent cartoon characters of the era, including Felix the Cat and Mickey Mouse (**FIG. 93**). By mimicking features of these beloved icons, Kogan aligned her clocks with the joy, amusement, and modern technology of animated cartoons.

Kogan's clocks not only looked modern in materials and design, their function assisted with (and reinforced) modernity's fast-paced lifestyle. International timekeeping, with twenty-four time zones based on the Greenwich meridian, was established in 1884 but met with massive resistance. While many in the United States started to follow the Greenwich Mean Time standard in the years that followed, it was not made law until the Standard Time Act was enacted on March 19, 1918. Soon after, the spread and growing reliability of electricity in the 1920s sparked great demand for small-scale electric clocks. No longer was the family reliant on the sole grandfather clock in the front hall; each member could have their own version, individually suited to their tastes. Warren Telechron's first alarm clock, the *Electrolarm*, with its skyscraper-inspired shape made out of Vinylite, was released in 1929 (**FIG. 94**). Such bedroom alarm clocks were marketed as essential for successful modern living. As one 1931 General Electric advertisement promised, a reliable alarm clock meant that "nobody at breakfast gets nervous indigestion for fear of missing the seven-forty. The children are off to school with minutes to spare. All the demands upon your time seem easier to meet. The course of life runs smoother."[44]

Warren Telechron unveiled Kogan's two clocks at the second annual National Electrical and Radio Exposition, which opened in New York's Madison Square Garden on September 19, 1934. Both the *Smug* and *Quacker* got prime billing in the Telechron booth, with two large cut-out images of the clock prominently displayed to draw visitors' attention. The exposition was well attended by manufacturers, retailers, and the general public, welcoming over one hundred thousand people during its ten-day run. An active marketing campaign followed that fall, with advertisements for the affordable clocks by both Warren Telechron and Plaskon in a range of journals and magazines, including *Jewelers' Circular Keystone*, *Hardware Age*, *Printers' Ink Monthly*, *American Home*, and *Business Week*. Warren Telechron would sell the *Smug* and *Quacker* for over four years, discontinuing the line in early 1939. During that time, they sold 18,569 units of the *Smug* and 10,422

BELLE KOGAN DESIGNER

of the *Quacker*.[45] Kogan's playful design brought a warmth and familiarity to plastics that resonated with consumers.

Kogan featured the clocks in her 1935 display at Rockefeller
Center's Annual Industrial Arts Exhibition, organized by the National
Alliance for Art and Industry (FIG. 95). In addition to three ducks—one
each in blue, yellow, and black—she included samples of her vanity
sets for Celluloid, her Trimatic Toaster in chrome with a molded plastic
base for Samson United, white ceramic tablewares for the Philadelphia
firm of Ebeling & Reuss, and more.[46] According to Alon Bement, director of the National Alliance for Art and Industry, the exhibition's goal
was "to show the progress that has been made in the manufacturing of
'articles of good appearance.'" For, as architect Harvey Wiley Corbett
said, "if any beauty is to come into the life of the masses of the people,
it must come through machine-made articles."[47] Kogan, who had long
embraced the affordability of mass-produced products, surely agreed.

By the end of the 1930s, Kogan had worked with a wide range of
the available plastics—as well as with silver, silver plate, ceramics, glass,
and metal household appliances. At the 1937 World's Fair in Paris, she
reported for *Modern Plastics* on the use of the material in wall cover-
ings, fashion, and display apparatuses. In 1940, she wrote an article, "A
Designer Looks at Plastics," for *Bakelite Review*.[48] She would continue
to work in the latest plastic technologies well into the 1940s and 1950s,
most notably with an extensive line of melamine dinnerware designed
for the Boonton Molding Company of New Jersey (FIG. 96).[49] Although
more expensive than many ceramic dinnerwares, Boontonware was
"virtually unbreakable" (it came with a guarantee) and available in a
wide range of colors.

A solo exhibition at the Philadelphia Art Alliance in 1946 was a
triumph for the intrepid, pioneering designer, despite being errone-
ously called a "One-Man Show." One reviewer noted that Kogan's
toiletry sets "satisfy a universal yearning for luxury, at low cost. They
don't have to last forever. She disapproves, in fact, of buying things to
last forever and thinks possessions ought to grow and change with
their owners"—a modern concept made possible by the mass production of inexpensive consumer goods, including plastics.[50]

Belle Kogan, *Boontonware sugar, creamer, and tray,* 1950s

Notes

Modern by Design

1 Abbott Kimball, "Going Modern," *Printers' Ink* (November 8, 1928): 7–20; emphasis in original.
2 Some scholars argue that industrial design predates this time period, and starts with the rise of industrialized production. However, for the purposes of this book, we are using the term to refer to the modern American industrial designer whose role developed in the late 1920s and 1930s. For in-depth studies of industrial design in the United States, see John Heskett, *Industrial Design* (New York: Oxford University Press, 1980); and Jeffrey L. Meikle, *Twentieth Century Limited: Industrial Design in America, 1925–1939* (Philadelphia: Temple University Press, 1979).
3 "What Is Industrial Design?," Industrial Designers Society of America, https://www.idsa.org.
4 "Both Fish and Fowl," *Fortune* (February 1934): 40–41.
5 Rachel Elizabeth Delphia, "Design to Enable the Body: Thomas Lamb's 'Wedge-Lock' Handle, 1941–1962" (master's thesis, University of Delaware, 2005), 17–19; and Walter Dorwin Teague (office) Meeting Minutes, February 27, 1944, as quoted in Arthur Pulos, *American Design Adventure, 1940–1975* (Cambridge, MA: MIT Press, 1988), 200. Of the fifteen founding members of the SID, fourteen worked on the East Coast, while Brooks Stevens hailed from Milwaukee, Wisconsin.
6 Meikle, 13–14.
7 Ralph C. Epstein and Florence M. Clark, "Manufacture and Its Major Groups," in Ralph C. Epstein, assisted by Florence M. Clark, *Industrial Profits in the United States* (New York: National Bureau of Economic Research, 1934), 357.
8 Thomas C. Cochran, *The American Business System* (Cambridge, MA: Harvard University Press, 1957), 44.
9 Earnest Elmo Calkins, "Beauty the New Business Tool," *The Atlantic* (August 1927).
10 Christopher Long, *Paul T. Frankl and Modern American Design* (New Haven, CT: Yale University Press, 2007), 14–15.
11 Donald Deskey Associates was formally organized in early 1940s and flourished under Deskey's leadership for three decades until his retirement in 1976. The firm, now called Deskey Branding, still exists today. Viktor Schreckengost worked as a consultant for manufacturers such as American Limoges and Murray Ohio in the late 1930s. He continued to teach and design for over fifty years.

Skyscrapers

1 Paul T. Frankl, "The Modern Art of Interior Decoration," *Arts and Decoration* 5, no. 7 (May 1915): 269.
2 The most comprehensive source on Frankl and his designs is Christopher Long's *Paul T. Frankl and Modern American Design* (New Haven, CT: Yale University Press, 2007). Other important resources include articles by Long, as well as Frankl's own writings, including his autobiography, published (thanks to Long) in 2013. According to Long, Frankl regularly included his middle initial T (for Theodor) in his name to distinguish himself from Paul Frankl, the Prague-born art historian.
3 Paul T. Frankl, *New Dimensions: The Decorative Arts of Today in Words & Pictures* (New York: Payson & Clarke, Ltd., 1928), 52.
4 Paul T. Frankl, "Just What Is This Modernistic Movement?," *Arts and Decoration* (May 1928): 56.
5 Paul T. Frankl, Christopher Long, and Aurora McClain, *Paul T. Frankl: Autobiography* (Los Angeles: DoppelHouse Press, 2013), 73–74.
6 Frankl, Long, and McClain, 73–74.
7 Sarah Bradford Landau and Carl W. Condit, *Rise of the New York Skyscraper, 1865–1913* (New Haven, CT: Yale University Press, 1996), 382; and Andreas Bernard, *Lifted: A Cultural History of the Elevator* (New York: NYU Press, 2014), 19.
8 Frankl, *New Dimensions*, 55.
9 Frankl, Long, and McClain, 69.
10 FTIR (Fourier transform infrared) microscopy analysis confirms that there are at least four distinct layers of green paint initially applied to the interiors of the exposed compartments. These include a dark green primer, four layers of bluish-green featuring Prussian Blue pigment (each layer with some slight variation in the amount of pigment included), and a cellulose nitrate varnish on top. See object file in the Art of the Americas department, MFA. With thanks to Christine Storti, MFA Furniture and Frame Conservator, and Michelle Derrick of the MFA Scientific Lab for their analysis.
11 For architect Louis Sullivan's interest in using green (and other colors) on his buildings, see Lauren S. Weingarden, "The Colors of Nature: Louis Sullivan's Architectural Polychromy and Nineteenth-Century Color Theory," *Winterthur Portfolio* 20, no. 4 (Winter 1985): 243–60. For Raymond Hood's McGraw-Hill Building, see L. E. Cooper, "Helped to Change Skyline of Manhattan: Raymond Hood, Architect, Put Color into Office Buildings . . . ," *New York Times*, August 19, 1934, RE1.

12 Walter Rendell Storey, "Skyscraper Architecture Influences Furniture: Bookcases, Cabinets and Chests of Drawers Now Show Rectangular Forms and Pyramid Effect—Oak Again," *New York Times*, February 20, 1927, SM12.

13 Frankl, *New Dimensions*, 36, 62.

14 For a detailed discussion of the trends seen in Frankl's Skyscraper Furniture line, see Christopher Long, "Paul T. Frankl's Skyscraper Furniture," *Magazine Antiques* 173, no. 1 (January 2008): 162–71.

15 Lewis Mumford, *Sticks and Stones: A Study of American Architecture and Civilization* (New York: Boni and Liveright, Inc., 1924), 177.

16 Many commentators, including Frankl, compared skyscrapers to Egyptian pyramids. Frankl wrote: "The modern skyscraper is a distinctive and noble creation. It is a monument of towering engineering and business enterprise. It stands as a symbol of American life of today, much as the pyramids were symbols of the life of ancient Egypt." Frankl, *New Dimensions*, 56.

17 Francis Lorne, "The New Architecture of a Flamboyant Civilization," *Arts & Decoration* (November 1925): 58–59, 90.

18 H. I. Brock, "Lesser Cities Also Lift Their Towers: The Skyscraper of Manhattan," *New York Times*, May 26, 1929, SM4.

19 Frankl, *New Dimensions*, 17.

20 Frankl, 76.

21 Frankl, 76.

22 Frankl, 18, 75.

23 Sarah D. Coffin suggests Frankl may have also become interested in lacquer for his Skyscraper Furniture through his contact with Donald Deskey, himself recently returned from the 1925 Paris Exposition, where he saw the lacquer work of French artist Jean Dunand. Coffin, "Melting Pot Modern," *Magazine Antiques* 184, no. 2 (March/April 2017): 110–17.

24 Elizabeth Collins Cromley, *Alone Together: A History of New York's Early Apartments* (Ithaca, NY: Cornell University Press, 1990), 62, 65; and Charles H. Israels, "New York Apartment Houses," *Architectural Record* 11, no. 1 (July 1901): 476–508.

25 Israels, "New York Apartment Houses," 477.

26 Frankl, *New Dimensions*, 21, 45.

27 Walter Rendell Storey, "Making the Most of a City Apartment," *New York Times*, May 13, 1928, 79.

28 *New York Times*, March 27, 1929, 25.

29 "Housewife Learns Furniture Can Jibe with Limited Space: Boston Museum of Fine Arts Puts Collection on View to Show How Needs of Modern Housing Can Be Met." *Christian Science Monitor*, January 26, 1926, 1.

30 Storey, "Making the Most of a City Apartment," 79.

31 "Housewife Learns Furniture Can Jibe," 1.

32 Edwin Avery Park, *New Backgrounds for a New Age* (New York: Harcourt, Brace and Company, Inc., 1927), 72.

33 For refrigerator history, Shelley Nickles, "'Preserving Women': Refrigerator Design as Social Process in the 1930s," *Technology and Culture* (October 2002): 693–727.

34 Lucien Bernhard, "Magical Use of Space in Today's Apartment," *Arts & Decoration* XXIX, no. 4 (August 1928): 52–53, 86–87.

35 Paul T. Frankl, *The Arts & Decoration Home Study Course covering the Modern Movement as applied to Interior Design and Kindred Subjects* (New York: Arts & Decoration Publishing Company, 1928), 19.

36 Paul T. Frankl, "Furniture of the Fourth Dimension: Designed for the New Interior," *House and Garden*, February 1927, 76–77, 140.

37 Walter Rendell Storey, "Old Decorative Ideas Return: Painted Screens Find a Place in Modern Homes," *New York Times*, May 23, 1926, SM13. Also see Walter Rendell Storey, "When a Room Becomes More than One: Decorators Find New Ways to Divide Up a Space without Use of Walls," *New York Times*, February 25, 1934, SM14.

38 For privacy concerns of apartments, see Cromley, *Alone Together*.

39 Storey, "Old Decorative Ideas Return," SM13; and Walter Rendell Storey, "The Oriental Screen Finds Favor Again: Prized in the Early Days of the China Trade It is Now Put to New Decorative Uses," *New York Times*, August 28, 1927, SM16.

40 Nunnally Johnson, "The New Furniture Gives Every One His Own Skyline: Interior Creations of Mr. Paul T. Frankl Rise Aloft in Geometric Lines, with Step-Back and Economy of Space Modeled after Tall American Buildings," *New York Evening Post*, May 19, 1927, 3; and "American Modernist Furniture: Inspired by Sky-Scraper Architecture," *Good Furniture* 29, no. 3 (September 1927): 119–21.

41 "Furniture in the Modern Manner: A New Type of Architecture is Training the Eye to Appreciate Furniture of Modernistic Simplicity," *Vogue* 69, no. 6 (March 15, 1927): 84–85.

42 Park, 90, 168.

43 Storey, "Skyscraper Architecture Influences Furniture," SM12.

44 "American Modernist Furniture," 119–21.

45 Storey, "Making the Most of a City Apartment," 79.

46 Storey, 79.

47 Long, "Paul T. Frankl's Skyscraper Furniture," 170.

48 For example, the rounded corners seen on the dressers also appear on a Skyscraper bookcase/end table in the collection of the Philadelphia Museum of Art (2010-28-1).

49 Johnson, "The New Furniture Gives Every One His Own Skyline," 3.

50 Paul T. Frankl, *Machine-Made Leisure* (New York: Harper & Brothers, 1932), 70.

51 While others also mimicked the look of sky-scrapers for household products in the 1920s, Frankl's designs were the first to get widespread recognition in exhibitions and publications, therefore exerting the greatest influence on the trend that crested in 1928–29. On May 2–6, 1927, Frankl's Skyscraper Furniture was featured in the pioneering Art-in-Trades Club exposition. It garnered ample press attention both at home and abroad. Coverage for Frankl's work included articles in the *New York Times* (Storey, "Skyscraper Architecture Influences Furniture") and the European edition of the *New York Herald Tribune* ("Modern Art and Style Dictate in Furniture Field. Declares P.T. Frankl, American Authority Now Here," August 7, 1927). Images of Frankl's Skyscraper Furniture were also included in Eugene Clute's *The Treatment of Interiors*, published in 1926, and Edwin Avery Park's *New Backgrounds for a New Age*, which was released by June 1927.

52 Rice's design reveals the influence of both Frankl's furniture and Erik Magnussen's silver *Cubic* coffee set, released by Gorham late in 1927, which, according to critics at the time, was "poetically named 'The Lights and Shadows of Manhattan' because of its suggestion of metropolitan archi-tecture and the play of light over its variegated surfaces" (Walter Rendell Storey, "Lamps That Lend Harmony to the Home," *New York Times*, December 11, 1927, SM14). While Rice's forms, like Frankl's furniture, share the rectilinearity of the buildings themselves, his use of patinated trian-gles on his serving wares (though not seen on the example shown in fig. 16) evoke the multiple facets of Magnussen's Cubist-inspired design. In advertisements for Bernard Rice's Sons, Inc., the Apollo *Sky-Scraper* Line was advertised "with Black Smoke-Stacks as Handles." Advertisement reproduced in Jewel Stern, *Modernism in American Silver: 20th-Century Design* (Dallas: Dallas Museum of Art; New Haven, CT: Yale University Press, 2005), 78.

53 John Stuart Gordon provided the attribution to Jean George Theobald for Manning-Bowman's clock designs, sketches for which exist at the Meriden Historical Society, Meriden, Connecticut.

54 French designer Jules Buoy ran the New York showroom, known as Ferrobrandt, of the Paris metalworker Edgar Brandt. Long, *Paul T. Frankl and Modern American Design*, 62.

55 Long, 116.

Electric Light

1 For more on Deskey, see David A. Hanks and Jennifer Toher, *Donald Deskey: Decorative Designs and Interiors* (New York: E. P. Dutton, 1987).

2 "Saks is Very . . . ," *Fortune* 18 (November 1938): 126.

3 "Lighting and Display—Equipment and Supplies: Abstract Concepts Are Guiding Rule of Modernistic Sets, Says Deskey," *Women's Wear Daily* 36, no. 153 (June 30, 1928): 17.

4 "Lighting and Display," 17.

5 Gilbert Seldes, "Profiles: The Long Road to Roxy," *New Yorker Magazine*, February 25, 1933, 22–26.

6 Ernest Freeberg, *The Age of Edison: Electric Light and the Invention of Modern America* (New York: Penguin, 2013), 28; and David E. Nye, *Electrifying America: Social Meanings of a New Technology* (Cambridge, MA: MIT Press, 1990), 2.

7 *The Panama-Pacific International Exposition: San Francisco, California, U.S.A., February 20 to December 4, 1915* (Chicago: C. Teich & Company, 1915); and Frank Morton Todd, *The Story of the Exposition: Being the Official History of the International Celebration held at San Francisco in 1915 to Commemorate the Discovery of the Pacific Ocean and the Construction of the Panama Canal*, vol. 2 (New York: G. P. Putnam's Sons, 1921), 342.

8 Although designers had created artistic and beautiful electric lamps since the turn of the century, the 1925 Exposition marked a major increase of interest in directing rays of light, as well as the new modern design.

9 Margot Amory, "Electricity as an Influential Factor in Architecture," *House Beautiful* 62 (September 1929): 246, 294.

10 Walter W. Kantack, "Fundamentals in Providing for Good Lighting," *American Architect* 140 (September 1931): 49. Kantack, a leader in the field, also wrote extensively on electric lighting's possibilities in his journal *Kaleidoscope*.

11 Bassett (elsewhere written as Basset) Jones Jr., "The Relation of Architectural Principles to Illuminating Engineering Practice," *Transactions of the Illuminating Engineering Society* 3, no. 1 (January 1908): 30, 60.

12 For the idea of "luminous architecture" in the 1930s, see Dietrich Neumann, ed., *Architecture of the Night: The Illuminated Building* (Munich: Prestel, 2002), 61.

13 John McMullin, "Features: Modern Lighting," *Vogue* 73, no. 7 (March 30, 1929): 94.

14 In the 1930 census, Philip Vollner (note mis-spelling) listed his occupation as sales manager for a lamp manufacturer.

15 Dorothy Bent, "Small Tables Essential in Modern Decoration," *Arts & Decoration* 27 (August 1927): 76.

16 Earl F. Lougee, "Furniture in the Modern Manner," *Modern Plastics* 12, no. 4 (December 1934): 18.

17 For the spread of a national culture based on electricity, see Sandy Isenstadt, *Electric Light: An Architectural History* (Cambridge, MA: MIT Press, 2018).

18 While the Dynamotive Radio Corporation's *Dynergy* radio of 1924 preceded it, RCA's *Radiola 30* of 1925 is widely considered the first commercially successful wired radio, despite its traditional wooden cabinet form, complete with tall turned legs and inlay decoration. Quote from 1926 *Vanity Fair* advertisement for the *Radiola 30*, in Alan Douglas, *Radio Manufacturers of the 1920s, Vol. 3, RCA to Zenith* (Chandler, AZ: Sonoran Publishing, 1999), 38–39.

19 Sparks-Withington Company, "The New Sparton Equasonne" (about 1929), 2. Brochure available digitally from the Hagley Museum, John Okolowicz collection of publications and advertising on radio and consumer electronics.

20 *Radio Retailing* 20, no. 9 (September 1935): 12.

21 Sparton subsequently released several additional Teague-designed "sled" models in the same color scheme: see MFA objects 1996.352 and 1997.76.

22 Jim Linz, *Electrifying Time: Telechron and G.E. Clocks, 1925–1955* (Atglen, PA: Schiffer Publishing, 2001), 14.

23 Randy Juster, *Moderne Time: Lawson Art Deco Clocks* (Decopix Books, 2019), 132.

24 John Stuart Gordon, *A Modern World: American Design from the Yale University Art Gallery, 1920–1950* (New Haven, CT: Yale University Press, 2011), 65–66; and Karen Davies, *At Home in Manhattan: Modern Decorative Arts, 1925 to the Depression* (New Haven, CT: Yale University Art Gallery, 1983), 80.

25 "Have You a Radio in Your Home?," *American Lumberman*, February 18, 1922, 37.

26 It is possible the zigzag lamp was also produced in nickel plate, but no examples with nickel have been confirmed. Hanks and Toher, *Donald Deskey*, 39; and Robert Heide and Jon Gilman, *Popular Art Deco: Depression Era Style and Design*, (New York: Abbeville Press, 1991), 22. Both picture zigzag lamps said to be nickel-plated.

27 Silver-plated: MFA Boston (fig. 22), Sotheby's Auction December 16, 2015 (lot 86), and Rago Auction April 12, 2008 (lot 78). Chromium-plated: Metropolitan Museum of Art (2014.744) and High Museum of Art (2000.207). Author communication with John Stuart Gordon (October 26, 2020).

28 The term "artist-designer" is used by Helen Sprackling in her essay on the American Designers' Gallery, of which Deskey was founding member. Sprackling, "Modern Art and the Artist: The Farseeing Manufacturer Is Proving that He Appreciates the Value of the Artist," *House Beautiful* (February 1929): 151–55. The exhibition ran from November 1928 to March 1929, and was visited by, according to estimates at the time, more than twenty thousand people. Marilyn F. Friedman, "Defining Modernism at the American Designers' Gallery, New York," *Studies in the Decorative Arts* 14, no. 2 (Spring–Summer 2007): 79–116.

29 C. Adolph Glassgold, "The Decorative Arts," *The Arts* 14, no. 6 (December 1928): 341.

30 The MFA is the only collection to own both the zigzag lamp and the ashtray.

31 That the lamp was originally located in Crocker's apartment comes from Sotheby's catalog for its "Important Design" auction, December 16, 2015, lot 89, but the period photograph to which Sotheby's refers could not be located to confirm. According to design historian Mark McDonald, the MFA lamp and its partner came out of an estate in California. Author communication with Mark McDonald (September 25, 2020).

32 For Crocker's penthouse, see Mary Ashe Miller, "A Twentieth Century Apartment," *Vogue* 74, no. 3 (August 3, 1929): 30–35, 94. Some of Crocker's furnishings are now at the Metropolitan Museum of Art and featured in Jared Goss, *French Art Deco* (New York: The Metropolitan Museum of Art, 2014).

33 If chrome, the pair may be the examples now in the Metropolitan Museum of Art (2014.744) and Atlanta's High Museum (2000.207), which initially came on to the market together in New Haven, Connecticut. Author communication with Mark McDonald (September 25, 2020).

34 For photos of Breese's bedroom at his home (called the Orchards) in Southampton, Long Island, see *House & Garden*, July 1929, 81. Also see Ralph M. Pearson rug advertisements in *Creative Art* (April 1929 and August 1929), which include photographs of Breese's library (with a rug designed by Pearson) and bedroom (with rugs designed by Emily Reist and Helen Turquand), as decorated by Frances Tileston Breese Miller, with the assistance of architect Herbert Lippman.

35 Manuel Komroff, "Putting Modern Art in Its Place," *Creative Art* 12 (January 1933): 42.

36 Bassett Jones Jr., "Indirect Lighting," *The American Architect* 96, no. 1772 (Dec 8, 1909): 247. MFA collection includes a Deskey floor lamp likely from Radio City (2014.1384).

37 Donald Deskey, "The Rise of American Architecture and Design," *London Studio* 5 (April 1933): 266–73.

38 "Modernistic into Modern," *Arts & Decoration* 42 (November 1934): 11.

39 Deskey proposed his first lamppost in 1958, but it wasn't until 1959 that a modified version was accepted. By 1965, more than eleven thousand were on the streets. Hanks and Toher, *Donald Deskey*, 150–52.

Nightlife

1 Quote from paper sleeve of one of the Frisco Jazz (also spelled "Jass") Band's Edison recordings of 1917. Reproduced in Don Tyler, *Music of the First World War* (Santa Barbara, CA: ABC-CLIO, 2016), 213.

2 Several publications have documented Schreckengost's long and illustrious career as an industrial designer, including Henry Adams, *Viktor Schreckengost and 20th-Century Design* (Cleveland: Cleveland Museum of Art, 2000); Henry Adams, *Viktor Schreckengost: American da Vinci* (Windsor, CT: Tide-Mark Press, 2006); William Daley, "In Conversation: Viktor Schreckengost/William Daley," *American Craft* 57 (June/July 1997): 44–49, 70, 72; James Stubblebine and Martin Eidelberg, "Viktor Schreckengost and the Cleveland School," *Craft Horizons* 35, no. 3 (June 1975): 34–35, 52–53; and most recently, Mark Bassett, Heather McClellan, and Richard McClellan, "Learning by Doing: The Evolution of Viktor Schreckengost's Jazz Series," *Journal of the American Art Pottery Association* 33, no. 4 (Fall 2017): 12–28.

3 Schreckengost, quoted in Daley, 46, and Adams, *Schreckengost and 20th-Century Design*, 12.

4 On the 1931 Cleveland Museum of Art May Show entry form, Schreckengost spelled his first name with a *k*. Available on archive.org.

5 For Schreckengost's arrival in New York on August 28, 1930, from Cherbourg, France, on the SS *Europa*, see passenger arrival records on Ancestry.com.

6 The idea that Schreckengost spent the night in New York City on his way back to Cleveland from Vienna is an assumption based on a specific reference, made by Schreckengost, that he said was a particular inspiration for the *Jazz* bowl: "I thought back to a magical night when a friend and I went to see Calloway at the Cotton Club. My friend had only just arrived in New York from Vienna and he just flipped; he fell in love with the city, the jazz, the Cotton Club—everything. As I remembered that night, I knew I had to get it all on the bowl." Schreckengost, quoted in Christina Corsiglia, "Viktor Schreckengost" (unpublished manuscript, 1990s).

7 Corsiglia says it was his first project at Cowan, but this fact has not been confirmed.

8 According to Adams, *Schreckengost: American da Vinci*, 27, the *Jazz* bowl label developed with 1980s scholarship. The term is not used in Stubblebine and Eidelberg, "Viktor Schreckengost."

9 Stubblebine and Eidelburg, 52. Binder immigrated to the United States in 1934 and, through his artwork, lecturing, and teaching, was one of the most important influences on American graphic design of the era.

10 Schreckengost said, "At night, you can imagine for yourself what is on the signs." Quoted in Bassett, McClellan, and McClellan, "Learning by Doing," 26.

11 Bassett, McClellan, and McClellan, 16.

12 Stephen Graham, *New York Nights* (New York: George H. Doran, 1927), 65.

13 Eileen Beel, "Viktor Schreckengost: How Cleveland Heights 'Frightening Guest' Became a Legend," *View from the Overlook: The Journal of the Cleveland Heights Historical Society* 34 (Summer 2013): 10.

14 On the *Poor Man's Jazz* bowl, the third version, there are playing cards instead of dice.

15 Quotation from *Sterling Silver by Gorham* (Providence, RI: Gorham Company, 1929), cited in *Silver of the Americas: American Silver in the Museum of Fine Arts, Boston*, ed. Jeannine Falino and Gerald W. R. Ward (Boston: MFA Publications, 2007), 425–26.

16 Schreckengost, quoted in Bassett, McClellan, and McClellan, "Learning by Doing," 26.

17 On jazz's origin in New Orleans, see Ted Gioia, *History of Jazz* (New York: Oxford University Press, 2021). For more on the Great Migration and its impact, see James N. Gregory, *The Southern Diaspora: How the Great Migrations of Black and White Southerners Transformed America* (Chapel Hill: University of North Carolina Press, 2005).

18 See, for example, Alwyn Williams, "Jazz and the New Negro: Harlem's Intellectuals Wrestle with the Art of the Age," *Australasian Journal of American Studies* 21, no. 1 (July 2002): 1–18.

19 Anne Shaw Faulker, "Does Jazz Put the Sin in Syncopation?," *Ladies Home Journal*, August 1921, 16, 34.

20 For Ford's opposition to jazz and its xenophobic/anti-Semitic roots, see Peter La Chapelle, "'Dances Partake of the Racial Characteristics of the People Who Dance Them': Nordicism, Antisemitism, and Henry Ford's Old-Time Music and Dance Revival," in *The Song Is Not the Same: Jews and American Popular Music*, ed. Bruce Zuckerman (West Lafayette, IN: Purdue University Press, 2011), 29–70. For Edison's disdain for jazz, see Stuart Nicholson, *Jazz and Culture in a Global Age* (Boston: Northeastern University Press, 2014), 189; and Damon J. Philips, *Shaping Jazz: Cities, Labels, and the Global Emergence of an Art Form* (Princeton, NJ: Princeton University Press, 2013),

88. For details on the important role of Jewish Americans in promoting Black music and dancing, see Stephen J. Whitfield, "From Patronage to Pluralism: Jews in the Circulation of African American Culture," *Modern Judaism* 33, no. 1 (February 2013): 1–23.

21 As the *New York Times* reported in 1922, it was essential for a successful club to provide "the 'society' member a sprinkling of expensive naughtiness—or she might as well dance at home." Helen Bullitt Lowry, "New York's After Midnight 'Clubs,'" *New York Times,* February 5, 1922, 38.

22 Adams, *Schreckengost: American da Vinci*, 28.

23 See note 6 above.

24 Schreckengost, quoted in Daley, "In Conversation," 72.

25 Abel Green's first *Variety* magazine review of Ellington uses "torrid" to describe Ellington's music on March 21, 1928. *Variety*'s June 20, 1928, issue bears two references to Ellington's Cotton Club radio performances using the adjective "sizzling." Quotes taken from Chadwick Jenkins, "A Question of Containment: Duke Ellington and Early Radio," *American Music* 26, no. 4 (Winter 2008): 424–25.

26 Oral history interview with Archibald Motley, January 23, 1978–March 1, 1979, Archives of American Art, Smithsonian Institution, Washington, DC.

27 Ralph G. Giordano, *Social Dancing in America, Volume Two: Lindy Hop to Hip Hop* (Westport, CT: Greenwood Press, 2007), 53–64.

28 For the expansion of Cowan Pottery, including the New York City office, which opened in February 1930, see Corsiglia, "Viktor Schreckengost." For the Brownell-Lambertson Gallery, see Adams, *Schreckengost and 20th-Century Design*, 15.

29 For receivership and the firm's closure, see Adams, 15; and Corsiglia, which describes the studio atmosphere at Cowan in its final year.

30 In the 1931 Cowan Pottery catalog, "Dry Point" is described as "a process developed by Mr. Cowan," yet it appears to have come to Cowan with Arthur Baggs, who was using it at his Marblehead Pottery earlier in the 1920s. Bassett, McClellan, and McClellan, "Learning by Doing," 18–19.

31 For descriptions of the sgraffito technique as used on the *Jazz* bowl, see Bassett, McClellan, and McClellan, 18; Adams, *Schreckengost and 20th-Century Design*, 88–92; and Adams, *Schreckengost: American da Vinci*, 16, which includes an excerpt from a letter the designer wrote to Homer Kripke (February 15, 1954, Viktor Schreckengost Foundation), describing the method of making the bowl.

32 Bassett, McClellan, and McClellan, "Learning by Doing," 18.

33 Bassett, McClellan, and McClellan, 12.

34 According to Bassett, McClellan, and McClellan, Schreckengost created the form for the parabolic bowl while the flared bowl form was created by Guy Cowan in an attempt to minimize loss. Bassett, McClellan, and McClellan, 15.

35 Whitney Atchley (1908–1955), Edris Eckhardt (1905–1998), and Charles E. Murphy (1909–1994) were students at the Cleveland School of Art and worked at Cowan Pottery while in school. Thelma Frazier, later Thelma Frazier Winter (1903–1977), was a full-time employee at Cowan. Bassett, McClellan, and McClellan, 13. For Schreckengost's use of patterns and his encouragement of improvisation, see Bassett, McClellan, and McClellan, 25.

36 This third version was made in a green and black color scheme in addition to blue and black. For description of how the third version was made, see Bassett, McClellan, and McClellan, 24; and Adams, *Schreckengost and 20th-Century Design*, 92.

37 For locations of known examples, see Bassett, McClellan, and McClellan, "Learning by Doing," 13. According to Adams, *Schreckengost and 20th-Century Design*, Schreckengost estimated that around fifty of the first version were made, two or three examples of the second version, and approximately twenty of the molded third version. Adams, *Schreckengost: American da Vinci*, adds that, while the original order may have been for fifty of the first version, it is unlikely that was entirely filled, and he suggests a new estimate of about twenty-five sgraffito examples and another twenty-five *Poor Man*'s versions.

38 The *Night Club* bowl (with its dancing couple, akin to the *Danse Moderne* plate, with which it likely was meant to pair) is known only from a photo that depicts *Night Club*, *Rhythm in Blue*, and a *Poor Man's Jazz* bowl. The photo was published in *Crockery and Glass Journal* (December 1930) and then in *The Studio* (London) in the early 1930s. Bassett, McClellan, and McClellan, "Leaning by Doing," 22; Adams, *Schreckengost: American da Vinci*, 22–23. There was also a *New Yorker* plate to match the *Jazz* bowl, and there likely were other—no longer known—designs for plates and bowls that never went into production. The *Danse Moderne* plate appears in Cowan's 1931 catalog for $6 apiece, $72/dozen, and in multiple colors: "dark blue, green or yellow." Bassett, McClellan, and McClellan, "Learning by Doing," 19–20. For additional images of the various bowls, see *Viktor Schreckengost: The Jazz Series* (booklet published by Viktor Schreckengost Studios in 2006 and available online).

39 Bassett, McClellan, and McClellan, 19.

40 Eleanor Roosevelt paid $50 for the bowl. Adams, *Schreckengost: American da Vinci*, 17. Schreckengost quote from Mark Favermann, "Viktor Schreckengost: An American Design Giant,"

Journal of Antiques and Collectibles, January 2001, 27–29. At present, the whereabouts of the three original Roosevelt bowls are unknown.

41 Catherine Gilbert Murdock, *Domesticating Drink: Women, Men, and Alcohol in America, 1970–1940* (Baltimore: Johns Hopkins Press, 1998), 129–31.

42 FDR Presidential Library blog, "From the Museum," June 21, 2011. Available at fdrlibrary .wordpress.com; currently published on fdr.blogs.archives.gov.

43 "Jam Session," *Life* 15, no. 15 (October 11, 1943): 118. More information available at Life.com.

Transportation

1 Richard S. Tedlow, "The Struggle for Dominance in the Automobile Market: The Early Years of Ford and General Motors," *Business and Economic History* 17 (1988): 53.

2 For more on Harley Earl, see Ron Van Gelderen and Matt Larson, *LaSalle: Cadillac's Companion Car* (Padukah, KY: Turner Publishing, 2000); Michael Lamm and Dave Holls, *A Century of Automotive Style: 100 Years of American Car Design* (Stockton, CA: Lamm-Morada, 1996); Edson Armi, *The Art of American Car Design* (University Park: Pennsylvania State University Press, 1988); David W. Temple, *The Cars of Harley Earl* (Forest Lake, MN: CarTech, 2016); David Gartman, "Harley Earl and the Art and Color Section: The Birth of Styling at General Motors," *Design Issues* 10, no. 2 (Summer 1994): 3–26; Michael Lamm, "The Beginning of Modern Auto Design," *Journal of Decorative and Propaganda Arts* 15 (Winter–Spring 1990): 60–77; Sally Clarke, "Managing Design: The Art and Colour Section of General Motors, 1927–1941," *Journal of Design History* 12, no. 1 (1999): 65–79; and harleyjearl.com.

3 Christy Borth, "Harley J. Earl," *Ward's AutoWorld*, June–July 1969, 35.

4 Earl, quoted in Borth, 41.

5 "Arbuckle's Car Is A Genuine Knockout," *The Los Angeles Times*, May 2, 1920, 104.

6 http://www.harleyjearl.com/timeline.

7 Gartman, "Harley Earl," 12.

8 "La Salle Named for Noted Explorer," *The Boston Globe*, March 6, 1927, 90.

9 Including Gordon Buehrig, Raymond Dietrich, Thomas Hibbard, John Tjaarda, Phillip O. Wright, and more.

10 Lamm and Holls, *Century of Automotive Style*, 98.

11 Harley J. Earl, "I Dream Automobiles," *The Saturday Evening Post*, August 7, 1954, 82.

12 The MFA has models for some of these race cars, including Henry Segrave's Golden Arrow,

which broke the land speed record at Daytona Beach in 1929 (MFA, 2014.1243), and George Eyston's Speed of the Wind, which achieved long-distance endurance records in Utah in 1935 and 1936 (MFA, 2014.1244). The latter model bears markings from having been placed in a wind tunnel.

13 Waldemar Kaempffert, "Auto Racers Near Limit of Speed: Nerves of the Drivers, Air Resistance, and Other Conditions Stand in the Way of a Much Higher Velocity," *New York Times*, February 26, 1928, 130.

14 For more on this medal, which was designed by Geddes with the assistance of sculptor Rene Paul Chambellan and minted at Medallic Art Company, see Gordon, *Modern World*, 142. The medal was distributed at the 1933–34 World's Fair in Chicago.

15 Meikle, *Twentieth Century Limited*, 148.

16 Harley J. Earl, interviewed by Detroit journalist Stanley H. Brams in 1954; later transcribed by Michael Lamm on December 15, 1990. Interview available online at deansgarage.com.

17 Author correspondence with Hampton Wayt, July 16, 2021.

18 "Twenty-Seven Makes of Cars on View at Show: Great Variety of Mechanical Features and Body Designs among Many Models Offered to Motoring Public for 1934—Something for Every Taste—Company Products Listed Alphabetically," *New York Times*, January 7, 1934, 12A.

19 "Stage Stars Visit Automobile Show," *New York Times*, January 10, 1934, 15.

20 Armi, *Art of American Car Design*, 67.

21 Cadillac Motor Company, *The New La Salle 1934 Features of Construction*, 19. Available online through the General Motors Heritage Archive, gmheritagecenter.com.

22 Author correspondence with Hampton Wayt, July 16, 2021.

23 Armi, *Art of American Car Design*, 69.

24 Earl, "I Dream Automobiles," 18.

25 Earl, 19.

26 Lamm and Holls, *Century of Automotive Style*, 99.

27 Van Gelderen and Larson, *LaSalle*, 6. See David Temple, "The 1934 LaSalle, the car that was not supposed to be built!," *Old Cars Weekly*, December 19, 2019, for another version of the story in which Earl says "Gentlemen, if you decide to discontinue the LaSalle, this is the car you are not going to build."

28 Van Gelderen and Larson, *LaSalle*, date the GM executive meeting that saved the line to August 1933. Admittedly this timeline is tight for releasing a new car at the car show in January 1934. Yet, the authors explain that the problem of how to make the cars was fixed by having Fleetwood Body craft all of the 1934 LaSalles, since they otherwise largely were idle (as few people were buying Cadillacs during the Depression, but GM was hesitant to let their highly skilled Fleetwood craftsmen go). Also, they say that manufacture of 1934 LaSalles did not begin until March of 1934, with orders already piling up.

29 Cadillac Motor Company, *The New La Salle 1934 Features of Construction*, 22.

30 E. Y. Watson, "Scope for New Design: Streamline Idea Urged for Every Type of Power Vehicle," *New York Times*, April 22, 1942, XX10.

31 Alfred P. Sloan, letter to stockholders on GM's 1935 model styles, quoted in Meikle, *Twentieth Century Limited*, 151.

32 "The Streamliners—After Six Years," *Business Week*, February 10, 1940, 47 quoted in Meikle, 155.

33 Quote from William Stout of Trimotor, who also worked on—and was one of four men to receive a patent for—the Union Pacific M-10000 in Meikle, 160.

34 Earl, interviewed by Brams, 1954.

35 "Streamline Train Crossing New York: Makes Stop at Buffalo on Way Here . . . ," *New York Times*, October 25, 1934, 1.

36 Meikle, *Twentieth Century Limited*, 164.

37 *Recent Social Trends in the United States, Report of the President's Research Committee on Social Trends*, 2 vols. (New York: McGraw-Hill, 1933), 172.

38 Federal Highway Administration, Office of Highway Information Management, *Highway Statistics Summary to 1995*. Available online at fhwa.dot.gov.

39 Quoted in Meikle, *Twentieth Century Limited*, 164.

40 As seen in a second photograph by Gutmann of McDonnell's Drive-In (MFA, 2000.900).

41 J. George Frederick, "A New Life on the Road: The Motorist Now Finds Joy in Making Camp in the Wood," *New York Times*, July 28, 1935, XX10.

42 Catherine MacKenzie, "The Week-End Rush: When New York Starts for the Country City Streets Are Almost Empty," *New York Times*, July 28, 1935, XX1.

43 Robert W. Brown, "Vacation Pictures," *New York Times*, June 11, 1939, XX29.

44 "Camping Has Become Refined since the Motor Car Arrived," *New York Times*, June 7, 1925, XX2.

45 John R. McMahon, "Unspeakable Jazz Must Go," *Ladies Home Journal* 38 (December 1921): 34.

46 Virginia Scharff, *Taking the Wheel: Women and the Coming of the Motor Age* (Free Press, 1991), 138.

47 Ralph W. Sherman, quoted in Scharff, 117.

48 Earl, quoted in Harry J. Stathos, "Harley J. Earl Profile," International News Service, 1955, 1, from GM Design Library Technical Center.

49 "Women's Influence in Motor Car Designing: Closed Car Popularity," *New York Times*, January 6, 1924, A21.

50 Margaret Walsh, "Gendering Mobility: Women, Work and Automobility in the United States" *History* 93, no. 3 (July 2008): 376–395; and Scharff, *Taking the Wheel*, 135.

51 Walter Rendell Storey, "Linking Beauty to Machine Products: Familiar Things Are Shown in New Forms at an Exhibition in Philadelphia," *New York Times*, March 6, 1932, SM14.

52 "Art and Machines," *Architectural Forum* 60 (May 1934): 331.

53 David A. Hanks and Anne Foy, *American Streamlined Design: The World of Tomorrow* (Paris: Flammarion, 2005), 158–59, and Gordon, *Modern World*, 340.

54 According to Rachel Delphia, Jewel Stern, and Catherine Walworth, the pitcher was released in August 1935, two months after the ocean liner's triumphant first arrival in New York City's harbor. Delphia, Stern, and Walworth, *Silver to Steel: The Modern Designs of Peter Müller-Munk* (Pittsburgh: Carnegie Museum of Art, 2015), 48. Gordon dates it as "after 1935" (Gordon, *Modern World*, 340).

55 *Fiesta Ware* was designed in 1935 and released in 1936. The *Fiesta Disc* water pitcher was added to the line in 1938. "Fiesta 101: A course for beginner collectors. Part One, 1936" available at drivingfordeco.com.

56 Edward Alden Jewell, "High Spots of the Week: Industrial Art," *New York Times*, April 8, 1934, X7.

57 Henry Dreyfuss, *Designing for People* (New York: Grossman, 1974), 74–75.

58 *The Look of Things* is the title of a booklet made to accompany a film by Earl, 1952.

Plastics

1 "Time for All Ages—From Eight to Eighty," *Modern Plastics* 12, no. 3 (November 1934): 35.

2 "Time for All Ages," 35.

3 Kogan, quoted in Marcy Babbitt, "As a Woman Sees Design: An Interview with Belle Kogan," *Modern Plastics* 13, no. 4 (December 1935): 16.

4 Jane Corby, "Smart Girls: Designer of Household Utensils," *Brooklyn Eagle*, July 26, 1939, n.p.

5 Norton Levine, interview with Belle Kogan, Association of Americans and Canadians in Israel, 1992. Recording courtesy of Bernie Banet.

6 Levine, interview with Kogan.

7 Babbitt, "As a Woman Sees Design," 16–17.

8 "Belle Kogan Remembers: A Journey to Design," *Innovation: The Quarterly Journal of the Industrial Designers Society of America* 13, no. 2 (Spring 1994): 39.

9 Belle Kogan, "Changing the Kitchen Scene," *Modern Plastics* 29, no. 7 (March 1952): 104.

10 Babbitt, "As a Woman Sees Design," 17; Belle Kogan, "Making the Most of Materials," *Electrical Manufacturing*, October 1935, n.p.

11 Kogan, "Changing the Kitchen Scene," 104.

12 "Casein," The Plastics Historical Society, plastiquarian.com.

13 Jeffery L. Meikle, *American Plastic: A Cultural History* (New Brunswick, NJ: Rutgers University Press, 1995), 2, 5, 10–18.

14 "John Wesley Hyatt" and "Celluloid," The Plastics Historical Society, plastiquarian.com.

15 John Wesley Hyatt, "Address of Acceptance," *Journal of Industrial & Engineering Chemistry* 6, no. 2 (1914): 158–61.

16 Meikle, *American Plastic*, 10–30.

17 Meikle, 74.

18 Meikle, 58–60.

19 Attribution to Theobald courtesy of John Stuart Gordon. Author correspondence, August 2020.

20 "A Cloud No Bigger than a Lady's Wrist," *Modern Plastics* 12, no. 1 (September 1934): 28, 29.

21 Kathy Flood, *Things* (Bloomington, IN: Authorhouse, 2006), 78; Julie M. Fenster, "Bakelite Jewelry," *American Heritage* 52, no. 5 (May 2001); and "Cast Phenolics Aid the Vogue For Colorful Costume Jewelry," *Modern Plastics* 12, no. 6 (February 1935): 14–15, 51–54.

22 Meikle, *American Plastic*, 76.

23 Babbitt, "As a Woman Sees Design," 16–17, 49. Two images published in *Modern Plastics* a year earlier also show some of this same jewelry. One is included in the "Plastic in Pictures" section of the June 1934 issue (when the periodical was known as *Plastic Products*), in which the caption attributes the jewelry to Blefeld & Goodfriend. The other, in an article on cast phenolics published in November 1934, does not note the designer or manufacturer.

24 For a full account of the Toledo Scale Company's journey, see Meikle, *American Plastic*, 118–23.

25 Harold Van Doren, "A Designer Speaks His Mind," *Modern Plastics* 12, no. 1 (September 1934): 24.

26 Meikle, *American Plastic*, 115–16.

27 Franklin E. Brill, "What Shape Phenolics," *Modern Plastics* 13, no. 1 (September 1935): 21.

28 Meikle, *American Plastic*, 115–16.

29 "Eastman Introduces a Molded Camera," *Modern Plastics* 12, no. 1 (September 1934): 64.

30 Rachel Hunnicutt, "A Camera Worth a Thousand Words: Eastman Kodak's Baby Brownie and the Rise of Popular Photography," Cooper Hewitt Design Stories, cooperhewitt.org.

31 Paul T. Frankl, quoted in Frank E. Brill, "Our Homesick Plastics," *Plastics & Molded Products* 8, no. 6 (June 1932): 235.

32 Van Doren, "Designer Speaks His Mind," 24.

33 Babbitt, "As a Woman Sees Design," 49.

34 Gordon, *Modern World*, 285.

35 W. R. Brooks, "Ivory, Apes and Peacocks," *Outlook and Independent* 6 (March 1929): 383.

36 H. S. Spencer, "This Year," *Plastics & Molded Products* 8, no. 12 (January 1933): 451–52.

37 Meikle, *American Plastic*, 110–12.

38 Brill, "What Shapes Phenolics," 236.

39 *Modern Plastics* was originally founded in 1925 as *Plastics*, changed its name to *Plastics & Molded Products* in 1927 (shortened to *Plastic Products* in 1933), and then shifted again to *Modern Plastics* in September 1934. Meikle, *American Plastic*, 99–100.

40 Walter Dorwin Teague, "No Longer Substitutes," *Modern Plastics* 12, no. 1 (September 1934): 68.

41 Meikle, *American Plastic*, 99, 100.

42 Both toiletry sets were made of Amerith and were patented by Kogan, "assignor to Celluloid Corporation," on July 16, 1935 (Capri USD96261 and Continental USD96260).

43 Babbitt, "As a Woman Sees Design," 49.

44 General Electric ad reproduced in Jim Linz, *Electrifying Time: Telechron and G.E. Clocks, 1925–1955* (Atglen, PA: Schiffer Publishing, 2001), 161.

45 Pricing varies in different publications, from $3.50 to $5.25 for *Smug* and $4.95 to $6.50 for *Quacker*. Sales statistics from Linz, 185, 226.

46 For the *Trimatic* Toaster, see ad in *Modern Plastics* 12, no. 7 (March 1935): 41. Ad says the photo is courtesy of the Bakelite Corporation. The white, melon-shaped tea set with flower-petal platter at the center of the display was patented by Kogan for Ebeling & Reuss on March 19, 1935.

47 "Modern Art Held Quest for Truth," *New York Times*, February 5, 1935, 17.

48 Belle Kogan, "A Designer Looks at Plastics," *Bakelite Review* 11, no. 4 (January 1940): 6, 18; and Belle Kogan, "Noted at Paris Exposition," *Modern Plastics* 15, no. 5 (January 1938): 34–35, 64, 66.

49 Charles L. Venable, Ellen P. Denker, Katherine C. Grier, and Stephen G. Harrison, *China and Glass in America, 1880–1980: From Table Top to TV Tray* (New York: Harry N. Abrams, 2000), 151; and Gordon, *Modern World*, 401.

50 "One-Man Show Devoted to Industrial Designer Who Likes Best to Produce Chain Store Wares," *New York Herald Tribune*, April 12, 1946.

List of Illustrations

Unless otherwise noted, works of art come from the collection of the Museum of Fine Arts, Boston.

Skyscrapers

1
Paul T. Frankl at his desk, Woodstock, New York, mid-1920s
Photograph
Courtesy of Christopher Long

2
Frankl's son, Peter, with the first Skyscraper bookcase, Woodstock, New York, mid-1920s
Photograph
Courtesy of Christopher Long

3
Paul T. Frankl (American [born in Austria], 1886–1958)
Skyscraper desk and bookcase, about 1927–28
Walnut, walnut veneer, pine, birch plywood, core board, American beech, steel, paint, silver-plated brass handles, electrical wiring, and light bulb
210.8 × 123.8 × 54 cm (83 × 48¾ × 21¼ in.)
The John Axelrod Collection, 2011.1647

4
Detroit Publishing Company (American, active 1890s–1932)
Woolworth Building, New York, about 1913
Offset photomechanical on card stock
14 × 8.9 cm (5½ × 3½ in.)
Leonard A. Lauder Postcard Archive— Gift of Leonard A. Lauder, 2013.15258

5
Detroit Publishing Company
New York Telephone Building, 1926–30
Photograph
Library of Congress, Prints & Photographs Division, Detroit Publishing Company Collection

6
Alfred Stieglitz (American, 1864–1946)
The City of Ambition, 1910
Photogravure
34.1 × 26.2 cm (13⁷⁄₁₆ × 10⁵⁄₁₆ in.)
Gift of Miss Georgia O'Keeffe, 50.834

7
Max Weber (American [born in Russia], 1881–1961)
New York (The Liberty Tower from the Singer Building), 1912
Oil on canvas
46.35 × 33.34 cm (18¼ × 13⅛ in.)
Gift of the Stephen and Sybil Stone Foundation, 1971.705

8
M. Murray Leibowitz (American, 1903–1999)
Skyscraper, 1928
Wash, charcoal, and conté crayon on paper
111.8 × 90.2 cm (44 × 35½ in.)
Gift of Murray Leibowitz, 1983.198

9
Detail of *Skyscraper* desk and bookcase

10
Accessories Manufacturers Limited (Canadian)
Magicoal Electric Fire, late 1930s
Steel frame, wire mesh with crystal-like rubber coating, black paint, and electrical workings
31.8 × 46.4 × 22.2 cm (12½ × 18¼ × 8¾ in.)
The John Axelrod Collection, 2014.1464

11
The Hall China Company (East Liverpool, Ohio; founded 1903)
Phoenix water server, about 1938
Stoneware with Delphinium blue glaze
12.7 × 26.7 × 13.3 cm (5 × 10½ × 5¼ in.)
Gift of Barbara McLean Ward and Gerald W. R. Ward, 2015.2234a-b

12
Norman Bel Geddes (American, 1893–1958)
for Revere Copper and Brass Company (Waterbury, Connecticut; founded 1801)
Manhattan cocktail set, designed 1934; produced about 1939–41
Manufactured by Revere Copper and Brass Co. (American, founded 1801), about 1939–41
Chromium-plated brass
Shaker: H. 34.3 cm (13½ in.)
The John Axelrod Collection, 2014.1262.1-8

13
Donald Deskey (American, 1894–1989)
Screen, 1927–31
Wood, canvas, metal fittings, aluminum leaf,
and paint
194.3 × 148.6 cm (76½ × 58½ in.)
The John Axelrod Collection, 2011.1648

14
Paul T. Frankl
Pair of *Skyscraper* dressers, about 1927–28
Walnut veneer, soft wood, core board, paint,
and silver-plated brass
190.8 × 152.7 × 50.8 cm (75⅛ × 60⅛ × 20 in.)
The John Axelrod Collection, 2015.964.1-2

15
Julian de Miskey (American [born in Hungary],
1898–1976)
"Don't you just love my skyscraper furniture?"
New Yorker, March 10, 1928
de Miskey, Julian / The New Yorker Collection /
The Cartoon Bank

16
Louis M. Rice (American, dates unknown)
for Apollo Studios, a Division of Bernard Rice's
Sons, Inc. (New York; active about 1899–1959)
Sky-scraper coffee and tea service, designed 1928
Patinated silverplate
Coffee pot: 24.1 × 21 × 10.2 cm (9½ × 8¼ × 4 in.)
The John Axelrod Collection, 2014.1300.1-4

17
Possibly Jules Buoy (French, active in the
United States, 1872–1937) for Ferrobrandt (Paris
and New York; active early 20th century)
Cigarette lighter, about 1930
Nickel-plated and polished brass; clear plastic
and electrical wiring
41 × 12.9 × 12.9 cm (16⅛ × 5¹⁄₁₆ × 5¹⁄₁₆ in.)
The John Axelrod Collection, 2014.1266

18
RumRill Art Pottery Company (1931–42) for
Red Wing Potteries, Inc. (Red Wing, Minnesota;
active 1878–1967)
Manhattan Group vase, 1931–38
Glazed stoneware
17.1 × 17.8 × 7.6 cm (6¾ × 7 × 3 in.)
Gift of J. Parker Prindle, Jr. in honor of Carl Edwin
Prindle, 2014.1091

19
Paul T. Frankl for Johnson Furniture Company
(active 1908–83)
Cocktail table, about 1951
Cork and mahogany
36.8 × 119.4 × 88.9 cm (14½ × 47 × 35 in.)
Gift of Lillian Heidenberg, 2008.29

Electric Light

20
Donald Deskey, 1939
Photograph
Getty Images

21
Study room, Adam Gimbel apartment,
Park Avenue, New York, about 1927–28
Donald Deskey Archive, Cooper Hewitt,
Smithsonian Design Museum
© Smithsonian Institution

22
Donald Deskey for Deskey-Vollmer, Inc.
(New York; active 1927–31)
Table lamp, designed 1927–28; produced 1927–31
Silver-plated brass, glass, and electrical fittings
33 × 11.1 × 13.3 cm (13 × 4⅜ × 5¼ in.)
The John Axelrod Collection, 2008.1416

23
Alvin Langdon Coburn (American, 1882–1966)
Broadway at Night, about 1910
Photogravure
20.1 × 14.9 cm (7¹⁵⁄₁₆ × 5⅞ in.)
Gift of David H. McAlpin, 1972.333

24
Poul Henningsen (Danish, 1894–1967) for Louis
Poulsen & Co. (Copenhagen, Denmark)
PH table lamp, designed 1926
Bakelite, glass, and brass
44.5 × 34 cm (17½ × 13⅜ in.)
The Museum of Modern Art, New York
Estée and Joseph Lauder Design Fund, 27.2000
Digital Image © The Museum of Modern Art /
Licensed by SCALA / Art Resource, NY

25
Berenice Abbott (American, 1898–1991)
New York City Streets at Night, 1933
Photograph, gelatin silver print
15.3 × 12.4 cm (6 × 4⅞ in.)
Gift of Mrs. Jeanne Kanton Landon, 1973.524
Berenice Abbott / Getty Images

26

Walter von Nessen (American [born in Germany], 1889–1943) for Nessen Studio, Inc. (New York; founded in 1927)
Floor lamp, designed about 1928; produced 1928–31
Brushed and chromium-plated brass, cast iron, and electrical fittings
171.5 × 34.3 cm (67½ × 13½ in.)
The John Axelrod Collection, 1985.672

27

Donald Deskey for Deskey-Vollmer, Inc.
Desk lamp, designed about 1928; produced 1928–31
Chromium-plated metal, painted wood, green felt, and electrical components
The John Axelrod Collection, 2014.1382

28

William Lescaze (American [born in Switzerland], 1896–1969)
Counter-balance table lamp, designed about 1934
Chromium-plated metal and paper/parchment shade (replaced)
63.5 × 15.9 × 7.6 cm (25 × 6¼ × 3 in.)
The John Axelrod Collection, 2010.947

29

Reddy Kilowatt marketing sign, late 1940s
Enamel-coated metal
H. 127 cm (50 in.)
Collection of John Axelrod

30

Donald Deskey for Deskey-Vollmer, Inc.
Side table, designed about 1928; produced 1929–31
Vitrolite (glass) and chromium-plated steel
45.7 × 50.8 × 30.5 cm (18 × 20 × 12 in.)
The John Axelrod Collection, 2014.1272

31

Manning-Bowman Company (Meriden, Connecticut; active 1849–1945)
Coffee percolator, about 1928
Chromium-plated metal and Catalin (plastic)
H. 37.5 cm (14¾ in.)
Gift of J. Parker Prindle in memory of Florence Cheney Prindle, 2008.277.2a-c

32

Walter Dorwin Teague (American, 1883–1960) for Sparton Corporation (Jackson, Michigan; founded 1900)
Sparton Bluebird radio, designed 1934; produced 1935–36
Mirrored glass, chromium-plated metal, painted wood, and electrical components
10.8 × 36.8 × 35.6 cm (4¼ × 14½ × 14 in.)
The John Axelrod Collection, 1996.351

33

Paul T. Frankl for Warren Telechron Company (Ashland, Massachusetts; active 1912–92)
Modernique clock, designed 1928; produced 1928–31
Chromium-plated brass, glass, plastic (probably Bakelite), and enamel
19.1 × 14.9 × 9.5 cm (7½ × 5⅞ × 3¾ in.)
Museum purchase with funds donated by J. Parker Prindle, 2008.1038

34

Top row, from left:

Gilbert Rohde (American, 1894–1944) for Herman Miller Clock Company (Zeeland, Michigan; active 1926–37)
Electric clock, model no. 4082, designed 1933
Maidou burl, chromium-plated metal, white painted metal dial, and glass
17.5 × 33.7 × 6.4 cm (6⅞ × 13¼ × 2½ in.)
The John Axelrod Collection, 2014.1430

Gilbert Rohde for Herman Miller Clock Company
Electric clock, model no. 4090, designed 1933
Chromium-plated metal, enameled metal, and etched plate glass
27.9 × 31.8 × 8.9 cm (11 × 12½ × 3½ in.)
The John Axelrod Collection, 2014.1282

Jean George Theobald (American, 1873–1952) for Manning-Bowman Company
Mantel clock, 1929–31
Chromium-plated metal and black Catalin
24 × 28 × 9.5 cm (9⁷⁄₁₆ × 11 × 3¾ in.)
Gift of J. Parker Prindle in memory of Florence Cheney Prindle, 2008.278

Gilbert Rohde for Herman Miller Clock Company
Tide electric clock, model no. 6366, designed about 1933
Macassar ebony (or East India Laurel), chromium-plated metal, and glass
15.9 × 40.6 × 6.4 cm (6¼ × 16 × 2½ in.)
The John Axelrod Collection, 2009.5314

Gilbert Rohde for Herman Miller Clock Company
Electric clock, model no. 4708B, designed 1933
Blue-mirrored glass, polished and brushed
chromium-plated metal
16.2 × 15.2 × 8.9 cm (6⅜ × 6 × 3½ in.)
The John Axelrod Collection, 2014.1429

Paul Feher (American, 1898–1990) and
George F. Adomaitis (American, 1907–1982)
for Lawson Time (Pasadena, California;
active about 1934–about 1975)
Zephyr electric clock, designed 1937
Brass, copper, plastic (probably celluloid),
and glass
9.5 × 21.6 × 7.9 cm (3¾ × 8½ × 3⅛ in.)
The John Axelrod Collection, 2014.1263

Paul Feher and George F. Adomaitis for
Lawson Time
Arlington electric clock, 1936
Silver-plated brass, plastic (probably
celluloid or Lucite), alabaster, and glass
9.5 × 33 × 10.8 cm (3¾ × 13 × 4¼ in.)
The John Axelrod Collection, 2014.1449

Gilbert Rohde for Herman Miller Clock Company
Electric clock, model no. 6351, designed 1934–37
Aluminium, metal with black alumilite finish,
and glass
8.9 × 21.6 × 5.4 cm (3½ × 8½ × 2⅛ in.)
The John Axelrod Collection, 2014.1434

Gilbert Rohde for Herman Miller Clock Company
Electric clock, model no. 4704B, designed 1933
Harewood, chromium-plated metal, silver-plated
brass dial (replaced?), and glass
12.1 × 22.9 × 5.7 cm (4¾ × 9 × 2¼ in.)
The John Axelrod Collection, 2014.1436

Paul Feher and George F. Adomaitis for
Lawson Time
Highboy clock, designed about 1938
Chromium-plated metal (nickel?), plastic
(probably celluloid), and glass
16.5 × 9.8 × 7.6 cm (6½ × 3⅞ × 3 in.)
The John Axelrod Collection, 2014.1454

35
Raymond Hood (American, 1881–1934)
Table, 1931
Black glass, steel, wrought iron, brass and
brass-plated metal, and plywood
75.9 × 73.8 × 58.1 cm (29⅞ × 29¹/₁₆ × 22⅞ in.)
The John Axelrod Collection, 2014.1255

36
Ruth Reeves (American, 1892–1966) for
W. & J. Sloane (New York; active 1843–1985)
Electric coverlet, 1930
Cotton
188.3 × 104.46 cm (74⅛ × 41⅛ in.)
Yale University Art Gallery, 1995.49.1
John P. Axelrod Collection, B.A. 1968

37
Donald Deskey for Deskey-Vollmer, Inc.
Ashtray, designed about 1927; produced 1927–31
Chromium-plated metal
8.57 × 10.16 × 5.08 cm (3⅜ × 4 × 2 in.)
The John Axelrod Collection, 2008.1417

38
Jean Dunand (French [born Switzerland],
1877–1942)
Table, about 1927–28
Lacquered wood
59.1 × 34.9 × 34.9 cm (23¼ × 13¾ × 13¾ in.)
The Metropolitan Museum of Art
Gift of Mr. and Mrs. Peter M. Brant, 1977, 1977.226.7
© 2022 Artists Rights Society (ARS), New York
Image copyright © The Metropolitan Museum
of Art
Image source: Art Resource, NY

Nightlife

39
Viktor Schreckengost, 1931
Negative 12458B
The Cleveland Museum of Art Archives

40
Michael Powolny (Austrian, 1871–1954)
Bear, about 1935
Earthenware with white crackle glaze, and
dark brown and black glaze details
30.5 × 21 × 24.8 cm (12 × 8¼ × 9¾ in.)
The John Axelrod Collection, 2014.1333

41
Viktor Schreckengost (American, 1906–2008)
for Cowan Pottery Studio (Rocky River, Ohio;
active 1919–1931)
Jazz Bowl, designed 1930; produced 1930–31
Glazed porcelain with sgrafitto decoration
22.9 × 42.9 cm (9 × 16⅞ in.)
The John Axelrod Collection, 1990.507

42
Rollout of *Jazz bowl*

43
Joseph Binder (Austrian, 1898–1972)
New York World's Fair, 1939
Color lithograph poster
76.1 × 50.8 cm (29¹⁵⁄₁₆ × 20 in.)
Gift of Richmond G. Wight, 1970.626

44
Walker Evans (American, 1903–1975)
Times Square / Broadway Composition, 1930
Gelatin silver print
24.8 × 21.7 cm (9¾ × 8⁹⁄₁₆ in.)
The J. Paul Getty Museum, Los Angeles
© Walker Evans Archive, The Metropolitan
Museum of Art

45
Erik Magnussen (Danish, 1884–1961) for Gorham
Manufacturing Company (Providence, Rhode
Island; active 1865–1961)
Modern American cocktail set, designed 1928;
produced 1928–30
Silver
Shaker: 31.4 × 16.1 cm (12³⁄₈ × 6⁵⁄₁₆ in.)
The John Axelrod Collection, 1999.250.1-9

46
Russel Wright (American, 1904–1976) for Russel
Wright, Inc. (New York; active 1930–76)
Cocktail set, designed about 1930;
produced 1930–31
Polished pewter or silver-lined chromium-plated
metal
23.5 × 20.3 cm (9¼ × 8 in.)
The John Axelrod Collection, 2014.1296.1-8

47
Arthur Garfield Dove (American, 1880–1946)
George Gershwin—I'll Build a Stairway to Paradise,
1927
Ink, metallic paint, and oil on paperboard
50.8 × 38.1 cm (20 × 15 in.)
Gift of the William H. Lane Foundation, 1990.407

48
Norman Lewis (American, 1909–1979)
Harlem Jazz Jamboree, 1943
Oil on canvas
18 × 16 in. (45.7 × 40.6 cm)
Charles H. Bayley Picture and Painting Fund,
2007.5
© Estate of Norman W. Lewis; Courtesy of Michael
Rosenfeld Gallery LLC, New York, NY

49
Viktor Schreckengost
Harlem Hoofers, 1929–30

Glazed earthenware (red clay)
34.3 × 20.3 × 15.2 cm (13½ × 8 × 6 in.)
The John Axelrod Collection, 2014.1340

Harlem Melodies, 1929–30
Glazed earthenware (red clay)
30.5 × 23.5 × 20.6 cm (12 × 9¼ × 8⅛ in.)
The John Axelrod Collection, 2014.1335

50
Viktor Schreckengost
Blue Revel, 1931
Oil on canvas
127 × 81.3 cm (50 × 32 in.)
Gift of Vik Schreckengost 2000.127
The Cleveland Museum of Art
© Copyright 1931 by Viktor Schreckengost
Used with permission by American da Vinci, LLC

51
Archibald Motley (American, 1891–1981)
Cocktails, about 1926
Oil on canvas
81.3 × 101.6 cm (32 × 40 in.)
The John Axelrod Collection—Frank B. Bemis
Fund, Charles H. Bayley Fund, and The Heritage
Fund for a Diverse Collection, 2011.1859

52
Viktor Schreckengost for Cowan Pottery Studio
Danse Moderne plate, designed 1930–31
Glazed earthenware
2.5 × 28.3 cm (1 × 11⅛ in.)
The John Axelrod Collection, 2014.1339

53
Arthur E. Baggs (American, 1886–1947)
Vase, 1922
Wheel-thrown earthenware, glazed with sgrafitto
decoration
17.15 × 13.34 cm (6¾ × 5¼ in.)
The John Axelrod Collection, 2014.1292

54
Viktor Schreckengost for Cowan Pottery Studio
Vase, 1931
Earthenware with dry point decoration
17.15 × 13.34 cm (6¾ × 5¼ in.)
The John Axelrod Collection, 2014.1293

55
Gjon Mili (American [born in Albania], 1904–1984)
First Jam (Billie Holiday), 1943
Gelatin silver print
26.67 × 26.67 cm (10½ × 10½ in.)
Charles H. Bayley Picture and Painting Fund,
2008.678
© CORBIS / Corbis via Getty Images

Transportation

56
Harley J. Earl in a 1927 LaSalle at the car's unveiling,
Boston, 1927
Photograph
Courtesy of General Motors Archives

57
Ford Trimotor airplane model, about 1929
Metal
22.2 × 102.2 × 86.4 cm (8¾ × 40¼ × 34 in.)
Jean S. and Frederic A. Sharf Collection

58
Norman Bel Geddes
General Motors' 25th Anniversary medal, 1933
Silver-plated bronze
7.6 × .6 cm (3 × ¼ in.)
Collection of John Axelrod

59
Harley J. Earl (American, 1893–1969) for General
Motors (Detroit, Michigan; founded 1908)
Cadillac-LaSalle design model, 1930–33
Mahogany, painted black, chromium-plated
metal, and glass
38.1 × 45.7 × 137.2 cm (15 × 18 × 54 in.)
Jean S. and Frederic A. Sharf Collection

60
Margaret Bourke-White (American, 1904–1971)
La Salle, about 1935
Photograph
Margaret Bourke-White Papers, Special
Collections Research Center, Syracuse University
Libraries
© 2021 Estate of Margaret Bourke-White /
Licensed by VAGA at Artists Rights Society (ARS), NY

61
J. Friedrich Werner (American [born in Germany])
Kissel car model, about 1920
Maple, ash, and other woods
48.3 × 111.8 × 40.6 cm (19 × 44 × 16 in.)
Gift of Jean S. and Frederic A. Sharf, 2014.1239

62
Western Coil & Electric Company (Racine,
Washington; founded 1915)
Burlington Zephyr train model, designed about
1934; produced about 1934–40
Cast aluminum, plastic, paper, and electrical
components
5 × 4 × 39¼ in. (12.7 × 10.2 × 99.7 cm)
Gift of Jean S. and Frederic A. Sharf, 2014.1238.1-5

63
*110 Mile Per Hour—Union Pacific Streamlined
Passenger Train*, about 1934
Real photograph on card stock
8.9 × 14 cm (3½ × 5½ in.)
Leonard A. Lauder Postcard Archive—Gift of
Leonard A. Lauder, 2015.6309

64
International Silver Company (Meriden,
Connecticut; founded 1898)
American Airlines DC-3 Flagship flatware,
designed 1936
Silverplate
L. 16.5 cm (6½ in.)
Gift of Jean S. and Frederic A. Sharf, 2014.1247.1-37

65
Harry Callahan (American, 1912–1999)
Detroit, 1943
Gelatin silver print
27.9 × 35.6 cm (11 × 14 in.)
Gift of Barbara J. and Eugene P. Polk, 2013.1910
© The Estate of Harry Callahan; Courtesy Pace/
MacGill Gallery, New York

66
Iannelli Studios (1920–65)
Design for Standard Service Station, 1931
Graphite, pen and ink, and opaque watercolor,
with collage element
40.6 × 76.8 × 2.5 cm (16 × 30¼ × 1 in.)
Gift of Jean S. and Frederic A. Sharf, 2016.729

67
John Gutmann (American, 1905–1998)
*Car Hops, Early Drive-in Restaurant, Hollywood,
California*, 1935
Gelatin silver print
23.7 × 20.2 cm (9⁵⁄₁₆ × 7¹⁵⁄₁₆ in.)
Ellen Kelleran Gardner Fund, 1976.785
© Center for Creative Photography, Arizona Board
of Regents

68
Walter Dorwin Teague (American, 1883–1960)
for Eastman Kodak Company (Rochester,
New York; founded 1889)
Bantam Special camera, designed 1936;
produced 1936–48
White metal with plastic coating
8.3 × 12.1 × 5.1 cm (3¼ × 4¾ × 2 in.)
The John Axelrod Collection, 2014.1441

69
John Vassos (American [born in Romania],
1898–1985) for RCA Victor Co. (New York;
founded 1929)
RCA Victor Special portable phonograph,
about 1935
Aluminum, chromium-plated steel, and plastic
55.25 × 44.45 × 53.34 cm (21¾ × 17½ × 21 in.)
The John Axelrod Collection, 2014.1284

70
Viktor Schreckengost for Murray Ohio Company
(Cleveland, Ohio; active 1919–88)
Torpedo pedal car, designed about 1938–49
Steel, chrome, and enamel
L. 94 cm (37 in.)
Museum purchase with funds donated by
J. Parker Prindle in the name of Carson Edwin
Prindle, 2010.29

71
Viktor Schreckengost sculpting a pedal car,
about 1940
Photograph by Frank Aleksandrov
From the Cleveland Press Collections, courtesy of
the Michael Schwartz Library Special Collections,
Cleveland State University

72
Woman's scarf and hat set, 1925
United States
Printed silk plain weave (chiffon) and silk
thread fringe
Scarf: 129.5 × 25.4 cm (51 × 10 in.)
Hat: 15.2 × 22.9 cm (6 × 9 in.)
Gift of Francisca Smith Clark, 2008.720.1-2

73
Gilbert Rohde for Herman Miller Clock Company
Clock, Model No. 4082, designed about 1933
Maidou burl, chromium-plated metal, silver-
plated brass dial, glass, and electrical fittings
17.5 × 33.7 × 6.4 cm (6⅞ × 13¼ × 2½ in.)
The John Axelrod Collection, 2014.1430

74
Kem (Karl Emanuel Martin) Weber (American
[born in Germany], 1889–1963) for Air Line
Furniture Company (Los Angeles; active 1935–36)
Air Line chair, designed 1935
Birch, ash, metal, and Naugahyde
78.74 × 81.28 × 63.5 cm (31 × 32 × 25 in.)
The John Axelrod Collection, 2014.1276

75
Peter Müller-Munk (American [born in Germany],
1904–1967) for Revere Copper and Brass Co.
Normandie pitcher, designed 1935
Chromium-plated brass
30.48 × 8.26 × 25.4 cm (12 × 3¼ × 10 in.)
The John Axelrod Collection, 2014.1287

76
Walter Dorwin Teague (American, 1883–1960) for
Hamilton Beach Manufacturing Company (Racine,
Washington; founded in 1910)
Milkshake mixer, about 1940
Cast iron, porcelain, chromium-plated metal, and
stainless steel
48.3 × 15.9 × 21.6 cm (19 × 6¼ × 8½ in.)
The John Axelrod Collection, 2014.1442.1-2

77
Frederick Hurten Rhead (American [born in
England], 1880–1942) for Homer Laughlin China
Company (Newell, West Virgina; founded in 1873)
Fiesta Disc water pitcher, designed 1938; produced
1938–43
Earthenware with glaze
19.1 × 21 × 11.4 cm (7½ × 8¼ × 4½ in.)
Gift of Nonie Gadsden in honor of Brett Angell,
2014.1088

Plastics

78
Belle Kogan (American [born in Russia], 1902–
2000) for Warren Telechron Company
Smug clock, designed 1934
Plaskon, brass, glass, and clockworks
15.2 × 14.6 × 6.3 cm (6 × 5¾ × 2½ in.)
Gift of Clifford S. Ackley, 2021.565

79
Belle Kogan, 1947
Photograph
Courtesy of Bernie Banet

80
American Designers' Institute dinner, 1942 or 1943
Photograph
Courtesy of Bernie Banet

81
Comb, late 19th or early 20th century
Celluloid
16.5 × 12.7 × 4 cm (6½ × 5 × 1⁹⁄₁₆ in.)
Gift of Mrs. Edward Jackson Holmes, 54.1364

82
Rolmonica Music Company (Baltimore, Maryland; about 1925–?)
Automatic harmonica, designed 1928
Bakelite, paper, and metal
L. 10 cm (3¹⁵⁄₁₆ in.)
Helen and Alice Colburn Fund, 1984.311.1-6

83
Manning-Bowman Company
Cocktail set, about 1928
Chromium-plated metal and Catalin
3 × 46.4 cm (1³⁄₁₆ × 18¼ in.)
Gift of J. Parker Prindle in memory of Florence Cheney Prindle, 2008.276.1

84
John George Theobald for Manning-Bowman Company
Mantel clock K906, 1929–31
Aranium-plated metal and Catalin
Gift of J. Parker Prindle, Jr., 2015.3039

85
Hinge bracelet, about 1935
Phenolic resin and metal
Diameter: 22.9 cm (9 in.)
William E. Nickerson Fund and funds donated by Marc S. Plonskier, 2019.540

86
Belle Kogan
Two-tone bracelets, designed 1933–34
Bakelite
Diameter: 7.6 cm (3 in.)
Collection of Nonie Gadsden

87
Harold Van Doren (American, 1895–1957) and John Gordon Rideout (American, 1898–1951) for Air-King Products Company (Brooklyn, New York; active mid-20th century)
Air King radio, released 1933
Plaskon, black plaque insert, glass, and metal
29.85 × 22.54 × 19.05 cm (11¾ × 8⅞ × 7½ in.)
The John Axelrod Collection, 2014.1283

88
Walter Dorwin Teague for Eastman Kodak Company
Baby Brownie camera, designed 1934; produced 1934–41
Bakelite, metal, and glass
6.7 × 7.9 × 7.6 cm (2⅝ × 3⅛ × 3 in.)
Gift of Lewis A. Shepard, 2016.762

89 & 90
Belle Kogan
Patents for clock cases, 1934
United States Patent and Trademark Office

91
Paul T. Frankl for Amerith Division of Celluloid Manufacturing Company (Newark, New Jersey; active 1928–35)
Rond vanity set, designed 1928
Amerith, Amer-glo, mirrored glass, and bristles
Mirror L. 27.9 cm (11 in.)
The John Axelrod Collection, 2014.1269.1-3

92
Belle Kogan
Patent for *Continental* vanity set, 1935
United States Patent and Trademark Office

93
Mickey and Minnie on bicycles with their pals, 1936
Lithograph on card stock
8.9 × 15.2 cm (3½ × 6 in.)
Leonard A. Lauder Postcard Archive—
Gift of Leonard A. Lauder, 2014.9822
© Disney

94
Warren Telechron Company
Electrolarm clock, 1929–31
Vinylite, brass trim, metal dial, and electronic components
19.1 × 13.3 × 8.9 cm (7½ × 5¼ × 3½ in.)
Gift of J. Parker Prindle, Jr. in honor of Carl Edwin Prindle, 2014.1093

95
Belle Kogan display at the Annual Industrial Arts Exhibition, 1935
Photograph
Courtesy of Bernie Banet

96
Belle Kogan for Boonton Molding Company (Boonton, New Jersey; active 1920–81)
Boontonware sugar, creamer, and tray, 1950s
Melamine
Platter L. 35.6 cm (14 in.)
Gift of Barbara McLean Ward and Gerald W. R. Ward, 2010.540

Details
pp. 2–3: fig. 16; p. 4: fig. 84; p. 6: fig. 62; p. 8: fig. 8; p. 11: fig. 14; p. 12: fig. 13; p. 15: fig. 52; pp. 16–17: fig. 86.

Index

Page numbers in *italics* refer to illustrations.

Acknowledgments

The ideas and research for this publication began in 2008 when John P. Axelrod pledged to donate his outstanding collection of American modern design to the Museum of Fine Arts, Boston. I was assigned the enviable task of reviewing his holdings and recommending what would come to the MFA. I was not shy—the final list included nearly four hundred objects. Some works were already icons, not only of John's collection, but of the field as a whole. John had generously lent objects to several landmark exhibitions over the years, so his *Skyscraper* desk and bookcase by Paul Frankl and his painted screen by Donald Deskey are literally the ones in the books. But it was the depth of his collection that blew me away—fifteen works by Frankl, fourteen by Deskey, ten by Kem Weber, sixteen by Viktor Schreckengost, ten electric clocks by Gilbert Rhode, every color of soda syphon by Norman Bel Geddes—and numerous excellent pieces by unknown or lesser-known designers that helped to tell the story of early American modern design. John had researched each piece and loved to teach (usually in quiz form). He is the inspiration behind this book.

Yet, John would be the first to remind me that this book includes works given to the MFA by others as well. Fred and Jean Sharf; J. Parker Prindle; Cliff Ackley, Ruth and Carl J. Shapiro Curator of Prints and Drawings Emeritus; and others helped to grow the MFA's collection of American modern design in important ways. Together, these collectors have amassed one of the nation's best collections of this material. I am honored to have had the opportunity to work with and learn from each of them.

But as in any museum project, countless people are involved in making it possible. I am indebted to John Stuart Gordon, Benjamin Attmore Hewitt Associate Curator of American Decorative Arts at the Yale University Art Gallery, who engaged in numerous conversations, entertained countless questions, and provided essential feedback to early drafts. James Zemaitis, Mark McDonald, John Waddell, Christopher Long, Hampton Wayt, Bernie Banet, David Temple, and Karima Perry also graciously shared their knowledge and ideas. Additionally, I would like to acknowledge the generous support and assistance provided by Sheldon Steele at the Larz Andersen Automotive Museum, Christo Datini at the General Motors Archives, and Nilda Lopez at the Cooper Hewitt Archives.

From the MFA, I am grateful to Matthew Teitelbaum, Ann and Graham Gund Director; Elliot Bostwick Davis; and Ethan Lasser, John Moors Cabot Chair, Art of the Americas, for supporting this project, and to my many curatorial colleagues who generously shared their knowledge, including Erica Hirshler, Croll Senior Curator of American Paintings; Ben Weiss, Leonard A. Lauder Senior Curator of Visual Culture, Department of Prints and Drawings; Gerry Ward, Katharine Lane Weems Senior Curator of American Decorative Arts and Sculpture Emeritus; Dennis Carr; Meghan Melvin, Jean S. and Frederic A. Sharf Curator of Design; Patrick Murphy, Lia and William Poorvu Associate Curator of Prints and Drawings; Karen Haas, Lane Senior Curator of Photographs; Kristen Gresh, Estrellita and Yousuf Karsh Senior Curator of Photographs; Emily Stoehrer, Rita J. Kaplan and Susan B. Kaplan Curator of Jewelry; and Bobby Giglio, Pappalardo Assistant Curator of Musical Instruments. Jordan Barnes, Paul McAlpine, and Hee Jung Lee of the MFA Libraries and Archives were also enormously helpful. Others who contributed their impressive skills and expertise in studying the works and making them look their best include Gerri Strickler; Abigail Hykin, Robert P. and Carol T. Henderson Head of Objects Conservation; and William Mastandrea, Gale R. Guild and Henry R. Guild Fellow for Advanced Training, of the objects conservation department; Christine Storti and Gordon Hanlon of the furniture and frames conservation department; and Richard Newman of the scientific research lab. I am beyond thankful to Michael Gould for his stunning photography and to Carly Bieterman, Maggie Loh, and Meghan Anderson for making those photographs possible. And to the wonderful women of MFA Publications (past and present), my deepest gratitude for your boundless encouragement and guidance. Emiko Usui challenged me to find the right approach, Jennifer Snodgrass helped to shape the content, and Hope Stockton carried the project over the finish line. I also want to acknowledge the many MFA interns and volunteers who contributed research to this publication, including Meredith Crawford, Alexandra Polemis, Sophia Lufkin, Robina Mitchell, Betsy Upham, Jessica Nelson, Virginia Wilbanks, John Duval, Elizabeth Kendrick, Julia Carabatsos, and Lauren Spengler.

This publication would not have been completed without the brilliant mind, superlative research skills, beautiful writing, impressive attention to detail, and extraordinary dedication of Kate Lanford Joy. It's not easy doing research during a pandemic, but Kate always managed to find what we needed. She kept me going and kept it fun.

And lastly, my love and undying gratitude to my family for their patience, support, inspiration, and encouragement.

Nonie Gadsden
Katharine Lane Weems Senior Curator
of American Decorative Arts and Sculpture

mfa
BOSTON

MFA Publications
Museum of Fine Arts, Boston
465 Huntington Avenue
Boston, Massachusetts 02115
www.mfa.org/publications

Generous support for this publication is
provided by the Andrew W. Mellon
Publications Fund. Additional support
from John P. Axelrod.

© 2022 by Museum of Fine Arts, Boston

ISBN 978-0-87846-885-0
Library of Congress Control Number:
2022934504

While the objects in this publication
necessarily represent only a small portion
of the MFA's holdings, the Museum is
proud to be a leader within the American
museum community in sharing the objects
in its collection via its website. Currently,
information about approximately 400,000
objects is available to the public world-
wide. To learn more about the MFA's
collections, including provenance, publication, and exhibition history, kindly visit
www.mfa.org/collections.

For a complete listing of MFA publications,
please contact the publisher at the above
address, or call 617 369 4233.

Front cover: Donald Deskey, Desk lamp,
designed about 1928 (fig. 27)

Back cover; Walter Dorwin Teague,
Bantam Special camera, designed 1934
(fig. 68)

Illustrations in this book were photographed by the Imaging Studios, Museum
of Fine Arts, Boston, except where
otherwise noted.

Editing and production by Hope Stockton
Proofread by Dianne Woo
Principal photography by Michael Gould
Designed by Rita Jules, Miko McGinty Inc.
Typeset in Centra No. 1 and NN Nouvelle
    Grotesk by Tina Henderson
Printed on 150 gsm Perigord
Printed and bound at Verona Libri,
    Verona, Italy

Distributed by
ARTBOOK | D.A.P.
75 Broad Street, Suite 630
New York, New York 10004
www.artbook.com

FIRST EDITION
Printed and bound in Italy
This book was printed on acid-free paper.

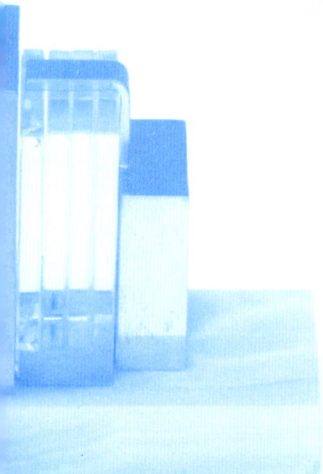

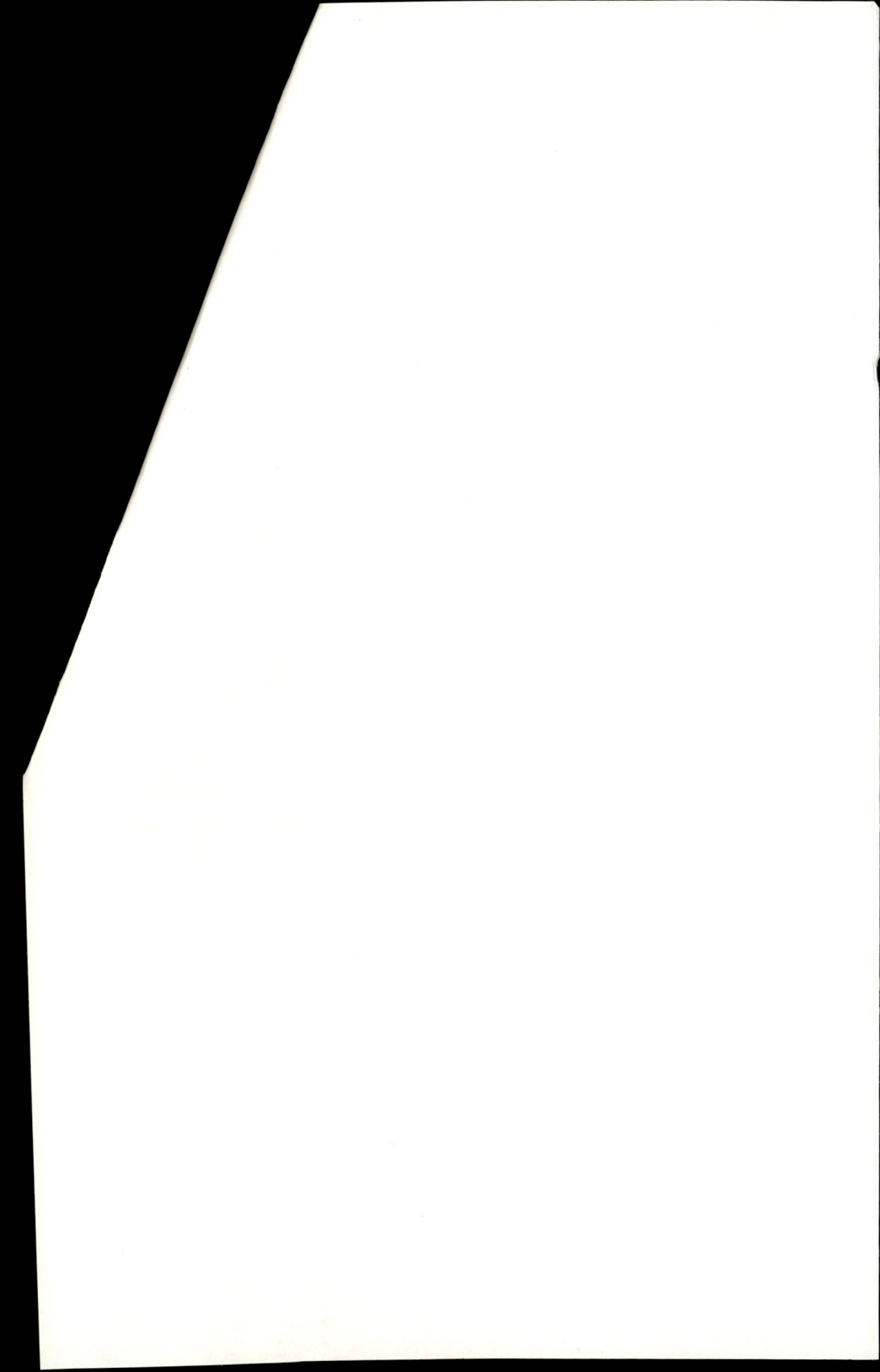

Bragging い

The Thrill of Resting in the Cross

It's unthinkable that I could ever brag about
anything except the cross of our Lord Jesus Christ.
Galatians 6:14a *(God's Word Translation)*

But we are the ones who are truly circumcised, because we
worship by the power of God's Spirit and take pride in Christ
Jesus. We don't brag about what we have done.
Philippians 3:3 *(Contemporary English Version)*

If you were to stand before God and if He were to say, "Why should I let you into my heaven?", what would you say?

If the first word out your mouth is the word "I…", you don't get it.

Dr. Bob Utley,
Teaching a sermon on **I John 1**.

Table of Contents

Preambles

I read an incredible story in Canadian news, February 2018.

The 465-year-old severed arm of a revered person in a particular religion was going on public display at some sites in Montreal and Ottawa. The officials had removed the right hand 60 years after he died in 1552 and kept it as a relic.

Flown first class from Europe to Canada, people flocked to the sites to see the arm. Some claimed to have experienced some spiritual closeness to God as a result of viewing it.

"Jesus came down in the form of the flesh - he became one of us," someone said. "Therefore, we also believe the flesh of Saints — even after they are dead, namely the relics, provide opportunities for us to receive graces from God."

You hear the sincere, well-intentioned zeal in those words, don't you? You know that human nature leans toward the fetish, the morbid in search of the supernatural, the divine. It's the most human of instincts.

I see this in my beloved Africa with native forms of religion. It is the same reason God took care of Moses' body Himself and did not let anyone know where. His body would have been an object of worship.

The Law of Moses offered man the chance to do his best in pleasing God. It was muchly a do-it-yourself religion.

Even with the best incentives from God, it ended in abject failure for man. This failure of the Law only points us to Christ.

Christ is the end of the law for righteousness to everyone that believeth. **Rom 10:4**

I feel a need to clarify one or two things before we enter this study of the Book of Galatians:

The Law

The term, "the Law" appears many times in Scripture and in the Book of Galatians. I have heard a number of interpretations of what people think the term means, especially in the context of this epistle.

"The Law" in the context of the Book of Galatians refers to the whole body of practices of the covenant given to Moses. This includes the 10 Commandments, the Sabbath, the sacrifices and the oblations, circumcision, the feasts such as Passover, Tabernacles, Pentecost.

"The Law" represents everything the Old Covenant or Testament stood for, everything from the Ten Commandments to the Feasts, the Priesthood, the sacrifices.

In **Exodus 19** (Paul references this in **Galatians 4: 24, 25**) the children of Israel arrived at the wilderness of Sinai in their journeys and were then given the Ten Commandments. In the next few chapters, they were also given other (a lot!) laws to follow. These laws included instruction concerning food, property, personal injury servants, the Sabbath, restitution and the list goes on.

Then, in the next few chapters Moses was asked to build the Ark of the Covenant and the Tabernacle after he had gone up to Mount Sinai. He was given the fine details of these articles and the order and process of approaching the presence of God including sacrifices, oblations, priestly garments, incenses and other things.

What is my point? That the whole of the transactions and commands at Sinai make up "the Law" which includes everything under Moses, every observance, practice, sacrifice, oblation, the Ten Commandments, the Tabernacle, circumcision.

In short, it is every effort to approach or effort to please God by our own performances, apart from Christ. "The Law" embodies this.

The Law, regardless of whether a person is a Jew or not, is Bible-speak for human effort and endeavor to please or win God's approval or righteousness, outside of Christ.

Paul's main concern in the book of Galatians, was not just about circumcision, like I have heard folks say. Paul was concerned about the Law being that which includes everything in the Old Covenant and tries to win God's righteousness through works or human effort.

I have heard one or two people say that Paul was primarily concerned about circumcision because it is not convenient to "circumcise adult men." Ridiculous.

And some others have said that although Christians don't have to be circumcised, they still need to keep the other parts of the Law. They mention things like the Feasts or the Sabbath; they say we still need to keep days like Yom Kippur, Passover etc.

Again, it is ridiculous for anyone to say that. These practices are all part of one entity. You don't get to choose or pick which one you obey.

It's just like the way the press or diplomats use the word "Washington". Washington DC is the capital of the U.S. government, but in news and diplomatic speak, "Washington" means the government, the political class, the Administration of the day, the presidency, the government's foreign policy stance, the White House.

"The Law" is also a reference to the Covenant made at Sinai.

> **Hebrews 10**
> 1For **the law** having a shadow of good things to come, *and* not the very image of the things, can never with **those sacrifices** which they offered year by year...
>
> 8Above when he said, **Sacrifice and offering and burnt offerings and** *offering* for sin thou wouldest not, neither hadst pleasure *therein*; which are **offered by the law**;

Notice carefully how Paul has associated sacrifices and offerings to the Law, showing that they are all part of the same Covenant. He says the *sacrifices and offerings were offered by the law.*

I will elaborate more on this later on in Chapter 2, but you will see that Paul rebuked Peter in quite a dramatic manner, over, - wait for it - having lunch with Gentile Christians and withdrawing when some Jewish folks came around.

So, Paul rebuked Peter over that? Over food? It's that serious?

One, it shows that this was not just about circumcision. This was about the whole Law including food and dietary laws. This was about human effort.

Two, it shows that this is all about the eternal destinies of the souls of men. Paul would later say this, down the chapter, still commenting on Peter's eating with the Gentiles and apparent hypocrisy:

> "16Knowing that a man is not justified by the works of the law, but by the faith of Jesus Christ, even we have believed in Jesus Christ, that we might be justified by the faith of Christ, and not by the works of the law: for by the works of the law shall no flesh be justified."

In other words, this is all about eternity, righteousness, justification and the eternal destinies of men.

Today, in many forms, the same situations are presented to Christians all over the world every day. People magnify the Law above the Cross. Folks talk more about Moses, human effort and the Old Covenant and relegate the work of Christ to the background.

Paul's sheer incredulity and angst at what was going on in these churches should be enough a cautionary tale for us.

Amen. The Lord cometh.

First Word

I like to tell this story about my son as a 2-year-old. I always liked to give him a shower and like most kids that age, he liked playing with the water.

Many times, when there's water and soap on his head and face, he, of course, had to close his eyes. That part he didn't like. No kid would like that part, right?

It was always funny to hear him say in two-year old tongues, eyes closed, a little panicked, "Who turned off the light? The light is off! Who turned off the light? Turn on the light!"

And then I would say, laughing, as I tried to quickly rinse the soap off his face, "No, nobody turned the light off! You closed your eyes! The light is on. Just open your eyes."

Sometimes, we act like that. There's light and revelation knowledge and direction in God's Word, and yet we ask why it is dark. Sometimes, we close our eyes willfully when light comes from the Word. Sometimes we are not just mature enough to tell the difference.

The issue is not that there are no answers in the Word or that the Word is dark, but that we need to open our eyes.

Thy word *is* a lamp unto my feet, and a light unto my path. (**Psalms 119:105**).

17

This book has come about as I studied the Book of Galatians in the fall of 2017. I was doing a bit of teaching from it speaking at our church on some Sundays – at my pastor's request.

My notes just got deeper and longer and, as I got more inspired as I wrote, I was convinced the Lord would have it become a book. This is the result. I had developed a slight passion for the Book of Galatians years before then and made quite a bit of reference to it in my first book, *Jesus My Righteousness*.

Then I learnt that Martin Luther, he of the Reformation, said this about the Book of Galatians, "The Epistle to the Galatians is my epistle. To it I am as it were in wedlock. It is my Katherine". Katherine was his wife, of course. This is the book, I understand, along with Romans chapter 4 that inspired Luther. I wondered a bit if Katherine would have enjoyed that.

The Book of Galatians has been called the "Magna Carta" of Christian freedom or liberty. It's been called the Christian's "Declaration of Independence" and "a formal declaration of liberty in Jesus Christ." You get the point.

There are, of course, a number of books, online videos and other resources that attempt to deal with Galatians, but I believe that the riches in God's Word will forever be mined and I'm trusting that this book will join the ranks of those that will be a useful resource and blessing to many as we keep looking into the perfect law of liberty.

I found out that some of the best sermons on the subject are, in my opinion, by a Baptist preacher and teacher. His name is Bob Utley. He has a real teaching anointing, and is a professor of Koine Greek, Hermeneutics and the Old Testament.

Dr. Utley's videos on YouTube are some of the clearest, cleanest teaching ministry gifts I have seen. I urge you to check out his videos on the Book of Galatians, though he has videos on other subjects too. They will bless you.

If you have a teaching call, I'm convinced you can learn a thing or two from Dr. Utley.

Bragging Rights

The Thrill of Resting in the Cross

Taiwo Oyadiran

New Creation Life Ministries

Modupe. *Anike.*

MoyosolaOluwa.
ModesolaOluwa.
Akinfolarin.

Èyí ni ìran àwọn tí ń ṣe àfẹrí Rẹ, Ọlọrun Jákọbù.

John, of Patmos.
Paul, of Tarsus.
Kenneth Erwin Hagin.
Essek William Kenyon.

The spirits of just men made perfect.

Man, of War

The dysrhythmia
Riding cherub wings
Slapping in
Terrible worship
Swift tear
Bending the copse
Brass gates smashed
Iron bars stranded.

Vanquished howls
Anterior seraphs tremble
Manic exultations
Cooking through
Abraham's bosom
The crazed jousting
Thunder, lightning
Hastening their
Salute to register.

Such calculi at
The Father's own
Fearsome declaration,
Terrible things attending,

"This day, I beget Thee…"
In trust, the stupendous,
"You will not leave My soul…",

Prostration,
It finds me prone –
The impossibility, Akinfolarin,
The ridiculous impossible eventuated…
 "You, you -
has He raised together…"

I will also recommend the series of sermons on Galatians from Stillwater Bible Church taught by their senior pastor, J.B. Bond. The video teachings are available on YouTube and are simple with incredible clarity and thorough scriptural references. They will surely bless you as they did me. The church is in Stillwater, OK.

The Why

In his epistle to the Galatians, Paul strenuously and vigorously lays out that irrevocable and most fundamental doctrine of Christianity of which there can be no negotiation: *Salvation by faith through grace.*

In simple terms, that is all there is to it. In sad terms, you will find that that when many people say, "Salvation by faith through grace", they mean many things but what Paul did.

In the mind of a lot of other people, it is, "saved by grace through faith *plus my consistency* or *plus my faithfulness* or *plus my not doing this or that.*" Some others see it as saved by grace through faith plus *keeping the Law of Moses* or plus *keeping the Ten Commandments.*

In many cases, Paul's admonition to "work OUT" our salvation with fear and trembling is often misread and misunderstood to be "work FOR" our salvation with fear and trembling.

This is where and why I hope this book will be useful to the Body of Christ. A proper reading of Paul in this epistle will show that putting the Christian under the Law of Moses with its laws, regulations, ordinances and practices or under human effort to achieve God's approval is a negation, not just a relegation of faith in Christ.

He put it this way: "You are cut off from Christ", and, "Christ will become of no benefit to you", and, "if righteousness *come* by the law, then Christ is dead in vain."

He was intolerant and very unapologetic about his rebuke of those who pushed this error. He treated it as a matter of eternal consequences.

19

It seems to me that all that Paul said in Galatians in brevity or summary, he expounds on in Romans and Hebrews. In a sense, Galatians is the capsule form of both Romans and Hebrews.

I am convinced that it is impossible to fully grasp or teach the Book of Galatians without copious reference to Romans and Hebrews. They all should go together. That is what I have tried to do in this book.

These books are the true and proper doctrinal books of the New Testament. In the case of Galatians, Paul wrote it with a certain apoplectic fever, and it seems to me that his angst should cause every Christian to pause and think or re-think things they have held on to that are not scriptural. I mean, his anger, at least, should make us curious, at the very least.

Galatians has only one theme, from start to finish. There's hardly any distraction, any straying from the subject matter.

I'm trusting the Lord that this book will be a useful resource and material to all who read it; that we would come to see, yet more, the glory of God reflected in the face of the Lord Jesus!

Even so, come, Lord Jesus.

Chapter 1

Just a few Sunday mornings ago, I couldn't find my phone. I checked everywhere – under the couch, on the bookshelf, on the kitchen counter, behind the TV stand. I just couldn't find it.

Then my daughter said something like, "What's that in your back pocket?" Well, it turned out that it was in my left back pocket – while I'd spent 5, maybe 7 minutes looking for it. In my pocket! I had it right with me all the time.

Ha. Tell me that has not happened to you too.

The same is true for salvation, I think. God has made a way for man, and we don't have to struggle for it. He has provided it and made a way and it is to be realized and received. In a sense, it is in "our pockets", and we can't work for it, or find it on our own.

In **Romans 10**, talking about the righteousness of faith, Paul interprets Moses's sermon from Deuteronomy 30 saying that we need not struggle in our own efforts to attain righteousness. We need not search in the high heavens or earth beneath as if it is impossible to have it.

But the righteousness that is by faith says: "Do not say in your heart, 'Who will ascend into heaven?'" (that is, to bring Christ down) "or 'Who will descend into the deep?'" (that is, to bring Christ up from the dead). How can this be done?

It is done in Christ and needs no struggle. It is near you. As close to you as your mouth and heart. It is faith in your heart.

"The word is near you; it is in your mouth and in your heart," that is, the message concerning faith that we proclaim: If you declare with your mouth, "Jesus is Lord," and believe in your heart that God raised him from the dead, you will be saved.

Galatians Chapter 1

Paul's letter to the Galatians begins with a palpable sense of angst, anger and frustration. He was angry to the point of not stopping to pray for them as he normally would in his other epistles.

For the Ephesians, he prayed that God would give to them the "spirit of wisdom and revelation in the knowledge of Him, the eyes of your understanding being enlightened…" **Ephesians 1:17**

For the Colossians, he prayed that they may be "filled with the knowledge of His will in all wisdom and spiritual understanding…" **Colossians 1:9.** For the Philippians that, "your love may abound in knowledge." **Philippians 1:9.**

You see that generally, in his epistles, he prayed for the churches. Today we call those prayers 'Pauline prayers'. These are obviously Holy Spirit inspired prayers.

That Paul did not pray for the Galatians in the same way is telling. He seemed to be upset, and it sounded like he was in a hurry to say what he wanted to say.

While we're wondering what is going on, what did Paul do next? He issues a curse. A curse? Yes, a curse. What was he so mad about? What could be so bad for this man of God to be so animated, so exercised?

I think if he had been speaking to them directly in a hall or in a synagogue, on Sunday morning, he would have raised his voice bigly.

If we or an angel from heaven preach to you another variation of the one that we delivered and taught you, let them be cursed!

Then he repeats the curse! An angel, a human being, an apostle – anyone at all, that tries to add to or give you a variant of the gospel, a curse be upon them!

We should pause and wonder and think. Why was he so mad? What has upset the man of God this much? What was so serious? The reason for his anger is the reason for the epistle and is the reason for this book. But I don't know about you, with all that Paul has said so far, it is critical for us as Christians to pay attention to the why of the epistle.

Our reading of Galatians, and indeed of Scripture must not be casual, although I am particularly considering the peculiarity and uniqueness of this book. You get the impression from the first few verses of this chapter that Paul's ministry, apostleship and even Christianity may have been called into question by some other Christians.

We find him establishing the legitimacy of his ministry and calling as he rehashed his life before and since getting born again. I guess that many people would have wondered about him - with good reason too - after all, he was, in a sense, a terrorist, persecuting Christians.

He was an enemy of the Cross.

> 13For you have heard of my previous way of life in Judaism, how intensely **I persecuted the church of God and tried to destroy it.** (NLT)

Thank God for His grace. Paul got born again. But I imagine that some people would have told him things like: "I was already in ministry 10 years before you got born again", "Where were you when we were called to preach, Paul? You were persecuting us", "Look, Paul, I was with the Lord Jesus. I spoke with Him personally and directly, you don't know what you are saying, you don't know what you're doing", "You are in no position to teach us."

In other words, they probably saw him as less than the other apostles. They probably were suspicious of him. It seems that is why he makes these statements in verses 11 and 12.

> 11But I certify you, brethren, that the gospel which was preached of me is not after man.

> 12For I neither **received it** of man, neither was I taught *it*, but by **the revelation of Jesus Christ**.

23

He seems to be saying that he was taught the gospel by the Lord Jesus by revelation. *I certify you. I assure you.* I know Him too. I know Him by revelation.

When he says, "by revelation", does that mean by a supernatural appearance of the Lord Jesus like by a vision, a dream or visitation? It could easily be.

But it could also easily mean that while he studied, revelation knowledge came to him. Light came, understanding came. The eyes of his understanding were enlightened. The Holy Spirit helped him along. And it could also be a combination of both.

But why am I saying this? You see, it is easy for some people to pick on verse 12 where Paul said, "...*I received it... by the revelation of Jesus Christ*" and use it as a premise to say that they received knowledge and direction supernaturally without cold-blooded scriptural vetting.

These days a lot of people say, "God told me this", "God told me that", and when you hear what "God told them", you see immediately that that was not quite the case. How do you know that? Because what they said "God" told them did not line up with Scripture.

I'll give you an example. I watched a preacher say that he had revelations and visions from God. He says Moses, Abraham, the Apostle John have all appeared to him. They told him prophetic things. They invited him into the "Council of Prophets". And people believe these things all the time. Well, you can't find Scriptures, properly interpreted, to support that.

That is immediately a slippery slope in the sense that we know that some people have based their entire doctrine and believing on a person saying they had an angelic vision or visitation without recourse to the Bible. Some people have said that the Lord Jesus appeared to them and told them to do things that do not line up with the Word. You could say, "Well, what he said did come to pass, though." A prophecy or prediction coming to pass should not be the basis for assuming that it came from the Lord. The Bible talks about "lying wonders." These are wonders, yes. But they are lies.

Joseph Smith, he of the Mormons, said an angel appeared to him and gave him instructions. We know that is from the devil. This is why I think Paul included supernatural visitations when he issued that curse:

> 8But though we, or **an angel from heaven, preach any other gospel** unto you than that which we have preached unto you, let him be accursed.

> 9As we said before, so say I now again, If any *man* preach any other gospel unto you than that ye have received, let him be accursed.

What's the point here? The fact that someone said they had a supernatural appearance or instruction, or visitation should not mean that that revelation is from God.

Though *we or an angel from heaven. Through a vision. An apparition. A dream. An appearance. A voice.*

Regardless of how spectacular or uber-natural it may be, if it is not the same as the gospel or line up with the gospel, let them be accursed. Beware of supernatural events, visitations, visions that do not line up with the gospel.

Do not let anyone come to you and say that an angel appeared to them and instructed them to do things that are not in line with Scripture. Don't let anyone say that they had a supernatural experience that will diminish the Cross. Anything that magnifies the Law above Calvary is not from God.

Evidently what Paul taught was backed up by Scripture. I lean towards believing that when Paul said he was taught the gospel by revelation of the Lord, he did not mean that he had visions or visitations from the Lord, though that is easily possible. I think he learnt it by revelation knowledge from the Word. That is the way we all will learn, right? I don't think the Lord would have made an exception with him.

This is what Paul said in **I Corinthians 15**

3For **I delivered unto you** first of all that which **I also received**, how that **Christ died for our sins according to the scriptures;**

4And that he was buried, and that **he rose again the third day according to the scriptures**:

I delivered to you what I received: *Christ died for our sins according to the scriptures. Christ rose again the third day according to the scriptures.*

The gospel that Paul preached, that we should and must preach must be **according to the Scriptures**. That is the point. The revelation that he had from the Lord was "**according to the Scriptures**." What Scriptures? The Scriptures of the Old Testament in Paul's case, and both the Old and New in our case.

That cannot be over-emphasized. Everything we believe must be according to the Scriptures. The Scriptures of the Old Testament promised the Messiah, while the New Testament unveils Him. When the Lord Jesus spoke to the two disciples on the road to Emmaus, He told them that the Law, the Prophets and the Psalms all talk about Him.

Luke 24:27, 44
27And beginning at **Moses and all the prophets**, he expounded unto them in all the scriptures the things concerning himself.

44And he said unto them, These *are* the words which I spake unto you, while I was yet with you, that all things must be fulfilled, **which were written in the law of Moses, and *in* the prophets, and *in* the psalms, concerning me**

Written in Moses, and in the prophets, and in the psalms. Concerning me.
It is instructive that repeatedly we find verses in the New Testament Gospels, that say something like, "*that it might be fulfilled which was written by the prophet…*"

I heard someone say that the New Testament is a commentary on the Old Testament. You can't get more accurate or profound than that.

The Old Testament is the type, the shadow, the outline, while the New is the reality, the body, the actual. We should be thankful for the epistles. The epistles are what explain to us the plan of redemption. They reveal what had been blind to man in the Old.

Paul tells a bit of his own history and emphasizes that now, he is saved, as saved as the rest of the other Christians.
But let us back up a bit.

Grace

Did you notice what the Apostle says in verse 3?

> **3Grace *be* to you and peace from God the Father, and *from* our Lord Jesus Christ,**

> 4Who gave himself for our sins, that he might deliver us from this present evil world, according to the will of God and our Father:

Grace be to you. Peace be to you from God. In the context of what he is going to say later on in this letter, it is remarkable that he still took time to establish God's disposition towards them.

Grace and peace be to you from the Father, and our Lord Jesus. Grace and peace are God's disposition toward us now. He is not mad at us. He is not looking to punish us. His outlook towards us is peace, not punishment, not retribution, not condemnation, not payback.

His disposition toward us is grace. What does grace mean? It means he is disposed to forgive us and help us, to favor us, to give us a "long rope", to be merciful toward us.

Do yourself a favor and go through all the epistles and check the greetings that start and end all of them. You will find out that there are 21 epistles and then the book of Revelation. Of the 21 epistles, about 18 of them have something like "Grace and peace be unto you", or "Peace be multiplied to you from God our Father and from the Lord Jesus" at their beginning or at their ends.

Paul wrote 13 epistles. All of them start with, "Grace and peace be unto you." All of them ended with the same declaration. *All.*

All I am trying to say is that we should notice the overwhelming declaration of God's love and affection for us. The epistles make that unmistakable. These are really love letters from a Father, to a daughter, to a son, declaring his love and care for them and letting them know of the provisions he's made for them.

God is not angry with sinners, let alone with His children! God is not angry with humanity. Is God angry with sinners? Absolutely not. Why do I say that? When I look at the Lord Jesus, I see that He was not.

You know that the Lord Jesus is the express image of the Father. He is the exact representation of His person. **Hebrews 1:3:**

> The Son is the radiance of God's glory and **the exact representation of his being**, sustaining all things by his powerful word. (NIV)

> The Son radiates God's own glory and **expresses the very character of God**. (NLT)

From the evidence of the gospels, He was not angry with sinners. There was the woman caught in adultery. The Bible says she was caught in the "very act". What was His reaction?

"I do not condemn you, either. Go, sin no more." **John 8:11.**

That is grace and peace. *Forgiveness. Mercy.*

Do you remember the woman the Lord Jesus spoke to at the well in Samaria? He knew she'd had five husbands. 5 husbands! Think about that folks. She was living with a sixth man!

He knew her life was a mess. Yet He spoke with her. He revealed Himself to her. That is in **John 4**. There was not a word of condemnation or revulsion or irritation from Him. That is grace and peace. God's character and nature are fully expressed in Christ.

He went to Zacchaeus' house without Zacchaeus asking. Zacchaeus the corrupt. Zacchaeus the nefarious. Zacchaeus the dubious.
He told him, "Salvation has come to you." That is grace and peace.

It is ridiculous for us to say that God is angry with sinners. If He was angry with sinners, which we all were anyways, He would not have come to save us in the first place. He would not have entered the womb of that sinner virgin.

That is grace and peace. On the cross, He still prayed, "Father, forgive them." That is grace and peace.

John 1:14 -18 give us cause for rejoicing.

> 14And the Word was made flesh, and dwelt among us, (and we beheld his glory, the glory as of the only begotten of the Father,) **full of grace and truth.**

He came full of grace and truth. That is what He brought us.

> 16And of his fulness have all we received, and grace for grace.

We receive grace upon grace as most other translations have it. Gracious blessing after gracious blessing.

> 17For the law was given by Moses, *but* grace and truth came by Jesus Christ.

You see the contrast with the Law, don't you? You can see that this verse is playing up the punishment and harshness of the Law of Moses against the grace of Jesus Christ.

> 18No one has seen God at any time; the only begotten God who is in the bosom of the Father, **He has explained Him.** (NASB,1977)

> The Passion Translation says, "Now he has unfolded to us the **full explanation of who God truly is!**"

Christ is the explanation of the Father, the elucidation of God. He is the express, unhindered, unmasking of God Himself: God naked, revealed, unveiled.

He has unfolded to us the full explanation of who God truly is!

In Christ, we see God's grace and peace extended towards us.

Even the Book of Revelation with all its apocalyptic imagery, starts with a reminder of God's gracious disposition toward us in Christ.

His magnanimity towards us is re-enforced in **Revelation 1:4**

> 4John to the seven churches which are in Asia: **Grace *be* unto you, and peace, from him which is, and which was, and which is to come**; and from the seven Spirits which are before his throne;
>
> 5And from Jesus Christ, *who is* the faithful witness, *and* the first begotten of the dead, and the prince of the kings of the earth. Unto him that loved us, and washed us from our sins in his own blood,

In spite of all the warnings and rebuke He would soon give to the 7 seven churches in Asia, He first said, "Grace and peace be to you."

From him which is, and which was, and which is to come (The Father); and from the seven Spirits (The Spirit); And from Jesus Christ (The Son).

You have all the 3 persons of the Godhead loving us, showing us grace and favor and peace and kindness. This is our God! Grace to you, peace to you.

It is inevitable that some folks will say, "Does that mean the sinners should keep sinning? Are you saying that God is happy for them to keep sinning?" If that is a question in your heart, you don't get it, yet.

Let's go back to **Galatians 1**.

Paul is later going to rebuke this Galatian church and blow a few gaskets, but he still starts saying, "Grace and peace to you, from Dad".

> 4Who gave himself for our sins, that he might **deliver us from this present evil world**, according to the will of God and our Father:

He delivered us from this present evil world.
This. Present. Evil. World.

He delivered us from the power of Satan. This is our present tense reality. It is comforting to know that it does not say, He delivered us from "this world". It says, "**This. Present. Evil. World.**" We have been delivered NOW.

Satan's authority over the believer has ceased to be. The believer is not under the dominion of the devil, sin and the grave. The Lord Jesus won the victory and set us free. That is a present reality.

> **Colossians 1:13**
> 13Who hath delivered us from the power of darkness, and hath translated *us* into the kingdom of his dear Son:

You have to notice that our deliverance is in the past tense. It has been done. *Has delivered us. Has translated us. It has happened. He delivered us from the power of darkness. He delivered us from this present evil world.*

It really means that we dominate this present evil world. It means that whatever forces of evil that are in this present evil world, they don't have any authority over us. How come? **Colossians 2:15**:

> 15Disarming the **rulers and authorities, he has made a public disgrace of them**, triumphing over them by the cross. (NET).
> 15In this way, he disarmed the spiritual rulers and authorities. **He shamed them publicly** by his victory over them on the cross. (NLT).

We are delivered, here and now. Our deliverance has happened. It is not when we get to heaven. It's not in the millennium. I hope you noticed the latter part of verse 4.

> 4Who gave himself for our sins, that he might deliver us from this present evil world, **according to the will of God and our Father**:

The Lord Jesus gave Himself for our sins, that He might deliver us from this present evil world. *According to the will of God, our Father.*

It is God's will for us to be delivered from evil. God made it His business for us to be delivered from evil. You find the same thing said in the 'Lord's Prayer': "Thy will be done on earth."

It is beyond sad that some folks believe that sickness, disease, tragedies can be the will of God. It is tragic that some Christians think that God brings hurricanes, tsunamis, typhoons and other natural disasters as acts of His will. Verse 4: our deliverance from this present evil world is the will of God!

What does that mean? What are the things in this present evil world? It means that sickness is not the will of God. Disease is not the will of God. A tsunami is not the will of God. Famines are not His will.

How can sickness be the will of love? Healing is always the will of God. Salvation is always the will of God. Our well-being is always the will of God. We have been set free from anything that is evil in this present evil world.

What is the will, wish, desire of God? Our deliverance, and that has been accomplished in Christ Jesus. Amen.

I like me best when I'm with you

As a part of an assignment for a doctoral thesis, a college student spent a year with a group of Navajo Indians on a reservation in the Southwest. As he did his research, he lived with one family, sleeping in their hut,

*eating their food, working with them and generally living the life of a
20th century Indian.*

*A close friendship developed between the student and the grandmother.
They spent a great deal of time sharing a friendship that was meaningful
to each, yet unexplainable to someone else. In spite of the language
difference, they shared the common language of love.*

*When it was time for him to return to the campus and write his thesis,
the tribe held a going-away celebration. It was marked by sadness, since
the young man had become close to the whole village and all would miss
him. As he prepared to get up into the pickup truck and leave, the old
grandmother came to tell him goodbye. With tears streaming from her
eyes, she placed her hands on either side of his face, looked directly into
his eyes and said, "I like me best when I'm with you."*

*Isn't that the way we feel in the presence of Jesus? He brings out the best
in us. We learn to see ourselves as worthy and valuable when we are in
His presence. The hurts, the cares, the disappointments of our life are
behind us when we look in His eyes and realise the depth of His love.*

*Our self-esteem no longer depends on what we have done or failed to do;
it depends only on the value that He places on us.*

From SermonCentral

Chapter 2

I just read the story of a certain man who, at the moment that he bought a winning lottery ticket, had only $25 to his name. He was in extreme poverty. He won $13 million.

I also read about a guy who was already a millionaire (worth $17 million) and then won $314.9 million.

Winning the lottery is a process of random selection supposedly. You can not do anything about it. You don't win because you are 18 or 80. You don't win because you are a good citizen or the worst criminal. It has nothing to do with being lazy or hardworking, nothing to do with being educated.

None of those who have won can boast or brag about what they did to win or how it came about. All they did was buy the ticket.

It was a free gift they got in spite of themselves.

We "buy" the ticket of faith and believing to gain access into God's righteousness. In Christ, we become "rich" in righteousness not because we deserve it or because we are good or bad. It is all because of what Christ has done. Our faith in what He did.

"God presented Christ as a sacrifice of atonement, through the shedding of his blood…" "…Rendered efficacious through faith in His blood." (NIV, Weymouth) **Romans 3:25**

It is purely by the grace of God - totally unmerited, not a reward for any kind of conduct. We come and stand by faith. We brag on Him, on His Blood, on His Cross. Only.

Galatians Chapter 2

Paul's angst begins to build up and he uses words that imply that he was going to say things against or about some people that they might not like. These people might have been people in leadership or people held in high esteem by many other people.

He begins to tell about Judaizers and false teachers who seemed to have "infiltrated" the churches. "They came to spy on our liberty which we have in Christ, so they can bring us into bondage". Verse 4.

I personally find the word "spy" serious and funny. Intriguing too. It means they are enemies. They are against us, not for us, and they pretend and appear to be like they are with us.

He says, "I don't care who they are or think they are or who people think they are. I will boldly say what I need to say."

> 10For do I now persuade men, or God? or do I seek to please men? for if I yet pleased men, I should not be the servant of Christ.

That is good stuff, won't you agree? I don't seek to please people. I report to God. I don't care for human opinion. I serve Jesus.

There is a time to speak up.

We should speak up at times like this. We must speak up in defense of the gospel. You don't have to be a minister to do this. It is the duty of every Christian to stand up for the truth and integrity of God's Word.

But, to back up to the first verses:

> 1Then fourteen years after I went up again to Jerusalem with Barnabas, and took Titus with *me* also.
> 2And I went up by revelation, and communicated unto them that gospel which I preach among the Gentiles, but privately to them which were of reputation, lest by any means I should run, or had run, in vain.

3But neither Titus, who was with me, being a Greek, was compelled to be circumcised:

I am not sure of the timeline of this epistle in line with the famous council meeting they had in Jerusalem in **Acts 15**. But it is easy to see that they are connected. I believe, in fact, that when Paul said he went up to Jerusalem, he was talking about that council in Jerusalem.

Acts 15
1And certain men which came down from Judaea taught the brethren, and said, **Except ye be circumcised after the manner of Moses, ye cannot be saved.**

2Paul and Barnabas had no small dissension and disputation with them.

Paul and Barnabas stood up against these false teachers and teaching who taught that "**it was needful to circumcise them, and to command *them* to keep the law of Moses**". (verse 5)

This brought Paul and Barnabas into **sharp dispute and debate** with them. (NIV)

Paul and Barnabas **disagreed with them, arguing vehemently**. (NLT)

Disagreed, arguing vehemently.

Galatians 4
4And that because of false brethren unawares brought in, who came in privily to spy out our liberty which we have in Christ Jesus, that they might bring us into bondage:

5To whom **we gave place by subjection, no, not for an hour; that the truth of the gospel might continue with you**.

We did not give in to these Judaizers and false teachers. We did not tolerate wrong doctrine! Verse 5 in the NLT:

5But **we refused to give in to them for a single moment.**
We wanted to preserve the truth of the gospel message for you.

We refused to give in to them for a single moment. We wanted to preserve the truth of the gospel. That the truth of the gospel might continue with you.

There is a time to resist. There is a time to stand up, to speak up. Sometimes, maybe too many times, we are too polite, too timid to stand up for the truth of the gospel.

You don't have to be a minister to do this. You just need to be a Christian. What is at stake are the lives and eternity of people.

But back to **Galatians 2**.

> 11But when Peter was come to Antioch, I withstood him to the face, because he was to be blamed.
>
> 12For before that certain came from James, he did eat with the Gentiles: but when they were come, he withdrew and separated himself, fearing them which were of the circumcision.
>
> 13And the other Jews dissembled likewise with him; **insomuch that Barnabas also was carried away** with their dissimulation.
>
> 14But when I saw that they walked not uprightly according to the truth of the gospel, I said unto Peter before *them* all, If thou, being a Jew, livest after the manner of Gentiles, and not as do the Jews, why compellest thou the Gentiles to live as do the Jews?
>
> 14When I saw that they were not following the truth of the gospel message, I said to Peter in front of all the others, "Since you, a Jew by birth, have discarded the Jewish laws and are living like a Gentile, why are you now trying to make these Gentiles follow the Jewish traditions? (NLT)

This is All About Food?

Paul starts to tell about his encounter with Peter: But when Peter came to Antioch, evidently after the meeting in Jerusalem of **Acts 15**, it seems, I withstood him to the face. He was to be blamed, he feared them which were of the circumcision.

Why was Peter to be blamed? What did he do wrong?

But when Peter came to Antioch, I withstood him to the face; he was to be blamed. For before that certain came from James, he did eat with the Gentiles: but when they were come, he withdrew and separated himself, fearing the Judaizers.

I confronted him. He was to be blamed. It was his fault. What did Peter do? What was Peter to be blamed for? He ate with the Gentiles before some influential Judaizers came around. Then he withdrew and separated himself, because he was afraid of or intimidated by them.

You say this big "fight" is all about food? This whole epistle is about Peter eating food with Gentiles? That would have been funny, but for the seriousness that Paul attached to it.

Paul saw it as a serious thing, in fact as a matter of life and death, or eternal salvation. It caused a fraction and division in the Church.

Why was Paul so exercised over this? *But when I saw that they walked not uprightly according to the truth of the gospel,* I confronted him *in front of them all.* You have to love and admire the ministry, boldness and focus of the Apostle Paul. He was sold out!

You notice that other people were affected by what Peter did. We should realize that other people will be affected by what we do or don't do. Lives can be changed one way or another by how much we live truly to the gospel.

And the other Jews dissembled likewise with him. "Dissembled" means playacting, pretense. In other words, they did not act true to what they believed. They acted below the level of knowledge they had. They knew better than to act the way they did. They did not walk uprightly. They became hypocrites.

They acted a certain way to please some certain people - the Judaizers. They did not want to "offend" the Judaizers. But it is a bit staggering to think that this was the same Peter who had the vision in **Acts 10,** where he was dramatically, supernaturally, spectacularly taught that salvation would now come to the Gentiles!

Evidently Peter knew better or so you would have thought. Peter was the one who had been led supernaturally to the house of Cornelius the Roman officer. When Peter got to Cornelius' house, he presented the gospel to them and the Bible says that while Peter was still speaking, the Holy Ghost fell on the people in the household, and they all began to speak with new tongues and to magnify God. All Gentiles!

Peter himself said, "...*God is no respecter of persons: But in every nation he that feareth him, and worketh righteousness, is accepted with him.*"

Peter was already living without the Law, like a Gentile. Or, we could say that he was already living like he was under the New Birth – not under the Law of Moses.

Paul said to Peter in front of all the others, "Since you, a Jew by birth, have discarded the Jewish laws and are living like a Gentile, why are you now trying to make these Gentiles follow the Jewish traditions? (NLT)

In other words, you already know that there is no more Jew or Gentile. In God's eyes, Jew and Gentile were always the same. God is no respecter of persons. Peter, you already know that. But he was now the one who acted hypocritically, instead of standing up for the truth that he knew.

So why was Paul so animated over this? What exactly was the problem?

When the Judaizers came around saying circumcision and the works of the Law of Moses were still necessary or to be added-on for salvation, Peter did not stand up to refute that. He still acted as if Christians are still subject to the dietary laws and ordinances of the Law of Moses.

Yes, Peter got carried away. He forgot what the Lord had told and demonstrated to him. He joined them. He temporarily reverted to Judaism. They set themselves apart from Gentile Christians as if, in Peter's own words, "God was a respecter of persons", as if God preferred or gave the Jew an advantage over the non-Jew.

They separated from the Gentile Christians, as if the Jews had a different covenant from them, as if Jews were superior. They set themselves apart from Gentile Christians as if it was not the same Jesus who died for them, as if they were not part of the same body.

By withdrawing from the Gentiles, Peter was following rules that presumed Jews to become unclean if they had dealings with Gentiles. In the vision that Peter had in **Acts 10**, the instruction to him was, "Don't call unclean or impure what God has called clean." (verse 15)

Well, the Jews no longer have a special covenant or arrangement with God than the rest of the Body of Christ. They used to. Not anymore. By withdrawing from the Christian Gentiles, Peter was upholding the Law and putting the Law above Calvary. He was inadvertently basing righteousness or justification on the Law, on our keeping it.

By withdrawing from the Christian Gentiles, Peter was putting himself under the Law, subjecting himself to the Law of Moses (not to touch the unclean). He was saying unconsciously that what Christ did was not enough, that the Law had a say in salvation.

This whole incident in itself shows us that the Christian is not and should not be a subject of the Law, no matter how simple the practice or ordinance. It shows that even seemingly minor practices of the Law are important. I mean as minor as eating food with the Gentiles, right?

The Law says that if you obey in one point, you must obey the whole of it. It also says you are cursed or condemned if you don't do *all* that is written or contained in it.

How Paul Saw it

Paul's reading of the incidence as simple as it seems, is that what Peter and the other folks did inadvertently or unwittingly amounted to a denial of salvation by faith through the grace of our Lord Jesus. You will see this in the verses that come after.

> 16Knowing that a man is not justified by the works of the law, but by the faith of Jesus Christ, even we have believed in Jesus Christ, that we might be justified by the faith of Christ, and not by the works of the law: for by the works of the law shall no flesh be justified.

Knowing that. By the works of the Law, shall no flesh be justified. We are justified by faith in Christ, not by the actions of the Law.

But perhaps, the curious question is: but Paul, it is not like Peter and the rest of these people 'denied' Jesus as the Savior and Messiah. It is not that they committed fornication or something bad like that. Going by Paul's reaction, this is like denying salvation by grace. Reverting to the Law constitutes a frustration of the grace of God.

> 19For I through the law am dead to the law, that I might live unto God.

> 20I am crucified with Christ: nevertheless I live; yet not I, but Christ liveth in me: and the life which I now live in the flesh I live by the faith of the Son of God, who loved me, and gave himself for me.

> 21I do not frustrate the grace of God: for if righteousness *come* by the law, then Christ is dead in vain.

I am dead to the Law. I am no more under the Law as a means of attaining righteousness. I have attained righteousness by faith through Jesus Christ. I do not frustrate the grace of God.

If I still need to do or something for righteousness, then Christ's death was pointless.
If I still need the Law for righteousness, then Christ's death was useless.
I am dead to the Law. I need nothing from the Law for me to attain righteousness.

Anything that seeks to gain or attain rightness or approval from God through the Law including ordinances and dates and sacrifice constitutes a tacit denial and rejection of the work of Calvary. *When I saw that they walked not uprightly according to the truth of the gospel, I spoke up.*

The Law, Briefly

I know I have already tried to give a clear definition of "the Law" in the Preamble chapter, but I think this bears repetition right here, in context. Some people try to make distinctions between the Law, circumcision, the Talmud, the Torah etc. But when Paul refers to "the Law", he's just referring to the Old Covenant – which includes, the Torah, Moses, the sacrifices, the feasts, the Sabbath, the priesthood, the Covenant ratified at Sinai and everything that had to do with it.

In the context of this epistle, it is all the same. It is all one. The Old Testament is the Old Covenant is the Law is the circumcision is the feasts is the Aaronic priesthood is the Torah. It's just like the way the press or diplomats use the word "Washington".

Washington DC is the capital of the U.S. government, of course. But in news and diplomatic speak, "Washington" means the government, the political class, the Administration of the day, the presidency, the government's policy.

"The Law" represents everything the Old Covenant or Testament stands for, everything from the Ten Commandments to the Feasts, the Priesthood. The Law is works is human effort is human wisdom is self-righteousness.

So here were Judaizers and proponents of the Law who have sneaked into Christian churches and wanted to bring them back into the Old Covenant, into the feasts, the Sabbath, the Aaronic priesthood, the Torah, Moses, the circumcision. They were magnifying human effort, (which means the Law) above the Cross.

If we are still under the Law, if we still need to keep the Law, why did the Lord Jesus come? What need was there for the Lord Jesus to die, if the Law was the way to righteousness? If the Law or the Old Covenant helped us, what need was there for a New Covenant, and a Savior?

43

Et tu, Barnabas?

Influence is a big deal. People like pastors and teachers and other ministers should be careful how they relate to God's people. You can see that it bothered Paul that his companion and fellow minister, Barnabas also got carried away by the effect this false doctrine was having on the church. *Even Barnabas. You too, Barnabas?*

Barnabas! Barnabas, of all people. He was the one who had more or less got Paul into ministry. This is how they started ministering together, and please note how Barnabas was particularly described.

> **Acts 11**
> 22Then tidings of these things came unto the ears of the church which was in Jerusalem: and they sent forth Barnabas, that he should go as far as Antioch.
>
> 23Who, when he came, and had seen the grace of God, was glad, and exhorted them all, that with purpose of heart they would cleave unto the Lord.
>
> 24For he was **a good man, and full of the Holy Ghost and of faith**: and much people was added unto the Lord.
>
> **25Then departed Barnabas to Tarsus, for to seek Saul**:
>
> 26And when he had found him, he brought him unto Antioch.

Barnabas was a spiritual, good man, full of the Holy Ghost and faith. He sought Paul out, found him, and brought him to Antioch where they served as teachers in the church where we were first called "Christians". Is that not remarkable? It was from Antioch that God called them to those great missionary journeys.

Barnabas likely had some years ahead on Paul in Christianity and ministry. Paul's alarm at what was going on was only exacerbated by the fact that Barnabas, his companion and spiritual 'big brother' was sucked into this thing! Barnabas!

As a result, other Jewish Christians followed Peter's hypocrisy, and **even Barnabas was led astray** by their hypocrisy. (NLT)

Notice how the "even Barnabas" illustrates Paul's annoyance and displeasure. "Even Barnabas" reflects his incredulity: "Barnabas, you too?" or "I can't believe Barnabas got carried away too."

What does that tell us? We should hold on to the Word. Don't let yourself get carried away by wrong doctrines. It also warns us to be careful of the kind of people we associate with. Barnabas was evidently influenced by the people around him, as was Peter. You pick up things from people around that influence you.

In verse 13, *"the other Jews dissembled likewise"* meaning that this was a group thing. It was not just Peter doing this. It was peer-pressure. We need to be careful of who we associate with. Many things are passed on by osmosis. We should particularly be careful about people we look up to spiritually. They can easily be wrong in their actions or doctrines. Respecting and loving someone should not mean that we should not be able to disagree with them.

Don't respect anyone that much. You must always retain your right to disagree with anyone when it comes to the Word and things of the spirit.

Judaizers Today

This reminds me of some folks today. I hear people these days say that the Jews have a different covenant with God apart from the gospel. That is another gospel that is cursed because there is only one gospel, only one covenant, only one Sacrifice for sin: The Lord Jesus.

How are these adherents to the Law manifest today? They are celebrating Yom Kippur and Passover and Tabernacles, and the Sabbath. Yes, they are observing the ordinances of the Law. And if you are a Jew practicing Judaism, that is fine. That is your religion. I have no issues with that just like I have no issues with any Muslim.

But you will see those who claim Jesus as Lord and Savior go the Wailing Wall to pray. You will see them go to pray at River Jordan, as if the presence of God was in those places. You will see them blowing horns or *shofars* and pray with "prayer shawls".

I have heard them say that you need to send money to partake of the "Jubilee". They say that the number 7 has a blessing attached to it. And it's not just the number 7. To them practically every number has a mystical and special meaning to it. They say 2018 is a prophetically important year, just because it is the 70th year after the creation of the 1948 state of Israel, and if you send in a monetary gift to a certain ministry, God will bless you specially

They talk about blood moons, and the "shemitah". They think there is going to be a third Temple built in Jerusalem. They are focused on the Law.

Paul said in verse 19, *I am dead to the Law. Dead to the Passover. Dead to dietary laws. Dead to Yom Kippur. Dead to sacrifices and oblations.*

Because I have been crucified with Christ. Christ is my Passover. I am no longer under or subject to the Law. If righteousness comes by the Law. If the blessing comes by what I do, what was the reason for Christ?

Today, some of them would call themselves "Messianic" or the "Hebrews Roots Movement". You hear them say things like "Jesus was a Jew", "the Hebrew roots of Christianity". They are, consciously or not, glorying in the flesh, in their race/tribe.

You see that this is *exactly* what Paul was against in this epistle. These are the EXACT things that Paul wrote this epistle against. Are you a Christian or not? Why are you a "Messianic Jew"?

Paul said this later **Galatians 6:14**:

> May I never boast except in the cross of…Jesus Christ. (NIV)

> But it's unthinkable that I could ever brag about anything except the cross of our Lord Jesus Christ. (God's Word)

To call yourself anything other than 'Christian' is to boast in a thing other than the Cross. Appellations like Jewish, Hebrew, European,

African is to unwittingly be glorying in the flesh, in your ancestry. Not unless you are doing it to simple identify your natural ethnicity.

The Lord Jesus was born a Jew. Yes. God used the Jewish race as an entry point into the earth, into the affairs of man. Yes. But to keep saying that He is Jewish now or to keep seeing Him as Jewish and not in the light of redemption is plain ridiculous and unscriptural.

What is important is He came! The greatness and magnitude of what He did totally overrules how He came!

This is what the Word says in **II Corinthians 5:16:**

> So from now on we don't think of anyone from a human point of view. **If we did think of Christ from a human point of view, we don't anymore**. (God's Word)

> So we have stopped evaluating others from a human point of view. **At one time we thought of Christ merely from a human point of** view. How differently we know him now! (NLT)

What's Paul saying? It's plain, isn't it? The Lord Jesus came to us in human form, in the flesh. But that's where that ends. In the light of all things properly considered, it is irrelevant how He came to the world. We don't see Him anymore in the flesh. We regard no one in the flesh anymore. We look at everyone from the spiritual point of view.

Put another way, we look at the Lord purely based on the finished work of Calvary, on the basis of what He accomplished in His death and resurrection. That is what is important.

It is laughable and unscriptural for people to keep referring to the Lord Jesus as Jewish. He came and died for the whole world! He belongs to the whole world. It is ridiculous to see Him otherwise.

Galatians 2
20I am crucified with Christ: nevertheless I live; yet not I, but Christ liveth in me: and the life which I now live in the flesh I

live by the faith of the Son of God, who loved me, and gave himself for me.

21I do not frustrate the grace of God: for if righteousness *come* by the law, then Christ is dead in vain.

I am crucified with Christ. My debt has been paid – in Christ. I am dead to the Law. I have Christ now and the Law is useless to me as a means of righteousness.

That is my new identification. My old sin, and sinful nature have been crucified with Christ. My old self.

Now in me lives Christ, though I still live. Christ and I, we are now one. I am absolutely absorbed into Him, and He into me. Paul makes it sound like I don't know where the Lord Jesus begins and I end, because we have become one. The believer's identification with the Lord is the story of Redemption.

Verse 20 is s seminal moment in this epistle.

Influence, A Story

Concerning the issue of Peter fearing those of the circumcision, I find it note-worthy that Paul prayed for *boldness to preach the gospel and to "speak as I ought to"*. In **Ephesians 6:18-20; Colossians 4:3-4**, he asked people to pray this for him. That is seriously important.

Is that what Peter lacked? Was it a lack of boldness that turned Peter into a hypocrite? After all, the Lord had spoken directly and in dramatic fashion to Peter about the Gentiles in **Acts 10**. But it seemed like he was too timid to stand up for the truth. Peter was "fearing them which were of the circumcision", verse 12.

It is possible for preachers to be intimidated by people to the point where they do not speak the truth, or do not speak the way they should or to even outrightly deny the truth. Like Paul said, "As I ought to".

It is easy to be intimidated by other ministers, senior ministers, church members, influential people. We must speak the truth.

There's a big story in the Old Testament about this. It's almost hidden away in there and it's easy to miss it. But let's take a bit of real estate to examine it here. I think it's a very important story to learn from.

In **1 Kings 13**, we read about a man of God who had gone to the king to deliver a prophecy. While he delivered the message, he had some supernatural manifestations confirming that he was really sent by God.

Afterwards, the king offered him food and drink, and this is what he said in reply to that offer:

> 8And the man of God said unto the king, If thou wilt give me half thine house, I will not go in with thee, neither will I eat bread nor drink water in this place:
>
> 9For so was it charged me by the word of the LORD, saying, Eat no bread, nor drink water, nor turn again by the same way that thou camest.

God had given him specific or exact instructions: don't go back the same way you came; don't eat anything; don't drink anything.

Now, there was an "old prophet" who lived around the same area and heard about this younger man of God. For some reason, the Old Prophet decides to go meet the man of God.

> 14And went after the man of God, and found him sitting under an oak: and he said unto him, *Art* thou the man of God that camest from Judah? And he said, I *am*.
>
> 15Then he said unto him, Come home with me, and eat bread. 16And he said, I may not return with thee, nor go in with thee: neither will I eat bread nor drink water with thee in this place:
>
> 17For it was said to me by the word of the LORD, Thou shalt eat no bread nor drink water there, nor turn again to go by the way that thou camest.

"Are you the man of God from Judah?"

"Yes, I am"

"Come home with me and have lunch. You look tired. You must be hungry"

"No, thanks. God told me not to do so. I have specific instructions. You should understand that – you are a man of God too. No, thanks."

I think that's a fair rendering of what happened there. There's a tragedy about to unfold soon, though.

> 18He said unto him, I *am* a prophet also as thou *art*; and an angel spake unto me by the word of the LORD, saying, Bring him back with thee into thine house, that he may eat bread and drink water. ***But* he lied unto him.**
>
> 19So he went back with him, and did eat bread in his house, and drank water.

But he lied to him. "Come on, man. I am a Prophet of God and you know it. I have been in ministry for 35 years. I have signs and wonders. I hear the voice of God clearly. I have more experience than you. I can teach you many things that you don't know anything about."

"I have preached many camp meetings. I have many TV programs."

"You should listen to me. God sent an angel to me to tell you that you should come with me to my house and eat and drink."
"Look at you all tired and fatigued."

"An angel appeared to me, I promise you."

So the man of God went with the prophet and disobeyed the instructions that God had given him. He ate and drank. You say what happened next?

> 20And it came to pass, as they sat at the table, that the word of the LORD came unto the prophet that brought him back:

21And he cried unto the man of God that came from Judah, saying, Thus saith the LORD, Forasmuch as thou hast disobeyed the mouth of the LORD, and hast not kept the commandment which the LORD thy God commanded thee,

22But camest back, and hast eaten bread and drunk water in the place, of the which *the LORD* did say to thee, Eat no bread, and drink no water; thy carcase shall not come unto the sepulchre of thy fathers.

23And it came to pass, after he had eaten bread, and after he had drunk, that he saddled for him the ass, *to wit*, for the prophet whom he had brought back.

24And when he was gone, a lion met him by the way, and slew him: and his carcase was cast in the way, and the ass stood by it, the lion also stood by the carcase.

What price, the fear of man. What price the fear of a "man of God"? How many times do we show more respect to a so-called "man of God", so-called, "spiritual father", so-called "apostle" or "prophet", than we show to God and His Word?

The fear of man is a snare. **Proverbs 29:25**

The same Old Prophet who told the man of God that an angel had appeared to him to tell the man of God to eat was the same one who prophesied his doom.

"Because you have disobeyed God, when He clearly instructed you not to eat and drink, you will die and not be buried with your fathers."

And when he was gone, a lion met him by the way, and slew him: and his carcase was cast in the way.

These are the days where folks talk about "spiritual fathers" all the time, everywhere. They say you must have a spiritual father. They say there are some blessings that you will not get if you don't have a "spiritual father".

I have heard folks say that you need to have a "prophet over your life." You need to find your "man of God." You need to locate the one that God has assigned to be "spiritual father" over you.

They say if you do not, then, you might or cannot make progress in life and ministry. If you don't, you are missing some "covering". Some "spiritual fathers" say they have "spiritual covering" over Christians they pastor or teach. This covering, they say they can remove at will.

By "spiritual covering" they mean the Christians are covered from attacks from the devil, poverty, sickness etc - the very same things Christ redeemed us from. These people say they have that covering over people and they can withdraw it whenever they choose to.

So, a Christian's covering and protection is from another Christian? What can a pastor or prophet give another Christian that Christ has not given them?

The truth is that a person called to ministry has nothing, absolutely nothing that makes them special and better than or superior to the ordinary Christian who seats on the pew or who serves as an usher in church. Being in ministry is just a call to serve. They are not your Lord! Some say they have the power to issue curses on individuals especially if you are their church member, or if you serve under them.

Such church members end up developing into Christians who practically pay more attention to these human beings than they do the Word. They end up not knowing the voice of the Lord. They show more respect to these "Old Prophets" than they do the Word of God and the witness and leading of the Holy Spirit in their own lives and hearts.

The consequence is always the same: getting "killed by a lion", so to speak. You can have someone you look up to for advice or guidance, that is really up to you. You ought to. It will help you. You can have people you run your visons and goals by. If you think you have some revelation from the Word, you should have people you can go to that can help you do some vetting of it.

There is nothing wrong with that – as long as they don't become God to you. As long as you don't put them ahead of the voice of the Holy Spirit speaking to you from the Word and your own heart.

You don't need a prophet over your life. That is a fallacy and a big fat lie from hell. You don't need to find "your man of God". Nobody, no human being has "spiritual covering" over you. The Lord Jesus does. Nobody, no prophet, no apostle can curse you. It is a big lie. The Lord Jesus is the only spiritual authority you need to submit to.

I hope you see what I mean. You should belong to a church, which means you will have a pastor. I submit to my pastors too within the context of church. You should submit to the authority in your church within the limits of the Word. You should respect them. We are commanded to respect them and to esteem them highly.

But that does not mean that they have the power to curse you. Or the power to remove the covering and protection from evil because that power and authority is the Lord Jesus'. They do not have the power to tell you what to do, or what decisions to make for your own life.

They can advise and guide and counsel you, but they are not your Lord. We submit to them only within the limits of their following the Word. Anything outside the Word we must not entertain. Jesus is your Lord and protector, not any man, no matter how anointed.

Don't, put a man of God, a prophet, an apostle above the Word or above the Lord. It can be costly. But that is not even the worst part of it. The real tragedy is that if you do, it shows that you don't have a correct appreciation of the work of redemption. The real greatness of the gospel is *Christ in you*. The Lord living in each one of us.

One last aspect of this as it relates to the subject of this book. Let's review some of the things that Paul said.

So just to back up a bit, Barnabas got carried away. He must have known better than he acted.

Peter definitely knew better than he did especially if Paul's rebuke of him happened after the events **Acts 10**.

16To reveal his Son in me, that I might preach him among the heathen; immediately **I conferred not with flesh and blood**:

17Neither went I up to Jerusalem to them which were apostles before me; but I went into Arabia, and returned again unto Damascus.

I did not ask the opinion of other people. I was sure of my calling. I did not seek their approval or endorsement. He did go to see Peter and James much later.

18Then after three years I went up to Jerusalem to see Peter, and abode with him fifteen days.

19But other of the apostles saw I none, save James the Lord's brother.

But back to our **Galatians 2:5**

5To whom **we gave place by subjection, no, not for an hour**; that the truth of the gospel might continue with you.

6But of these who seemed to be somewhat, (whatsoever they were, it maketh no matter to me: God accepteth no man's person:) for they who seemed *to be somewhat* in conference added nothing to me:

When it comes to the "truth of the gospel", we should not be respecter of persons. Why? That the truth of the gospel must continue.

They seemed to be somewhat. They had an attitude. They thought they were something. But I did not care what they thought they were. I cared for the truth of the gospel.

If we must disagree with anyone, it will have to be so "that the truth of the gospel might continue", especially if we have to do it in public. Anything else is frivolous, and it must be done in love and humility. We will get there later on, but look at what Paul said in **Galatians 6**:

1Brethren, if a man be overtaken in a fault, ye which are spiritual, **restore such an one in the spirit of meekness**; considering thyself, lest thou also be tempted.

In other words, if you are going to correct folks, or set them straight, do it in a nice, humble way, not arrogantly. Amen.

God Loves You

Tom Mercer writes, "Years ago, I heard an incredible story about a guy who, while walking through an intersection in a large city, noticed a police officer directing traffic in the middle of the street. As he walked by, the man sensed the Holy Spirit prompting him to go up to the officer and tell him that God loved him. The man dismissed the impulse and kept walking. Haunted by the continued sense that he had been disobedient to the Spirit, he finally walked back to that intersection, up to the officer, and said, "Excuse me, Officer, but God just told me to tell you that He loves you."

Tears began to trickle down from under the cop's mirrored sunglasses. Traffic stopped. With a broken voice, the officer said, "I prayed to God for the first time in a long time last night and told Him that, if He was real, the least He could do was to send someone to tell me that He was there for me." Within a matter of minutes, the officer called for backup and then prayed to receive Christ right there on that street corner.

And then he writes, "When I heard that story, I was mesmerized, to say the least. It was one of the most amazing and powerful conversion stories I had ever heard. The speaker closed his message to our group that evening, he said, 'Now go out and witness to people!' So we were all looking for cops all week!"

From SermonCentral

Chapter 3 ~ Part 1

My wife joined quite a while after I moved to live in Canada.
It was a "long" time, especially for me living in a country that
was new to me.

Within that time, we sent emails letters, pictures and gifts,
spent hours on the phone. Every opportunity we found with
someone coming or going either way, we sent something:
a picture, a card, a gift.

Then came the day I went to pick her up at the airport. She
was finally here. The wait was over. There was no
need to write those letters and send pictures anymore.
No more need for long -distance phone calls.

When I woke up the day after, she was right there!

The Old Testament - Moses, the Law, the prophets, the Psalms are essentially a description of all that God wanted to do in Christ. In burnt offerings. In the commandments. In prophecies. In Jonah. In David. In a thousand allegories, the Messiah was promised.

They had the shadow, the letters promising, the pictures projecting, the words assuring, hope stoked. We have the reality, the body casting the shadow. We are not in hope. We have arrived.

To look to the Law is to say that the Christ has not come. To look to Moses is to grab shadows.

The wife is here, no more pictures, letters or voice messages. The Christ is here, no more laws, shadows or allegories.

Galatians Chapter 3

Paul arrives at the meat of his epistle in this chapter. He quotes from the Old Testament more than 8 times in this chapter alone. Up to this point, he had not made express references to the Old Testament. You can see that this is where the rubber meets the road in his argument.

Paul quoted lavishly and copiously from the Old Testament in his epistles. By my own personal count, he quoted from the Old Testament at least 50 times in the epistle to the Romans. Think about that. 50 times! He laid solid foundations for doctrine. He could defend every slant he had, every stand he took from the Word.

I believe he did the same in the letter to the Ephesians about 7 times, again, by my count. I noticed also that the writer of the epistle to the Hebrews did the same, quoting the Old Testament about 24 times.

But I want you to note that this is not just about quoting. It is really about drawing out the spirit of the Word from the Old Testament. It is about drawing out sound doctrine from the Word. This is about teaching, explaining, about light and revelation from the Word as revealed by the Holy Spirit.

If there was an attribute in Paul that we can copy or learn from, it is this. Maintaining our stand based on the counsel on the Word.

Well, back to the letter to the Galatians.

He calls the Galatians foolish, stupid, senseless as different translations have it. "Thoughtless, mindless". "Are you under a spell? Are you out of your mind?" Who has bewitched you?

You understand he only means that in a metaphorical sense. He's just frustrated at these folks. His incredulity got the better of him.

> 1O **foolish Galatians, who hath bewitched you**, that ye should not obey the truth, before whose eyes Jesus Christ hath been evidently set forth, crucified among you?

2This only would I learn of you, Received ye the Spirit by the works of the law, or by the hearing of faith?

3**Are ye so foolish**? having begun in the Spirit, are ye now made perfect by the flesh?

4Have ye suffered so many things in vain? if *it be* yet in vain.

5He therefore that ministereth to you the Spirit, and worketh miracles among you, *doeth he it* by the works of the law, or by the hearing of faith?

Here is another translation (God's Word):

1**You stupid people of Galatia! Who put you under an evil spell?** Wasn't Christ Jesus' crucifixion clearly described to you?

2I want to learn only one thing from you. **Did you receive the Spirit by your own efforts to live according to a set of standards or by believing what you heard**?

3**Are you that stupid**? Did you begin in a spiritual way only to end up doing things in a human way?

4Did you suffer so much for nothing? [I doubt] that it was for nothing!

5Does God supply you with the Spirit and work **miracles** among you through your own efforts or through **believing** what you heard?

And in rebuking them, he tells them that everything we receive is all about and through faith. Miracles, receiving the Spirit, walking in holiness and indeed, every other thing we receive, we receive by faith. It will never be by what we do or don't do. It will always be by faith.

The Paradigm, The Promise

6Even as Abraham believed God, and it was accounted to him for righteousness.

7Know ye therefore **that they which are of faith, the same are the children of Abraham**.

8And the scripture, foreseeing that God would justify the heathen through faith, preached before the gospel unto Abraham, *saying*, In thee shall all nations be blessed.

9**So then they which be of faith are blessed** with faithful Abraham.

Paul takes off by presenting Abraham as a paradigm, a template, an allegory, a description, an illustration, a prototype, a model or pattern of the way we become righteous before God, of what God wanted to do with all of humanity.

How did Abraham arrive? Abraham believed God and God counted it for righteousness. All who follow the faith of Abraham are the children of Abraham and are blessed with the blessing of Abraham.

Even as Abraham believed God. Just like Abraham believed God. *In the same way* that Abraham believed God.

In like manner. Abraham is a paradigm, an example, a template of how a man was made or counted righteous before God. How?

Just like Abraham believed God, and it was accounted to him for righteousness, in the same way I want you to know that everyone who has faith is a child of Abraham, and has the same blessing that Abraham had.

The blessing of righteousness. Believing is how we are made righteous. Believing was how Abraham was made righteous. If we have the same kind of faith that Abraham had, we will be counted righteous.

In verse 8, Paul says that God preached the Gospel (which means good news) to Abraham. Why? How?

Because God was going to justify the heathen through faith. How did God preach the Good News to Abraham? What did He say to Abraham? *"In you, Abraham, will all the nations of the earth be blessed."*

How is the Gospel in this statement? What is the Good News in it? Because it is talking about Christ and our redemption prophetically.

First, I want you to consider that when God spoke this to Abraham, the whole world would have been considered *heathen.* There were no Jews. There were no Greeks, Gentiles or Yorubas. This promise was made to Abraham the *very first time* God spoke to him as documented in Scripture. **Genesis 12**.

> 1Now the LORD had said unto Abram, Get thee out of thy country, and from thy kindred, and from thy father's house, unto a land that I will shew thee:
>
> 2And I will make of thee a great nation, and I will bless thee, and make thy name great; and thou shalt be a blessing:
>
> 3And I will bless them that bless thee, and curse him that curseth thee: and **in thee shall all families of the earth be blessed.**

What I hope you see is that this promise of the whole world being saved and redeemed was made to Abraham from Day One of God's enterprise with him, and that this has nothing to do the Israel or Jews – in the light of our Redemption in Christ.

Also, notice that all these promises and blessings were given to Abraham without pre-conditions. It seemed to be a spontaneous outpouring of love from the Father. He said nothing like, "I will make your name great **if** you…" Or, "I will bless you **if** you sacrifice…" No. "**If** you pray all night…" No.

It does not say that Abraham was blessed because he had done something. The blessing of righteousness was not a reward for something! Not a reward for good behavior or a good sacrifice. Not a reward for tithing.

We are not even told that Abraham prayed before God gave these blessings. He just said "I will bless you, I will make you great", period, showing His penchant and willingness and spontaneity to bless.

This shows us, one, that God's only wish for us, for man, for humanity is for us to be blessed. That is the heart of the Father God. It is the highest tragedy to doubt or question this.

Two, it shows us that we cannot earn the blessings of God. We only come by faith. This is the only thing that pleases Him. This was how Abraham came.

Genesis 12:3 has absolutely nothing to do with the 1948 Nation of Israel *in Christianity*. Some folks would quote it today to substantiate the reason why Israel exists in the Middle East.

Frankly, that is purely a geo-political issue that is really none of my business. As a Christian, 1948 Israel is none of my business any more than Angola, Brazil, Oman or East Timor is.

To put it in a better way still, 1948 Israel is as much my business as Nepal, Jordan, China or Paraguay are.

I hope and pray for the salvation and wellness of the Jews as I pray for the salvation and wellness of the Chinese, the Palestinian and the Trinidadian.

I am saying that God preached the Good News to Abraham when the whole world was *heathen*. He did it when Jews were heathen, and He had the whole world in mind when He said it.

That Good News is Jesus. That is my point. That Promise is Christ.

God said, "**in thee shall all families** of the earth be blessed". It was about all the world.

Paul reflects on this in **Galatians 3:8**, *"the scripture, foreseeing that God would justify the heathen through faith, preached before the gospel unto Abraham"*. *God would justify the heathen.*

At this point, the Jew was heathen, the Gentile was heathen. In that sense, everyone was Gentile, without God in the world.

It is a bit farcical to use these terms two here at this point because they would not be defined for the next few hundreds of years, but I hope you get my point. With his use of the word "heathen" in verse 8, Paul has included everyone in this calculus.

It is sad, really, that all some Christians see today in **Genesis 12** is the natural, the carnal. All they see is the modern nation of Israel in the Middle East.

Foreseeing that He would justify the heathen or the godless through faith, God said, *"In you, Abraham, will all the nations of the earth be blessed."* This is the gospel, the good news that the blessing was going to come.

It is good news - available to everyone, and effectively, Paul has concluded all under sin, categorizing the whole world as godless, with God promising to use Abraham as a conduit to redeem all of mankind.

Abraham's Discovery

In **Romans 4**, Paul tells us that in Abraham's walk with God, he made a discovery, a finding: how a man can be made right with God.

> 1What shall we say then that **Abraham our father, as pertaining to the flesh, hath found?**

Abraham found something, made a discovery. What did he find? What did he discover?

> 2For if Abraham were justified by works, he hath *whereof* to glory; but not before God.

Was Abraham justified by doing something? No.

> 3For what saith the scripture? Abraham believed God, and it was counted unto him for righteousness.

4Now to him that worketh is the reward not reckoned of grace, but of debt.

5But to him that worketh not, but believeth on him that justifieth the ungodly, **his faith is counted for righteousness**.

Abraham found out that the way to be made righteous with God is only by faith. To him that believes, *his faith is counted for righteousness.*

You notice that in verse 5, Paul says God is the One that "justifieth the ungodly" and counts people righteous who put their faith in Him. That is what Abraham found. Man is counted right with God by faith.

Just like in **Galatians 3:8**, you find the words "justify", "heathen", "ungodly", "faith" in **Romans 4:5**.

Galatians 3:8 *"…God would justify the heathen through faith…"*

Romans 4:5 *"…To him that worketh not, but believeth on him that justifieth the ungodly, his faith is counted for righteousness."*

Justify the heathen…justify the ungodly. They are saying the same thing. In other words, Abraham was ungodly and heathen, a Gentile when God counted him righteous. Based on faith.

Through Faith

I hope you see what I see. I hope you noticed the two words, *"through faith"*. God was going to justify the heathen, the *world through faith*.

He was going to use Abraham as the agency for His plan, but the plan was always to save the whole world on the basis of faith. It had nothing to do with Abraham's natural lineage.

This reminds us of **Romans 3:25** in reference to the Lord Jesus.

25Whom God hath set forth *to be* a propitiation **through faith** in his blood, to declare his righteousness for the remission of sins that are past, through the forbearance of God;

Weymouth's New Testament has this verse as, "He it is whom God put forward as a Mercy-seat, **rendered efficacious through faith in His blood.**"

The NET version: "God publicly displayed him at his death as the mercy seat **accessible through faith.**"

Paul then makes a minor conclusion in view of the things he just said: *"So then they which be of faith are blessed with faithful Abraham."*

They which be of faith. So then. He is making a conclusion, as a result of things he's said previously. *So then.*

Since God counted Abraham's faith for righteousness, and since God said that the *whole world* would be blessed in Abraham, so then you can see that they which are of faith *anywhere in the world*, from *any corner of the world*, those are the ones that get the same blessing of Abraham.

From any and every corner of the world, as long as they have the Abraham kind of faith, they would be counted righteous too, and thus have the blessing of Abraham. You understand that this promise is about all the nations of the earth. You see that they which are of faith, these are the children of Abraham.

It is through faith we get the blessing that Abraham got. *They which be of faith are blessed with faithful Abraham. It is only through faith.* It belongs to those who are of the faith of Jesus Christ.

And the blessing is righteousness.

I recently watched something online in which a woman pretty much said that the way Christians are blessed or can be blessed is because they give financially to Israel, the nation.

These people say that nation who have anything against Israel are cursed. They even say that Christians who don't give to Israel are not blessed. They base this on *"I will bless those who bless you, and curse those who curse you"*.

You see these days, there are so many people flooding the online space who say they are prophets and prophetesses. They do all these so-called "prophetic" conferences and meetings. And all they talk about is the politics of the United States or Israel, how there will be war in the Middle East, how they want to see the Muslim nations destroyed.

They talk about earthquakes and hurricanes and eclipses of the moon and sun. I just personally feel sorry for their ignorance of God's Word.

God does not destroy nations, as these folks think He would do to Muslim and unbelieving nations. You get the sense that these people want to see unbelievers, especially Muslims, wiped out in a great "righteous" war.

They want to see, in their misinterpretation of Scripture, all the nations around Israel wiped out and destroyed. God is not like that. He has no pleasure in the death of sinners. The Bible says that there is great joy in heaven for every sinner that repents. He does not want to destroy people or nations. He makes His sun and goodness and mercy to fall on men everywhere.
Besides, Israel is not more righteous than its neighbors. It is not more special to God than its neighbors.

Yes, we must stand against the destruction of Israel. She has a right to exist and prosper in peace. But that is a purely geo-political issue.

In the same way, we also stand against the destruction of Indians, Pakistanis, Nigerians, Palestinians, Afghans, Canadians. We must stand against the mistreatment of any people anywhere – Aboriginal, British, African, Aztec, Gypsy, European or Jamaican.

God's love for the Jew is exactly the same for the Palestinian. God's love for Netanyahu is exactly the same for Ahmadinejad and Saddam Hussein. He did not prefer the David Ben-Gurion to Abdel Nasser.

"I will bless those who bless you, and curse those who curse you" is not about Israel. It is about the Christ and the Body of Believers in Him. When God made that statement to Abraham, there was no Isaac, no Jacob, let alone Israel. That Promise was made to Abraham and his seed. That seed is Christ.

"I will bless those who bless you, and curse those who curse you" is figure of speech for "I will give you the ultimate blessing." This is about how much of a blessing in Christ God was going to bring to the world through the seed of Abraham - in Redemption!

That promise is for those who emulate Abraham's faith and belief in that they also repose their faith and righteousness in the work and righteousness of Jesus Christ, the true Seed of Abraham.

They which be of faith are blessed with faithful Abraham. They which be of faith are blessed with the blessing promised and given to Abraham – the blessing of righteousness.

Every promise, every blessing that God made to him was/is for those that are of faith. Those that trust in Christ. I want you to notice that Paul will start to make his point by juxtaposing the promise to and faith of Abraham against the Law (of Moses), the effort of the flesh to earn God's righteousness.

Paul begins to make the case against trusting in the Law.

> 9**So then they which be of faith are blessed** with faithful Abraham.

> 10**For as many as are of the works of the law are under the curse**: for it is written, Cursed *is* every one that continueth not in all things which are written in the book of the law to do them.

You see the comparison, the contrast he is painting in verses 9 and 10?

"…of faith are **blessed.**"

"…of the Law are…**cursed.**"

To be under the Law is to be under a curse. To walk in faith, like the one that Abraham walked in, is to be blessed.

The demands of the Law are relentless, and you never stop doing them. These are demands that you could never meet in totality. In fact, if you obey one part of the Law and offend in another one, you have broken the whole Law.

This means that there will always be punishment with the Law. Paul continues to compare these two systems in the next verses.

> 11But that no man is justified by the law in the sight of God, *it is* evident: for, The just shall live by faith.
>
> 12**And the law is not of faith**: but, The man that doeth them shall live in them.

No man is justified in the sight of God by their **actions or works.** On the contrary, the one who is justified before God gets it by **faith.** Did you notice verse 12? *The Law is not faith.*

> 12*This way of faith is very different from the way of law.* (NLT).

Works versus faith. They do not mix. They are mutually exclusive. The righteous, just like Abraham, are justified by faith.

In the middle of talking about the Law, Paul inputs this: *the just shall live by faith.* **Galatians 3**.

> 11But that no man is justified by the law in the sight of God, *it is* evident: for, The just shall live by faith.
>
> 12And the law is not of faith…

What many of us have failed to realize is that even in the Old Testament, the just were not, were never justified by anything other than faith. Pleasing God by faith was always the plan.

The just shall live by faith. The Law is not of faith.

The just shall live by faith. The Law is not of faith. If the just live by faith, then, the just don't live by the Law.

If God never changes, if He was the God in the Old Testament, as He is in the New, and He tells us in the New Testament that we are justified by faith only, it means that faith has always been the way that anyone was justified by Him.

This means that the just have always been justified by faith. So was the case with the elders mentioned in **Hebrews 11** that received a good report by faith. This is the whole point of the Book of Hebrews.

This is the reason these heroes of faith are mentioned or listed. So that we can see that it is our faith and believing that saves us, and also that faith has always been the way that God justified man.

An overview and summary at the Book of Hebrews will show us the approach that the writer takes to make the case.

The Covenant Explained in Hebrews

Let's take a sizeable detour to the Book of Hebrews, then, to return later to verse 13 in **Galatians 3**.

You will notice that in **Hebrews 1**, he makes the case that the Lord Jesus is the Son of God, and incomparably superior to angels. The writer said this particularly because he is speaking to Hebrews who know that the Old Covenant was ratified in "the hand of an angel".

Then in later chapters he makes it clear that the Lord Jesus is superior to Moses (chapter 2). He talks about the Aaronic priesthood and insists that there is a new Priesthood of which the Lord Jesus is the High Priest! This priesthood lasts forever under the likeness of Melchizedek's, not Aaron's priesthood.

He talks about entering into the rest of God by ceasing to depend on our own work or efforts, and to rest in what God has done. He tells us in no uncertain terms that the Israelites of Moses' day did not enter the rest of God, because they did not walk by faith. They were in unbelief. Chapters 3 and 4.

He shows us that there is now a *new* Covenant in force. He argues that if there's a new Priest, then it means that there must be a new Law, and a new Covenant. If there's a new order of Priesthood, it means that there has got to be a change of the Law, a change of the Covenant.

Then in the 10th chapter, he maintains that God's real plan had never been the Law because that Old Covenant could never have brought salvation. That Old Covenant was just a type and shadow of the real plan of God.

Hebrews 10 is a rebuke to all who hold on to the Law!

> 5Wherefore when he cometh into the world, he saith, **Sacrifice and offering thou wouldest not, but a body hast thou prepared me:**
>
> **6In burnt offerings and** *sacrifices* **for sin thou hast had no pleasure.**
>
> **7Then said I, Lo, I come (in the volume of the book it is written of me,) to do thy will, O God.**

Look closely as he quotes from **Psalm 40.**

You have no pleasure in burnt offerings and sacrifices. That is not what you want. The Lord Jesus is the real sacrifice God wants.

> 8Above when he said, Sacrifice and offering and burnt offerings and *offering* for sin thou wouldest not, neither hadst pleasure *therein*; which are offered by the law;

A repudiation and rejection of the Law. Sacrifice and offering thou wouldest not.

> 9Then said he, Lo, I come to do thy will, O God. **He taketh away the first, that he may establish the second.**
>
> 10By the which will we are sanctified through the offering of the body of Jesus Christ once *for all*.

What is this saying? God never had pleasure in the Law. Never had pleasure in burnt offerings and sacrifices. Jesus was always the will of God as the sacrifice for sin.

In other words, he is saying that the Law (burnt offerings and sacrifices) was not the will of God.

He was saying, "I am the sacrifice that is acceptable to you! My body is what You, God, really wants as the acceptable sacrifice and offering. I have come to do Your will, O God".

Then said I, "Lo, I come (in the volume of the book it is written of me,) to do thy will, O God". I come to do Your will, which is to offer my body as offering and sacrifice.

Chapter 10 ends with the statement, "The just shall live by faith." This is where this connects to the Book of Galatians. This is exactly what Paul had said in **Galatians 3:11**

> 11But that no man is justified by the law in the sight of God, *it is* evident: for, The just shall live by faith.

This is the way to be justified in the sight of God. Can you see that all his arguments from chapter 1 to chapter 10 (Hebrews) was leading up to Chapter 11, the "faith" chapter?

"**Now, faith is…**" It is faith that justifies us. It is faith that has always justified man before God. The Book of Hebrews strains to explain to us that what God really desires are a people who walk with Him by faith and faith alone, not by sacrifices or observance of the Law.

"**Now, faith is…**" He defines what faith is and then shows us that the Old Testament saints lived by faith. Before and after the Law came on the scene, it was always their faith that got them God's approval.

For by it the elders obtained a good report. Without faith, it is impossible to please God.

It was their faith that made them approved before God, and in their hearts, what they sought was the presence of God. What they sought for was a relationship with God.

Without faith, it is impossible to please Him. Abraham, justified by faith, sought for a city in God. Moses esteemed the riches of Christ greater than the treasures of Egypt. He saw Christ in His dealings with God, "endured, as seeing him who is invisible." That is faith.

By faith Abel. By faith Enoch. By faith, Abraham. By faith Sarah. By faith Isaac. By faith Moses. By faith Rahab. By faith Jacob.

> **Hebrews 11**
> 13These all **died in faith**, not having received **the promises**, but **having seen them** afar off, and were persuaded of *them*, and embraced *them*, and confessed that they were strangers and pilgrims on the earth.
>
> 14For they that say such things declare plainly that they seek a country.
>
> 15And truly, if they had been mindful of that *country* from whence they came out, they might have had opportunity to have returned.
>
> 16But now they desire a better *country*, that is, an heavenly: wherefore God is not ashamed to be called their God: for he hath prepared for them a city.

Please don't just look at these verses casually. Slow down and digest what they are saying. *They died in faith, but they* **saw** *the promises; they were* **persuaded** *of the promises; they* **embraced** *the promises; they* **confessed** *what they believed.*

It must be faith for you to **see, be persuaded, embrace, and confess** something you never saw or touched physically. Their faith. They walked with God by faith. Their focus was on the unseen. They focused on the God they didn't see but walked with.

They lived like strangers and pilgrims on the earth. In other words, they were more conscious of the heavenly and spiritual realm than they were of natural, physical things. Notice the contrast: strangers on the earth versus desiring a heavenly home.

A casual look at the list of those saints would probably leave you with the impression that he was only talking about the folks that came **before the Law**. He mentioned Abel, Enoch, Abraham, Sarah, Isaac.

> 32And what shall I more say? for the time would fail me to tell of Gedeon, and of Barak, and of Samson, and of Jephthae; of David also, and Samuel, and of the prophets
>
> 33**Who through faith** subdued kingdoms, wrought righteousness, obtained promises…

David, Barak, Samuel, Gideon. These ones came after the Law. **Who through faith.** All these received a good faith report, even though they were under the Law.

The Promise, the Curse and the Blessing

Verses 13 and 39 pretty much echo each other. Notice the similarities.

> 13These all died in faith, **not having received the promises**, but having seen them afar off, and were persuaded of *them*, and embraced *them*…
>
> 39And these all, having obtained a good report through faith, **received not the promise:**

What promise(s)? The promise of the Christ. The promise of

Galatians 3:22
22But the scripture hath concluded all under sin, that **the promise by faith of Jesus Christ** might be given to them that believe.

Christ was the promise. The same Christ who is now our reality. They saw the Christ in their hearts, though He did not come in their lifetime.

The promise was the promise of Christ's coming and the redemption that would come through Him. Over the centuries, through the prophets, through the Law all through Scripture, again and again, God promised the Messiah.

These saints had a form of knowledge of what God wanted to do and accomplish. They obviously did not know the fine details, but they knew that a Redeemer was coming, bringing with Him our emancipation. Something in their hearts bore witness to this.

This was what made them approved before God. The real and ultimate longing of their heart was the promise of the Messiah, the Savior.

This has been the only way He justifies humanity. The Law was **never** meant to be the means to justify man. It's not, like some people say, that the Old Testament folks were justified or made righteous by the Law and New Testament folks are justified by faith.

I used to think that was the case myself. It was, has always been, will always be by faith – Old or New Testament, but the Promised Savior of Abel's, Enoch's, Abraham's, Moses's and David's dream, hope, expectation and faith is now here.

Christ, who was hope and promise to them, is now our reality. All of God's dealings with man culminated in Christ. Christ was the essence of it. It was always going to anchor at the harbor of Christ.

Back to **Galatians 3**, Paul continues his comparisons between the curse and the blessing or between faith and the works of the Law:

> 13Christ hath redeemed us from the curse of the law, being made a curse for us: for it is written, Cursed *is* every one that hangeth on a tree:
>
> 14That the blessing of Abraham might come on the Gentiles through Jesus Christ; that we might receive the promise of the Spirit through faith.

Christ has redeemed us from the curse of Law. The Law ends up brining a curse.

Do you want to be under the curse? Think about this. Just think about it in the context of what he's been talking about, of his whole argument.

Christ has redeemed us from the curse of the Law so that the blessing of Abraham might come on us. Through faith. Again, he is juxtaposing *the curse* against *the blessing.* He's using that comparison again. He is juxtaposing works against faith.

Christ has redeemed us from the curse. So, the blessing might come to us. Again, he goes back to Abraham. So that the promise that God had made to Abraham would come to pass. So that that original way of being justified before God through faith might stand.

You notice the phrase *through faith.* We receive the promise *through faith.* The promise of the Spirit? You can see that the promise of the Spirit is actually in Christ Jesus.

It is the same promise that God had made to Abraham when he said that it was in or through Abraham that the nations or families of all the earth would be blessed.

"In you shall all the nations of the earth be blessed". This is what Paul called, "The blessing of Abraham" in verse 14. Today we know that that blessing is salvation and righteousness in and through Christ Jesus, *through faith.*

The Law, a Curse

I feel the need to address the issue of Paul saying that the Law is a curse or brings a curse before I continue with the study.

Why on earth would Paul call the Law a curse? *A curse?!*

You can "understand" from statements like this why the Jews and Judaizers would have hated Paul. They tried to kill him many times. Here, he just called the Law of Moses a curse!

If the Law brings a curse, then why was it introduced? What was the point? You will find, looking through Scripture, that Paul describes the Law in other places in the New Testament in very, very strong language that will shock the average Jew and the average Evangelical Christian today.

Let me show you what Paul said about the Law in **II Corinthians 3**:

6Who also hath made us able ministers of the new testament; not of the letter, but of the spirit: **for the letter killeth**, but the spirit giveth life

7But if **the ministration of death, written *and* engraven in stones**…

9For if **the ministration of condemnation** *be* glory, much more doth the ministration of righteousness exceed in glory.

So, in addition to calling the Law a curse in Galatians, Paul, in these passages, says the Law *kills*, and is the *ministration of death* and *condemnation.*

Why has he resorted to describing the Law with these words? The Law of Moses, written and engraved in stones, the ministration of death?

Written and engraven in stones. That is surely the 10 Commandments. The Law given to Moses with supernatural signs and wonders is the ministration of condemnation? It's a curse?

How is the Law the ministration of death and of condemnation? In **Romans 7**, Paul addresses the issue directly.

7…*Is* **the law sin? God forbid**. Nay, I had not known sin, but by the law…

8Sin, taking occasion by the commandment, wrought in me all manner of concupiscence…**without the law sin *was* dead.**

9For I was alive without the law once: but when the commandment came, sin revived, **and I died**.

10…The commandment, **which *was ordained* to life, I found *to be* unto death.**

11For sin, taking occasion by the commandment, deceived me, and by it **slew *me.***

76

> 13Was then that which is good made death unto me? God
> forbid. But sin, that it might appear sin, working death in me
> by that which is good; that sin by the commandment might
> become exceeding sinful.

> 14For we know that the law is spiritual: but I am carnal, sold
> under sin.

Let's take a bit of time to digest and summarize all that Paul is saying
here. Is the Law sin? Is the Law bad? Is the Law a curse? Why does the
Law minister death and condemnation? Was the Law really the
problem?

Paul says the Law is not bad. The Law is not sin. There's nothing really
wrong with the Law, the Law is not the problem.

The law is holy, and the commandment holy, and just, and good. In verse 10
Paul says that although the Law was ordained to life, it became the
death of me.

In verse 13, he tries to wrap it all up, in a sense.

> 13Was then that which is good made death unto me? God
> forbid. But sin, that it might appear sin, **working death in me**
> by that which is good; that sin by the commandment might
> become exceeding sinful.

In essence Paul is saying that sin, not the Law, was the problem. The
Law was what produced sin in me, and that sin killed me. It was the
Law that smoked out the sin that was in me. It gave sin its potency.

Sin is what killed me, the Law was the agency that brought sin out. I
died spiritually. It slew *me*.

Because of my fallen nature, because I have been sold under sin, it
took advantage of the Law and killed me spiritually, condemned me.

Sin worked death in me by the Law. The Law was not the problem. Sin was the problem. My fallen sinful nature was the problem. The Law made sin look like what it exactly was.

> 7Nay, I had not known sin, but by the law:

> 7Well then, am I suggesting that the law of God is sinful? Of course not! In fact, it was the law that showed me my sin. (NLT)

> 7What should we say, then? Are Moses' laws sinful? That's unthinkable! In fact, I wouldn't have recognized sin if those laws hadn't shown it to me. (God's Word)

The Law served to identify sin, and, in that sense, condemned and killed man. In that sense, the Law was a curse. There was no way that I was going to be righteous in the eyes of the Law.

In view of the Law's relentless requirements and demands, I died spiritually. The strength (or power) of sin is the Law.

Let me show you one place in the Word that tells us the intent of the Law. This is from **Hebrews 10**.

> 1For the law having a shadow of good things to come, *and* not the very image of the things, **can never with those sacrifices which they offered year by year continually make the comers thereunto perfect**.

> 2For then would they not have ceased to be offered? because that the worshippers once purged **should have had** no more conscience of sins.

> 3But in those *sacrifices there is* a **remembrance again** *made* **of sins every year.**

I hope you see what I see from these verses. Paul is saying that the Law was never meant to make people perfect or righteous. It could not. It did not have the power to do it, otherwise, it should have cleansed man's conscience.

78

Then, the fact that the sacrifices had to be done continually means that your sins are **remembered year in year out** which means that the Law only serves to **remind you** of your sinfulness and spiritual depravity. The Law was designed to remind you of your sins, not cure you of them.

But in those sacrifices, there is a remembrance again made of sins every year. That you have to sacrifice continually is an indicator of your slavery to sin.

This is the purpose of the Law. Make sin stand out, obvious.

The Law brought us to Christ

Something Paul said in **Romans 10:4** will help us along here:

> 4For Christ *is* the **end** of the law for righteousness to everyone that believeth.

"End", in English can have two meanings also viz. It can mean termination, conclusion. It can also mean the point of, the essence, the goal.

From Strong's, the Greek word translated "end" in **Romans 10:4** is "Telos": **5056** *télos* (a neuter noun) – properly, consummation (the *end-goal, purpose*), such as *closure* with all its *results*.

Consummation. End-goal. Purpose. Aim.

Christ is the consummation, the end goal and purpose of the Law meaning that the Law aimed for us to look at Christ for righteousness.

It aimed to bring us to trust and place our faith in Christ for righteousness. Its purpose was to point us to Christ, its design to lead us to Christ, Christ being the Promised Seed.

He is the ultimate goal of the Law. *How many ways can I say this?* He is the conclusion and termination of the Law. He is, was always, the result and purpose of the giving of the Law. Paul confirms all this later down the road in **Galatians 3**.

23But before faith came, we were kept under the law, shut up unto the faith which should afterwards be revealed.

24Wherefore **the law was our schoolmaster *to bring us* unto Christ, that we might be justified by faith.**

The Law was to bring us unto Christ, that we might be justified by faith. Showing us the sinful state and depravity that we were in, the Law pointed us to Christ, to our need for a savior. It brought us to Christ, to justification by faith.

This is a scream.

Christ is the end of the Law for righteousness for those that believe. The Law brought us to Christ. *Christ is the end of the search for righteousness by the Law and the commandments.*

Let's take another useful detour.

In **Deuteronomy 30,** just after all the commandments and commitments were given to the children of Israel, Moses said a most curious thing to the people. He just got through telling (actually, reminding) them about the demands of the Law and the horrible, horrible consequences that would befall them if they failed to obey.

But hear what he says here:

> 11For this commandment which I command thee this day, it *is* not hidden from thee, neither *is* it far off.
>
> 12It *is* not in heaven, that thou shouldest say, Who shall go up for us to heaven, and bring it unto us, that we may hear it, and do it?
>
> 13Neither *is* it beyond the sea, that thou shouldest say, Who shall go over the sea for us, and bring it unto us, that we may hear it, and do it?
>
> **14But the word *is* very nigh unto thee, in thy mouth, and in thy heart, that thou mayest do it.**

Paul quotes these verses in the middle of talking about the righteousness of faith in **Romans 10**. He does something vital, curious: he explains Moses' real goal by inserting "Christ" into the verses.

> 5For Moses describeth **the righteousness which is of the law**, That the man which doeth those things shall live by them.
>
> 6But **the righteousness which is of faith** speaketh on this wise, Say not in thine heart, Who shall ascend into heaven? **(that is, to bring Christ down *from above*:)**
>
> 7Or, Who shall descend into the deep? **(that is, to bring up Christ again from the dead.)**
>
> 8But what saith it? The word is nigh thee, *even* in thy mouth, and in thy heart: **that is,** the word of faith, which we preach;

This is Moses describing both kinds of righteousness. The righteousness which is of the law which is up to your performance. *The man which doeth those things shall live by them.* Good luck with that.

Then, the righteousness which is of faith and is not up to your performance.

But what is Paul saying? What was he trying to do inserting Christ into the middle of this quote from Moses? He was saying that the commandments given to the children of Israel were impossible, absolutely impossible to do! They could not possibly be doers of it. It was too much for them.

He was also saying that Moses was really talking about salvation coming to man only in Christ.

"Who shall ascend into heaven?" That's figure of speech for "this is too much, this is impossible, this is too hard."

"Who shall descend into the deep?" *Who can do this? How can anyone do these things? How can we ever meet up with these demands?*

81

That was what the Israelites were thinking. That is what anyone would think if you were given so many laws and rules to obey. It was impossible! Or is it?

Do not to think like that. *"Say not in your heart, "This is impossible""*. Watch carefully how Paul navigates us through this.

> 6But **the righteousness which is of faith** speaketh on this wise, Say not in thine heart, Who shall ascend into heaven? (that is, to bring Christ down *from above*:)
>
> 7Or, Who shall descend into the deep? (that is, to bring up Christ again from the dead.)

The righteousness of faith says don't say it is impossible to do. That means that Moses was speaking about faith. It means that Moses was telling them how to become righteous, how to please God. By faith.

Who is going to bring the savior down from heaven? This, they were thinking, is as hard as someone going to heaven. Who is able?

This is as hard as going into hell and coming back. Impossible. *Who shall ascend into heaven? (that is, to bring Christ down). Who shall descend into the deep? (that is, to bring up Christ).*

By inserting Christ into it, he was saying that it is only in and through Christ that you can attain righteousness. These commandments are only accomplished in Christ. He will fulfill the requirements of the Law. Christ is the end, the doing, the obedience of the Law for those who believe.

The righteousness of faith says don't say it is impossible; you just need Christ.

Christ is righteousness. Christ is obeying God. Christ is pleasing God. Say not in your heart that it is impossible to do it, and don't repose confidence in your own effort. Don't trust in your own efforts.

He is saying that Christ will fulfill the Law and commandments for us.

Accepting Christ means that we have attained unto the righteousness of faith, the righteous requirements of the Law being fulfilled. Accepting Christ is righteousness, is the fulfillment of the Law.

Paul calls what Moses told them in a hidden form, the "Word of Faith". He is saying that believing it and confessing it is the way to be a doer of all that God requires from man. Faith is what it takes!

Moses was actually saying, "You think it's hard, don't you? You think it's too tough. But you will be surprised how much close to you the key to it is. It is the faith in your heart. It is the confession of your mouth." Let's quote Moses exactly: "**The word *is* very nigh unto thee, in thy mouth, and in thy heart**".

The Word of faith is nigh thee. The solution is near you. In your heart and in your mouth. Just by believing it! It is only hard without faith.

It is the faith in your heart! It is near you! Just believe it in your heart, confess it with your mouth.

The Word of Faith which we preach. In other words, this was always about faith! Even in giving them the commandments of the Law, God was telling them that the way to be a doer of it was by faith!

It's not far from you, it's not far-fetched. It actually is not hard. It's in your heart and mouth! It is hard when you depend on your own effort. You don't have to work for it. You don't have to struggle for it. It is by believing. It is by faith.

> 9That if thou shalt confess with thy mouth the Lord Jesus, and shalt believe in thine heart that God hath raised him from the dead, thou shalt be saved.
>
> 10For *with the heart man believeth unto righteousness; and with the mouth confession is made unto salvation.*

With the heart, you believe. With the mouth, you confess. The word is nigh thee. The solution is near you. How near? It is as easy as the words in your mouth and the faith in your heart. Being righteous or pleasing to God, is all about Christ and Calvary, and not works.

It tells us that Moses preached the same Gospel, preached Christ. It is the same message from Genesis to Revelation.

Back to **Galatians 3**.

> 18For if the inheritance *be* of the law, *it is* no more of promise: but God gave *it* to Abraham by promise.

This means that ethnic Jews that ignore the righteousness of faith through Christ Jesus are not the true sons of Abraham.

If they were, the promise God made to Abraham is nullified, because He gave it to Abraham by faith. When God made His promise to Abraham, Abraham did not have the Law.

> 13Christ hath redeemed us from the curse of the law, being made a curse for us: for it is written, Cursed *is* everyone that hangeth on a tree:

He became a curse for us, hanging on the cross. The Pharisees wanted Him to be crucified because they wanted Him to be cursed.

Cursed *is* everyone that hangeth on a tree. They wanted Him accursed by God. So, they insisted on His being crucified. In that, He became a curse indeed. So that the blessing, the promise of (to) Abraham might (has) now come on the Gentiles. Therefore, they that are of faith, the same are the children of Abraham.

Because I'm Yours
The little girl who finally went to Disney World

I never dreamed that taking a child to Disney World could be so difficult or that such a trip could teach me so much about God's outrageous grace. Our middle daughter had been previously adopted by another family. I [Timothy] am sure this couple had the best of intentions, but they never quite integrated the adopted child into their family of biological children. After a couple of rough years, they dissolved the adoption, and we ended up welcoming an eight-year-old girl into our home.

For one reason or another, whenever our daughter's previous family vacationed at Disney World, they took their biological children with them, but they left their adopted daughter with a family friend. Usually — at least in the child's mind — this happened because she did something wrong that precluded her presence on the trip.

And so, by the time we adopted our daughter, she had seen many pictures of Disney World and she had heard about the rides and the characters and the parades. But when it came to passing through the gates of the Magic Kingdom, she had always been the one left on the outside. Once I found out about this history, I made plans to take her to Disney World the next time a speaking engagement took our family to the southeastern United States.

I thought I had mastered the Disney World drill. I knew from previous experiences that the prospect of seeing cast members in freakishly oversized mouse and duck costumes somehow turns children into squirming bundles of emotional instability. What I didn't expect was that the prospect of visiting this dreamworld would produce a stream of downright devilish behavior in our newest daughter. In the month leading up to our trip to the Magic Kingdom, she stole food when a simple request would have gained her a snack. She lied when it would have been easier to tell the truth. She whispered insults that were carefully crafted to hurt her older sister as deeply as possible — and, as the days on the calendar moved closer to the trip, her mutinies multiplied.

A couple of days before our family headed to Florida, I pulled our daughter into my lap to talk through her latest escapade. "I know what you're going to do," she stated flatly. "You're not going to take me to Disney World, are you?" The thought hadn't actually crossed my mind, but her downward spiral suddenly started to make some sense. She knew she couldn't earn her way into the Magic Kingdom — she had tried and failed that test several times before — so she was living in a way that placed her as far as possible from the most magical place on earth.

In retrospect, I'm embarrassed to admit that, in that moment, I was tempted to turn her fear to my own advantage. The easiest response would have been, "If you don't start behaving better, you're right, we won't take you" — but, by God's grace, I didn't. Instead, I asked her, "Is this trip something we're doing as a family?"

She nodded, brown eyes wide and tear-rimmed.
"Are you part of this family?" She nodded again.
"Then you're going with us. Sure, there may be some consequences to help you remember what's right and what's wrong — but you're part of our family, and we're not leaving you behind."

I'd like to say that her behaviors grew better after that moment. They didn't. Her choices pretty much spiraled out of control at every hotel and rest stop all the way to Lake Buena Vista. Still, we headed to Disney World on the day we had promised, and it was a typical Disney day. Overpriced tickets, overpriced meals, and lots of lines, mingled with just enough manufactured magic to consider maybe going again someday.

In our hotel room that evening, a very different child emerged. She was exhausted, pensive, and a little weepy at times, but her month-long facade of rebellion had faded. When bedtime rolled around, I prayed with her, held her, and asked, "So how was your first day at Disney World?"

After a few moments, she opened her eyes ever so slightly. "Daddy," she said, "I finally got to go to Disney World. But it wasn't because I was good; it's because I'm yours."

That's the message of outrageous grace. Outrageous grace isn't a favor you can achieve by being good; it's the gift you receive by being God's. Outrageous grace is God's goodness that comes looking for you when you have nothing but a middle finger flipped in the face of God to offer in return. It's a farmer paying a full day's wages to a crew of deadbeat day laborers with only a single hour punched on their time cards (Matt. 20:1 — 16). It's a man marrying an abandoned woman and then refusing to forsake his covenant with her when she turns out to be a whore (Ezek 16:8 – 63; Hosea 1:1 — 3:5).

But here's what's amazing about God's outrageous grace: This isn't merely what God the Father would do; it's what he did do. God could have chosen to save anyone, everyone, or no one from Adam's fallen race. But what God did was to choose a multi-hued multitude of "someones," and — if you are a believer in Jesus Christ — one of those "someones" was you. God in Christ has declared over you, "I could have chosen anyone in the whole world as my child, and I chose you. No matter what you say or do, neither my love nor my choice will ever change." That's grace that's truly amazing. (Pgs. 81-84)

From SermonCentral

Chapter 3 ~ Part 2

Last winter my furnace stopped blowing hot.
Well, that's a critical thing in a Canadian winter.
I tried a thousand things to fix the issue, spoke to friends
who'd had issues with theirs, checked
YouTube videos for DIY solutions to no avail.

The engine itself revved up and started when
I turned it on. The vents still had forced air
coming out of them. It just wasn't warm air.

Finally, I spoke to a technician on the phone who suggested that
the motor may have been damaged. He helped me order new
parts and I was able to replace the old one myself.

The old one, when I took it out, was damaged,
the blades in the fan all collapsed
and broken up. That wasn't obvious till I opened it up.

No amount of fixing, cleaning or DIY tips would have restored it. The damaged motor just had to be replaced. Exteriorly, it looked well.

The real evil in man's fall lies in the fact that he became a child of the devil, his spirit, corrupted, damaged. This was something the Law could not fix. *Could not*, was not meant to.

It was powerless to change man's condition. The epistle to the Romans says, "what the law was *powerless* to do because it was weakened by the flesh", God has done through His Son.

The spiritual death and corruption are wiped out. I became what I'd dared not dream: perfect before God.

Galatians Chapter 3

I would like to explore Paul's statement about the Law a bit further. In verses 13 and 14 of Chapter 3, he said this:

> 13Christ hath redeemed us from the curse of the law, being made a curse for us: for it is written, Cursed *is* every one that hangeth on a tree:

> 14That the blessing of Abraham might come on the Gentiles through Jesus Christ; that we might receive the promise of the Spirit through faith.

Christ has redeemed us from the curse of the Law. Think about it.

The Curse, Burden and Yoke of the Law

It seems to me that you can look at this in two different ways. In **Deuteronomy 28**, there is a catalogue of curses reserved for those that break the Law. It's a list of evils, catastrophes and tragedies reserved for those that break the Law. It is a scary read.

Here's a sampling:

> 15But it shall come to pass, if thou wilt not hearken unto the voice of the LORD thy God, to observe **to do** all his commandments and his statutes which I command thee this day; that all these curses shall come upon thee, and overtake thee:

> 16Cursed *shalt* thou *be* in the city… and in the field.

> 17Cursed *shall be* thy basket and thy store.

> 18Cursed *shall be* the fruit of thy body…and fruit of thy land…

> 45Moreover all these curses shall come upon thee, and shall pursue thee, and overtake thee, till thou be destroyed; because thou hearkenedst not unto the voice of the LORD thy God, to

90

keep his commandments and his statutes which he commanded thee:

46And they shall be upon thee for a sign and for a wonder, and upon thy seed forever.

These are the curses of the Law. Christ has redeemed us from these. He has redeemed us from the curse and punishments due for breaking the Law. He has redeemed us from the curse of sickness, disease, poverty and calamities.

Himself took our infirmities and bore our sicknesses. The Lord has laid upon Him the iniquity of us all. The chastisement of our peace, wellness and well-being were upon Him.

But I want you to consider the "curse of the Law" in another sense that also agrees with the spirit of Paul's discourse before and after verse 13.

Christ redeeming us from the curse of the Law also means He has freed us from the burden, the weight of having to *obey every commandment, every observance, every ordinance.*

He has released us from trying to obey the demands and commands of the Law. He liberated us from dos and don'ts that made the Law impossible.

The Law was a curse in terms of its requirements and unattainable demands. Christ has released us from that.

Think about it. If you break just one of hundreds of rules and commandments, you have broken them all. Your punishments ranged from being stoned to death, to being sent into the wilderness, to being ostracized, to horrible sickness and disease, to losing your children, back to being struck dead by supernatural power.

That is not a slight thing to live under. They lived under the curse and threat of the Law. The threat of punishment, death, sickness, tragedy made the Law a curse. They were constantly watching their backs, needing to be sure they had done everything right.

They had to be perfect. They had to be detailed and precise. That is a huge yoke. They were under the burden and curse of performance yet knew that no performance was ever going to be enough.

Christ has redeemed us from the burden and curse of performance. He freed us from the burden of trying to earn our own righteousness which was never going to be enough anyways.

He has liberated us from the need to live up to the standard of the Law, which, in summary, was really against us. He freed us from the curse of performance and doing.

> **Colossians 2**
> 14Blotting out the handwriting **of ordinances that was against us, which was contrary to us,** and took it out of the way, nailing it to his cross;

> **Ephesians 2**
> 15Having abolished in his flesh **the enmity, *even* the law of commandments** *contained* in ordinances; for to make in himself of twain one new man, *so* making peace;

He blotted out, abolished the ordinances, "the Law of commandments", that stood against us. They were contrary to us in the sense that we could not, could never meet its requirements.

Did you notice that **Ephesians 2:15** calls the Law, the "enmity" contained in ordinances and ceremonies and rites?

Christ Jesus saved us from the tyranny of the Law in every way. The burden and onus of earning God's righteousness is no more on us which immediately means that we are also delivered from the "organic" curses and punishments of the Law.

The Law was a burden, a curse, a weight, a yoke too heavy, too hard to bear not just for Israel, but for all humanity. As a means of attaining righteousness, it was too much.

Christ has redeemed us from the curse so that the blessing of Abraham has come on the Gentiles to receive the promise of the Spirit.

14That the blessing of Abraham might come on the Gentiles through Jesus Christ; that we might receive the promise of the Spirit through faith.

I am convinced that the word "Gentile" here is better translated "heathen" just like the same Greek word was so translated in verse 8.

Remember that the Promise was made to Abraham before ever there was a Jew or the Law of Moses.

I believe that "Christ has redeemed us from the curse so that the blessing of Abraham has come on the *Gentiles*" is a reference to the whole world, not just non-Jews. It is a reference to the heathen, to the godless, to the sinner which means the whole world, Jew or Gentile.

I believe it could really read: "*Christ has redeemed us from the curse so that the blessing of Abraham has come on the heathen.*"

I say this because the blessing was promised to Abraham for the whole world when there were no Jews.

Instead of being under the Law, instead of the burden of the dos and don'ts of the Law, instead of the punishment of the Law, we have received the Spirit, we have received salvation.

The Promise

Back to the rest of the Book of Galatians, Chapter 3.

15Brethren, I speak after the manner of men; Though *it be* but a man's **covenant**, yet *if it be* confirmed, no man disannulleth, or addeth thereto.

16**Now to Abraham and his seed were the promises made**. He saith not, And to seeds, as of many; but as of one, And to thy seed, which is Christ.

17And this I say, *that* the **covenant**, that was confirmed before of God in Christ, the law, which was four hundred and thirty years after, cannot disannul, that it should make the promise of none effect.

18For if the inheritance *be* of the law, *it is* no more of promise: but God gave *it* to Abraham by promise.

Paul now goes back to talking about God's dealing with Abraham and implies that it was actually a covenant - that is a covenant between Abraham and God. You see that in verse 15.

Paul compares God's covenant to the human experience of signing of contracts or agreements. When we do contracts or legal agreements, that process is completed when we sign, right? After the signatures are appended, it is signed, sealed and delivered. It becomes binding on all parties. It would be illegal to tamper with such a document.

Now to Abraham and his seed were the promises made. So, we know for sure that Paul is talking about God's covenant with Abraham.

God's promises to Abraham essentially constituted an unbreakable covenant. What promises? Remember that in verses 6 to 8, Paul had told us what God said to Abraham and what Abraham's response was.

God had told him that in him (Abraham) all the families or nations of the earth would be blessed. Abraham had believed what God told him and his faith was counted to him for righteousness.

Let's go to Genesis to see what was in the promises or covenant.

Genesis 12
3And I will bless them that bless thee, and curse him that curseth thee: and **in thee shall all families of the earth be blessed**.

Then, in **Genesis 15**

5And he brought him forth abroad, and said, Look now toward heaven, and tell the stars, if thou be able to number them: and he said unto him, **So shall thy seed be**.

94

6And he believed in the LORD; and he counted it to him for righteousness.

7And he said unto him, I *am* the LORD that brought thee out of Ur of the Chaldees, to give thee this land to inherit it.

After going through the rituals of cutting a covenant, we are told:

18In the same day **the LORD made a covenant with Abram,** saying, **Unto thy seed have I given this land,** from the river of Egypt unto the great river, the river Euphrates:

In reporting or commenting on all these Paul rightly says, "*Now to Abraham and his seed were the promises made.*" That is rather obvious.

Now here is the important part as a teaching anointing descends on the Apostle Paul.

He says that in making the promises to Abram or Abraham, God used the word "seed", not "seeds", that is, in a singular form, not a plural one. In other words, God was not talking about a multitude. Let's extend that. He was not talking about a nation. He was not talking about a people. He was not talking about the nation of Israel. He was talking about Christ.

Of course, the word "seed" also means "descendant" or "offspring", and I have heard and read people try to play down Paul's argument or position here by saying the Greek word was mistranslated or something like that.

Descendant or offspring, the vitality of what Paul was trying to say does not change. God was specifically talking about Christ, not a crowd of people.

In other words, this is not about Israel. Period. This would be hard for many people to swallow. It is beyond Israel.

Now to Abraham and to Christ were the promises made.

We can easily, then read it this way. In other words, what God really promised Abraham was salvation, redemption and deliverance for the whole world though Christ.

In you shall all the nations of the earth be blessed. Now to Abraham and to Christ were the promises made.

Unto thy seed have I given this land. *Unto Christ have I given this land.*

This is all about Christ, folks. This is not about Israel, the nation. Do you see that? Do you see that salvation was the focus of the promise and covenant of God to and with Abraham?

It is to be regretted that many a Christian sees these promises only in terms of the nation of Israel. It is about redemption and salvation in Christ.

> 16Now to Abraham and his seed were the promises made. **He saith not, And to seeds, as of many;** but as of one, And to thy seed, which is Christ.

He saith not, And to seeds, as of many. Not a multitude, or a people, or a nation. The promises were in Christ. *But as of one, And to thy seed, which is Christ.*

God gave the children of Israel the land in the Old Testament. He fulfilled that promise in the physical. That is done with. He has also fulfilled the spiritual part of the same promise by bringing salvation through Christ Jesus!

It meant land and well-being for the children of Israel at that time, yes. It does not mean "land" in the vitality and the in-Christ New Testament interpretation of it.

In the light of Christ being the seed, the "land" in the promises to Abraham is just figure of speech. You say figure of speech for what?

You know that for example, when the Bible uses imagery like, "a land that flows with milk and honey", you can see that that is figure of speech. It is not literal. It is hyperbole for a land that is full of richness, good and prosperity.

96

And there is a lot of imagery and figure of speech like that in the Old Testament. The Psalms are full of them. Many times, David calls God his "Rock", his "Shield", his "Dwelling Place". He says, "He will deliver me from the snare of the fowler", "I will trust under His wings". These are all figures of speech of spiritual realities. They are ways to express spirituals facts and thoughts using human words and comparisons.

The Bible says, "*Every valley shall be exalted, and every mountain and hill shall be made low: and the crooked shall be made straight, and the rough places plain:*" in **Isaiah 40**, in a prophecy concerning John the Baptist. You see that that is figure of speech. It is not literal. It means things will be fixed and made right.

In the same way, the "land" with reference to the Promises made to Abraham is figure of speech for a place, a state of being or existence, a life. In other words, while God was saying that they would live good, rich, blessed, prosperous life in the Old Testament, in the New Testament today, we are blessed, we have the Spirit of promise and live in the land of promise. That promise is our reality. The "land" is being in Christ!

In the Old Testament God asked them to sacrifice sheep, goats and other animals for the atonement of their sins, yes. Was God concerned about the animal or the people? Was God interested in the animal used for sacrifice or was He concerned about the sins and the forgiveness of the people?

Was He not concerned only about the lives and ways of the people?

Was it that the blood actually washed away sins? Or was the shedding of the blood of the animals a symbolism signifying God's grace towards them? Was their sin a material that blood could wash away?

We should be able to see that the sacrificing of the animals and the performance of those ceremonies only served as a physical material demonstration and assurance to man that God's grace was **already** extended to him. It was essentially symbolic. It was for man to see and understand.

97

That God asked them to do the sacrifice in itself is proof of His grace.

I Corinthians 9:9:

> "For it is written in the Law of Moses: "Do not muzzle an ox while it is treading out the grain." Is it about oxen that God is concerned?" (NIV)

The KJV has this as, "*Does God care for oxen?*" You notice in that verse, Paul, quoting from the Old Testament, was just saying that God used an ox to illustrate a point. He used the ox as a figure of speech to make a point. His interest is not the ox!

In this case Paul was talking about taking care of the material or physical needs of those men and women who work in the ministry. He was saying that because they give and sacrifice their time and life serving the Gospel, we should not "muzzle the ox that treads out the corn." In other words, they are allowed to have their needs taken care of from the proceeds of working in the ministry.

But Paul says while God told them this in the Old Testament, what He really was focusing on was the minister, not the ox or the mule that works in your livestock farm. *Does God care for oxen?*

In other words, don't misinterpret a parable. Don't over-analyze what is a simple figure of speech. You would be missing the point and the purpose of the parable.

When God said He would give the land to Israel, is the physical piece of land what He was concerned about? Is He into real estate business? Is the earth not the Lord's, and the cattle on a thousand hills? *Does God care for land?*

The land, in proper New Testament context, is figure of speech. It is a parable. Israel itself was a parable and a metaphor. God does not love the Israeli more than He loves the Palestinian or the Mayan or the Belgian. He is as much the God of the Zulu as He is the God of the Malaysian and the Finn.

God's concern is not about a physical piece of real estate! His concern is about the destiny, life and eternity of the whole world, not just a section of the world. Not just the Jews.

The Jews were the pipe or agency through which Jesus our Savior was delivered to the world. And that is what *"in thee shall all the nations of the earth be blessed"* means. In other words, I will send Christ through you. I will send the savior of the world through you. This Promise was about the Christ!

Note that I am talking to Christians.

If the "land" is literal and the Promise still belongs to the natural DNA Jew, then the sacrifice and killing of bulls and goats for forgiveness of sins is still relevant today. It must be – by that logic. If the "land" is not just symbolic, then the sacrifice of animals was not symbolic.

If the land is still relevant to God's plans in Redemption, then the blood of bulls and goats in sacrifices is still relevant today. Do you see my point?

The sacrifices were symbolic of the death and suffering of Christ. The promised land is symbolic of redemption and arriving in righteousness, of peace with God, of living in the righteousness of Christ.

The Covenant in Christ

But let's move on to the next few verses in **Galatians 3**.

> 17And this I say, *that* the **covenant**, that was confirmed before of **God in Christ**, the **law**, which was four hundred and thirty years after, cannot disannul, that it should make the **promise** of none effect.

> 18For if the inheritance *be* of the **law**, *it is* no more of **promise**: but God gave *it* to Abraham by promise.

You notice the words "covenant", "law", "promise". Paul continues to compare faith (read that as "promise") and the law. He is now comparing them as covenants. We could say that the covenant with

Abraham is justification by faith, couldn't we? In verse 17, Paul says that that *Covenant of Faith* preceded the *Covenant of the Law*, and it has precedence, primacy or superiority over it.

The Covenant of the Law came into effect 430 years after the Covenant of Faith and it cannot override it. That means that being justified by faith was always the plan of redemption that God had always planned.

The Law came four hundred some years after the Abrahamic covenant, and it cannot override it because just like in human agreements or contracts, it was signed, sealed and delivered and it cannot be changed or amended.

Now let's dwell a bit on verse 17. I have used the King James version primarily in this book with the occasional reference to other versions.

So, did you notice that in verse 17, Paul says that the covenant that God made with Abraham was *in Christ*?

This I say, that the **covenant***, that was confirmed before of God* **in Christ***. This was all about Christ. God confirmed His covenant with Abraham in Christ.*

The covenant being confirmed of God in Christ means "with a view to Christ", "to find its fulfilment in Christ", according to one commentator. Paul saying that agrees with the general spirit of the discussion, does it not?

The covenant finds its fullness or fulfillment in Christ Jesus. It was with a view to Christ. It always had Christ in its mind, as its goal, its end. I'm saying that because I was surprised to note that most other translations do not have that "in Christ" phrase as the KJV does. Even with that phrase missing, I don't see any injustice to Paul's point.

I found out that of the about 24 translation or versions I checked, only about 3 apart from the King James had the phrase in them.

Again, back to the next verse of **Galatians 3**.

So, then, verse 18 says that if the people that get blessed or obtain righteousness or receive the blessing from God are those that follow the Law or those that do not come by faith, God would be breaking his covenant with Abraham. And that is not going to happen.

> 18For if the inheritance *be* of the **law**, *it is* no more of **promise**: but God gave *it* to Abraham by promise.

If the Jew inherits the promises of Abraham just because they are the natural children of Abraham, and not by faith, then God would be breaking the Covenant of Faith. And that will not happen.

If the ones who approach God by their own human efforts or those who follow the performance of the law are approved by God, then that nullifies the covenant with Abraham.

If God would be true to Abraham, if God would honor his covenant with Abraham, then those who come to him and get his righteousness must come the same way Abraham came, by faith, by the promise of the Christ.

God gave it to Abraham by promise (of salvation through Christ). God did not give it to Abraham by the Law. The Law will not override the Promise.

We continue in verse 19.

Paul then asks the perfect, most logical follow-up question: if the Law was/is a curse, then what was the purpose of the Law? Why was the Law introduced? We have already discussed some of this.

> 19Wherefore then *serveth* the law? It was added because of transgressions, till the seed should come to whom the promise was made.
>
> 19Why then was the Law given? It was imposed later on **for the sake of defining sin**, until the seed should come to whom God had made the promise…(Weymouth)
>
> 19Why, then, was the law given? It was given alongside the promise to **show people their sins** (NLT)

The Law was given for the purpose of sin. It was to identify what sin was, to show people their sin, to define sin, to make sin become "exceedingly sinful".

This immediately destroys the notion that we are still under the Law or that we should remain under the Law.

Man was not meant to and could not keep the Law. It was impossible to keep the whole Law. It was not designed to be kept. It was, in a sense, a diagnostic tool. To identify sin, convince or convict man of his sin and sinfulness.

You could also say that the Law was designed to keep man in check in his sinfulness, and it was put in place until the Promised One came.

Let's keep moving.

> 20Now a mediator is not *a mediator* of one, but God is one.
>
> 21*Is* the law then against the promises of God? God forbid: for if there had been a law given which could have given life, verily righteousness should have been by the law.
>
> 22But the scripture hath concluded all under sin, that the promise by faith of Jesus Christ might be given to them that believe.

I think the NLT version explains verse 20 better than the KJV:

> 20Now a mediator is helpful if more than one party must reach an agreement. But God, who is one, **did not use a mediator when he gave his promise to Abraham.**

God did not use a mediator when He gave His promise to Abraham. God, who is one, was the only party doing the doing when He made the promise.

In other words, God spoke directly to Abraham, without a mediator, when he cut that covenant with Abraham. That is a statement that has powerful implications. Thank God for other translations of the Bible.

You realize, looking at the discussion in context, that Paul is comparing and contrasting the two covenants.

He is implying that in the case of the Law at Sinai, angels administered it with Moses as the go-between or intermediary. Whereas, with the Abrahamic covenant Jehovah Himself cut the covenant, all by Himself alone. Abraham was in on the covenant, but God cut it, in a sense, unilaterally. In other words, God took sole, unitary responsibility for the covenant. Abraham's role was to believe it.

It was in **Genesis 15** that God cut that covenant with Abraham. If you read that account closely, you will notice that God asked Abraham to cut up the animals for the covenant as was done in those days. Typically, parties cutting a covenant will cut up the animals into two parts down the middle. Then the parties will walk together down the middle with the parts separated on either side.

God did not ask Abraham to walk with Him in the middle of the separated emblems. It was the presence of God only that did that as the covenant was sealed and ratified.

It tells us that God was taking responsibility for the covenant. In other words, He would fulfill both Abraham's and His sides of the covenant.

> 17And it came to pass, that, when the sun went down, and it was dark, behold a smoking furnace, and a burning lamp that passed between those pieces.
>
> 18**In the same day the LORD made a covenant with Abram**, saying, Unto thy seed have I given this land, from the river of Egypt unto the great river, the river Euphrates:

You say what is the point of all this? This is about **Galatians 3:20**: "But God, who is one, did not use a mediator when he gave his promise to Abraham."

God was one of the "parties" of the covenant, and in making that covenant with Abraham, He did so directly with him, no mediator involved. He took on the full responsibility for the covenant. He was the only One who walked between the covenant emblems.

The Promise. The Covenant. The Oath.

You find a breath-taking moment in God's enterprise with Abraham in **Genesis 22**, just after Abraham almost sacrificed Isaac.

> 16And said, **By myself have I sworn**, saith the LORD, for because thou hast done this thing, and hast not withheld thy son, thine only *son*:
>
> 17That in blessing I will bless thee, and in multiplying I will multiply thy seed as the stars of the heaven, and as the sand which *is* upon the sea shore; and thy seed shall possess the gate of his enemies;
>
> 18**And in thy seed shall all the nations of the earth be blessed**; because thou hast obeyed my voice

Your heart almost stops beating when you realize the immensity and implications of what God just said to Abraham.

"I swear by Myself."

So then, these are the reasons that the Abrahamic covenant was never going to be broken. God was not, would not break it. The Law, which came 430 years later could not annul it. His enterprise and commitment to Abraham was solidified in 3 ways.

First, **the Promise** itself. "In thee shall all the nations of the earth be blessed." In itself, we all know this was more than enough!

Second, **the Covenant**. He made the covenant with Abraham. Unbreakable!

Third, **the Oath**. I swear by Myself.

The writer of the Book of Hebrews commenting on this said God did this so that we, here today knowing that it is impossible for God to lie, we can rest in Him. **Hebrews 6:13-19**

13For when God made promise to Abraham, because he could swear by no greater, he sware by himself,

In giving His oath, He wanted to show us, "the heirs of promise the immutability of His counsel."

In the context of the Law and justification by faith as the subject matter of this book, you can see that God has gone to extreme extents to show that it is by faith that we are made right with Him.

So, you can see what Paul said in **Galatians 3:17** in a new light.

17And this I say, *that* the **covenant**, that was **confirmed before of God** in Christ, the law, which was four hundred and thirty years after, cannot disannul, that it should make the promise of none effect.

The Abrahamic covenant was *confirmed* of God. In Christ. *The Promise* was backed up by *the Covenant* and was confirmed by *the Oath*.

There was no way God was going to back away from the covenant of faith with Abraham for the covenant at Mount Sinai which the Israelites broke. The covenant with Abraham was the *Covenant of Faith*. You can see that it is an assurance against the false lies of the Judaizers who want you to believe that there's something else to do to achieve God's approval after or over what the Lord has done.

If anyone achieves righteousness apart from the faith of Jesus Christ, or because they obey or just because they are Jews, then faith is void.

God Keeps His Promises

Roger Simms shared this testimony in a book:
May 7 the day Roger was discharged from the army. He couldn't get a
bus so he decided to hitchhike his way home. Carry his heavy suitcase
and in his army uniform, he flashed for the on-coming car. It was a
luxurious, black Cadillac. To his surprise the car stopped.

He thanked the well-dressed man and entered the front seat.
He was heading to Chicago so it was along the way.
"I have a business there. My name is Hanover."

After talking about many things, Roger, a Christian, felt a need to
share with this 50-odd-year old successful businessman about Jesus
Christ. But he kept putting it off, until he realized he was just 30
minutes from his home. It was now or never. So, Roger cleared his throat
and said, "Mr. Hanover, I would like to talk to you about something
very important." He then proceeded to explain how his life has been
changed by Christ, the way of salvation, and finally asking Mr.
Hanover if he would like to receive Christ as is Saviour.

To Roger's surprise, the man pulled over to the side of the road. Roger
thought he was angry and wanted to ask him to get out of his car. But
the businessman bowed his head and said he wanted to pray. So, he
received Christ, and then thanked Roger. "This is the greatest thing that
has ever happened to me."

Five years went by, Roger married, had a two-year-old boy, and a
business of his own. Packing his suitcase for a business trip to Chicago,
he found the small, white business card Hanover had given him five years
before. In Chicago he looked up Hanover Enterprises, the company Mr.
Hanover works in.

A receptionist told him it was impossible to see him now, but he could
see Mrs. Hanover. A little confused as to what was going on, he was
ushered into a lovely office and found himself facing a woman in her
fifties. She extended her hand and asked, "You knew my husband?"

Roger told how her husband had given him a ride five years ago. She
asked, "Can you tell me when that was?"
"It was May 7, the day I was discharged from the army." He went on to
share what they talk about and how her husband prayed to receive
Christ into his life.

Mrs. Hanover began to weep. Roger was surprised. She said,
"I had prayed for my husband's salvation for years.
I believed God would save him."
"And where is your husband?" Roger asked.

"He's dead. He was in a car accident after he let you out of the car. He never got home. You see - I thought God had not kept His promise." She cried and then added, "I stopped living for God five years ago because I thought He had not kept His word!"

From SermonCentral

Chapter 3 ~ Part 3

Kids. The other day at the mall I watched a father trying to fix his 2-year-old son's broken toy car while the little boy threw a big tantrum. The toy was broken and had come apart.

The father is frantically trying to put it back together for his son. The son is extremely annoyed, is screaming and struggling to take it out of his father's grip. Hasn't that happened to you? I can't tell you how many times that's happened to me with my kids when they were that age.

You are trying to fix the toy car, or mend the dress on the doll, but they just can't see that you're trying to help. So they throw major fits or tantrums even when you try to explain that you're just trying to get it back to work.

They think you're probably trying to take it from them. At that age they have neither the patience nor the understanding to see that you were indeed trying to help.

Isn't this like the relationship between man to God? *Notice I did not say it's like God's relationship with man.* He is trying to help, trying to fix things. Sent the Lord Jesus. Sent the Holy Spirit. Gave us His Word.

Many times, we don't see what he is trying to do to help us. We are not spiritually aware or mature enough to see that He is trying to help us. Curse. "Christ has redeemed us from the curse of the Law."

Why would you want to be under a curse?

Galatians Chapter 3

L et's move on in Chapter 3 from the 21st verse.

21*Is* the law then against the promises of God? God forbid: for if there had been a **law given which could have given life, verily righteousness should have been by the law.**

22But the scripture hath concluded all under sin, that the promise by faith of Jesus Christ might be given to them that believe.

The Law could not Give Life

In view of all that we have discovered about the Law. In view of all that the New Testament has said about the Law, it is a good point to ask if the Law was against God's plan of redemption.

It seems that it is contrary to it. Are they opposite or opposed to each other? They seem not to agree.

Paul answers the question himself. No, the Law is not against the promises of God. The truth, Paul says, is that the Law couldn't just give life. I want you to notice something Paul said in **Romans 3:21:**

21But now the righteousness of God without the law is manifested, being **witnessed by the law and the prophets**;

This redemption in Christ Jesus is witnessed to by both the Law and the writings of the prophets of the Old Testament. They bear witness to the Gospel. They witness to Jesus as Messiah. They point to Jesus as the answer.

The Law establishes the legitimacy of Jesus as Messiah, to righteousness by faith alone.

We establish the Law. How? Because the Law is fulfilled in Him. *Because Christ is the end goal of the Law for righteousness.* Because the Law pointed us to our need for the Lord Jesus.

We concur with the Law that righteousness was always about faith. Thus, we establish the law, or the goal and the purpose of the Law, which was to point to Christ. The Law's purpose has been done and served.

The Law pointed us to Christ. That purpose is fulfilled and done. The Law showed man his helplessness and spiritual depravity. That purpose has been done and fulfilled.

We establish the Law. We do not make void the Law. That does not mean that the Law is in effect in the sense that we still need to observe its ordinances and rules. **Romans 3:31.**

We are saying that the effectiveness of the has been fulfilled. The Law has served its purpose. We are no more under the Law.

In saying that justification comes by faith only, we are corroborating, establishing and fulfilling the work and purpose of the Law. This righteousness by faith in Christ Jesus, Paul said, "is witnessed by the Law and the Prophets." In other words, the Law agrees and testifies that righteousness comes only by faith.

This is what the Lord was alluding to in **Matthew 5:17**

> 17Think not that I am come to destroy the law, or the prophets: **I am not come to destroy, but to fulfil.**
>
> 18For verily I say unto you, Till heaven and earth pass, one jot or one tittle shall in no wise pass from the law, till all be fulfilled.
>
> 19Whosoever therefore shall break one of these least commandments, and shall teach men so, he shall be called the least in the kingdom of heaven: but whosoever shall do and teach *them*, the same shall be called great in the kingdom of heaven.

A lot of folks use verse 17 to say that the Lord Jesus did not abolish or cancel the Law. They think this verse means that the Christian is still under the Law. That is a misinterpretation and misunderstanding of the intent of that verse.

If you consider the totality of God's plans and intent, you will understand it better. If you consider the purpose of the Law and why it was given, you will see that the Law found its fulfillment and purpose in showing man his sin and sinfulness. That purpose and goal of the Law came to an end because it showed man his helplessness in the face of sin, thus pointing us to our need of a Savior.

In that sense, when He said the Law would not pass away, He was just saying that the goal of the Law, the intent of the Law would come to pass as the Law finds its fulfillment and requirements fully met in Himself.

Many people who quote the Lord in verse 17, "Think not that I am come to destroy the law, or the prophets: *I am not come to destroy, but to fulfil*" don't seem to quote or mention the whole context of it. Looking at verses of Scripture in context cannot be overemphasized if we will understand its counsel.

In verse 20, the Lord said this as a continuation of **Matthew 5: 17-19**:

> 20For I say unto you, That except your righteousness shall exceed *the righteousness* of the scribes and Pharisees, ye shall in no case enter into the kingdom of heaven.

For I say unto you. *I am now telling you the reason I said what I said above.* In other words, you cannot enter the kingdom of God by obeying the Law. The righteousness of the Law is exemplified by the strictest adherents and observers of it. These are the scribes and the Pharisees. They obeyed every letter of the Law. Yet the Lord is emphatically saying that that righteousness would not save them.

Verse 19 says, "…but whosoever shall do and teach *them*, the same shall be called great in the kingdom of heaven…" Is the Lord saying that we are to preach the Law? Does He mean that we should keep teaching the Law of Moses?

That cannot be the case because of what He said in verse 20.

From verse 21 and following, He began to more or less dismantle or deconstruct the Jewish Laws. He began to raise the bar and standard of righteousness. He began to tell the real intent of the Law.

Moses said, but I say this. The Law tells you to do this, but I tell you the real truth. It has been said of old, but I, the Ancient of Days, I say this. Any eye for an eye? I say walk in love. Divorce? I say that is not God's will for you. Adultery? I tell you that you don't have to have done it physically to have committed it.

In other words, the problem is not obeying the Law, the problem is the sin nature and heart of man. The Law may have tried to deal with man's conduct and behavior, but the real target of God's heart is the heart and very being of man from the inside.

Do you see that, "Think not that I am come to destroy the law, or the prophets: **I am not come to destroy, but to fulfil" does not mean that we should keep ourselves under the Law of Moses?**

For sure, the Law is not against the Promises of God, not against the Abrahamic covenant. It is not opposed to justification by faith. It explains it. It bears witness to it as the way of salvation and righteousness.

You can see, if you look carefully, the intent and purposes of the Law. We have discussed this already. You realize that the ordinances, feasts, sacrifices all pointed to Christ. They all looked to the Messiah's arrival.

So, remember the question is: The Law and faith, are they against each other? Paul says faith, salvation by faith, establishes or upholds the Law. It confirms what the Law has said. The Law points to Christ.

The Law always pointed to salvation by faith as we have seen and was not designed to give life or righteousness.

Verse 22 of **Galatians** 3 in our text is key to understanding this.

But the scripture hath concluded all under sin, that the promise by faith of Jesus Christ might be given to them that believe.

Jesus is the Promise.

Let's put it this way: *The Law has concluded all under sin so that we can put our faith in Jesus Christ.*

The intent of the Law was to point us to Christ, by underlining our sinfulness and inability to do anything about it on our own. The Law could not give life and therefore, could not give righteousness.

Man's fall into sin meant that his spirit died or was cut off from God. In a sense, he was born again into spiritual death and sin.

He was dead, period. The Law could not make him come alive spiritually. The Law could probably curb his behavior but was helpless and powerless to change his spiritual nature now.

This is what was needed to redeem man. A change and re-birth of his spiritual nature.

Romans 8:3 is a direct echo of **Galatians 3:21**

> The law of Moses was unable to save us because of the weakness of our sinful nature. **So God did what the law could not do**. He sent his own Son in a body like the bodies we sinners have. And in that body God declared an end to sin's control over us by giving his Son as a sacrifice for our sins. (NLT)

> For what the law was powerless to do because **it was weakened by the flesh**, God did by sending his own Son in the likeness of sinful flesh to be a sin offering. And so he condemned sin in the flesh. (NIV)

What couldn't the Law do? Change the spiritual nature of man, drive out spiritual death, give man spiritual life. It was defeated by that sinful nature. It was rendered powerless in its inability to deal with sin.

The Law was made impotent because it could not change, reform or deal with the fallen nature of man.

114

What did God do? Sent His only begotten Son to deal with the sin problem, to drive out the spiritual death and give man life, and therefore righteousness.

The Son dealt with the sin problem, cast sin out of man's spirit. He condemned sin in the flesh.

In continuing with **Galatians 3**, in verse 22, Paul said we become partakers of the Promise by the faith of Jesus Christ when we believe. We believe and become partakers.

Continuing with the rest of the chapter.

> 23But before faith came, we were kept under the law, shut up unto the faith which should afterwards be revealed.
>
> 24Wherefore the law was our schoolmaster *to bring us* unto Christ, that we might be justified by faith.
>
> 25But after that faith is come, we are no longer under a schoolmaster.

These three verses easily help us decide on what the purpose of the Law was and what our relationship with it should be in the New Testament.

You should pay some attention to the tenses.

We were kept in custody of, or under guard of the Law, before faith, the real plan was revealed. Faith was always the plan. The Law was temporary.

We *were*, it says. The Law was our school master, the custodian, *to bring us to Christ* so that we can be justified by faith.

The Law *was*, it says. The Law led us to Christ, brought us to faith. But after Christ has come, we are no longer under the school master. We are no longer under the Law. Why? We have been justified by faith.

I know folks who would argue with everything they've got when you tell them that the Christian is no longer under the Law. To say that, for some people, is sacrilege. Does that mean we can do anything we want? Does that mean we can live in sin? These are some of the questions they would ask.

Yet these verses are simple and clear in what they say. We are no longer under the Law of Moses. What is there to disagree about in what they say?

Ye are Abraham's Seed and his Heirs

Let's conclude the rest of the chapter then.

> 26For ye are all the children of God by faith in Christ Jesus.
>
> 27For as many of you as have been baptized into Christ have put on Christ.
>
> 28There is neither Jew nor Greek, there is neither bond nor free, there is neither male nor female: for ye are all one in Christ Jesus.
>
> 29And if ye *be* Christ's, then are ye Abraham's seed, and heirs according to the promise.

After painting an image of being slaves under the Law as school master, Paul draws up a contrasting image of what we have now become in Christ.

You are now children of God by faith in Christ Jesus – meaning that we are no longer slaves under the Law. It is our faith that makes us the children of God. **Faith in Jesus Christ**.

This here is important, what Paul is trying to say. He is implying that no one becomes a child of God by any means other than faith in Christ. With the background story of this church and the reason for the epistle in the first place, it is not difficult to see why he is saying this.

He had the Jews and the Judaizers in mind. I don't know about you, but I have heard some Christians say that Jews have a special place with God. Some have said that Jews do not need to accept Jesus as Lord and Savior.

You are not a child of God based on any reason other than faith in Jesus. You are not a child of God because you are a Jew or because you obey the Law. Or because you have Abraham's DNA. **John 1:12**

> 12But as many as received him, to them gave he power to become the sons of God, *even* to them that believe on his name:
>
> 13Which were born, not of blood, nor of the will of the flesh, nor of the will of man, but of God.

Not of blood. Not of the flesh. Not by the will of man. As many as received Him, even to them that believe on His Name.

It is salvation by grace, not by race. It has nothing to do with blood relations or DNA or ancestry. In Christ, there is no Jew, no Greek or Gentile. No one is special. We all are. Anyone who has faith in Christ in the inheritor of the Promise of God to Abraham! This has nothing to do with the Jews.

There is absolutely no advantage or disadvantage to being a Jew! There is no advantage or disadvantage being Greek or Gentile. This was never about being a Jew anyhow. God's plan always has the whole world in mind.

"In thee, Abraham, shall all the nations of the earth be blessed." That was always the intent: *all the earth.*

You see, really, "the Jew" of the Old Testament, in the final analysis, is a paradigm, a figure of speech, a parable. A paradigm of what? A paradigm of being in a covenant relationship with God, of being a child of God.

Romans 2:

28For he is not a Jew, which is one outwardly; neither *is that* circumcision, which is outward in the flesh:

29But he *is* a Jew, which is one inwardly; and circumcision *is that* of the heart, in the spirit, *and* not in the letter; whose praise *is* not of men, but of God.

Just like Abraham is an example or paradigm of being righteous in God's eyes by faith, so is the Jew, so is Israel.

You can see the way that Paul has used the term "Jew" here: in an impersonal, objective metaphorical, allegorical way. He is defining a state, an existence, a typology.

"Jew" is not outward in the flesh, not natural. Not by birth. Not by genealogy. Not by circumcision.

"Jew" is inward, in the heart, in the spirit, not in the letter of the Law. It is a spiritual reality or definition only.

It is the person that has faith in Christ Jesus that is the Jew. It is he or she that has faith in Christ that has the blessings of God and that is the child of God. The natural Jew is not.

Christians still say that natural DNA Jews are "God's special people". Not anymore. It is the one that is born again by faith in Jesus that is the special one. No Jew or Greek, no male, no female in Christ!

29And if ye *be* Christ's, then are ye Abraham's seed, and heirs according to the promise.

If you are Christ's, then the Promise that God made to Abraham of the whole world being blessed in him finds its fulfillment.

You are the fulfillment of the Promise. Know ye therefore that they which are of faith, the same are the children of Abraham.
They that are of faith. Faith in Jesus Christ. These are the ones that are the heirs of the Promise of Abraham. There is neither Jew nor Gentile; male nor female; bond nor free in Christ.

118

The Law

My friend Dr. Roy Gustafson has the finest illustration of justification...there was a man in England who put his Rolls-Royce on a boat and went across to the continent on holiday.

While driving around Europe, something happened to the motor of his car. He cabled Rolls-Royce back in England, "I'm having trouble with my car; what do you suggest I do?"

Well, the Rolls-Royce people flew a mechanic over! The mechanic repaired the car and flew back to England...the man to continue his holiday. As you can imagine, the fellow was wondering, "How much is this going to cost me?" When he got back to England, he wrote the people a letter, asked how much he owed them. He received a letter that read: "Dear Sir: There is no record anywhere in our files that anything ever went wrong with a Rolls-Royce." That is justification.

Did Christ finish His work? How dangerous it is to join anything of our own to the righteousness of Christ, in pursuit of justification before God! If He has finished the work, what need is there of our additions? And if not, to what purpose are they?

Can we finish that which Christ Himself could not complete? No, no; Christ is no half-Savior. It is a hard thing to bring proud hearts to rest upon Christ for righteousness. God humbles the proud by calling sinners wholly from their own righteousness to Christ for their justification.

From SermonCentral

Chapter 4

Imagine that you leave your kids with a babysitter or at a daycare center for a few hours, so you can quickly run some errands or because you have to work. We all do it, don't we?

Then at the appointed time you come back to get the kids. But what if the kids refuse to leave the babysitter and come home with you? They want to stay and live with the babysitter.

The babysitter herself tells the kids, "Kids! You need to go home with your parents. I am not your mother. They just had me here to look after you, for 3 hours. I can't take care of you more than I have." You try everything to get the kids back, but they refuse to leave the babysitter and go home with you.

Imagine the annoyance, the frustration.

The Law was a babysitter, holding man in check until the appointed time. It was not the way of salvation and has served its purpose. This is the tragedy of the folks who hold on to the Law and ignore grace.

Paul tells us that, "before faith came, we were kept under the law, and the law was our schoolmaster to bring us unto Christ, but after that faith is come, we are no longer under a schoolmaster."

Christianity and Judaism don't mix. Do you sense Paul's incredulity and frustration at these Christians: Can't you see that there's no freedom in the Law? Don't you want to be free? You want to stick to feasts, ceremonies, rules and regulations?

Daddy is here! *You observe days, and months, and times, and years. I am afraid for you.* **Galatians 4:11**

Galatians Chapter 4

A s a new creation in Christ Jesus, the believer is now no more under the bondage of the Law and the Old Covenant. Instead, God has sent His Spirit into our hearts.

This is what constitutes our freedom.

The Law was a Babysitter

Paul continues to compare and portray the two covenants as slavery and freedom, curse and blessing, slave and child, works and faith.

> 1Now I say, *That* the heir, as long as he is a child, differeth nothing from a servant, though he be lord of all;

> 2But is under tutors and governors until the time appointed of the father.

> 3Even so we, when we were children, were in bondage under the elements of the world:

> 4But when the fulness of the time was come, God sent forth his Son, made of a woman, made under the law,

> 5To redeem them that were under the law, that we might receive the adoption of sons.

> 6And because ye are sons, God hath sent forth the Spirit of his Son into your hearts, crying, Abba, Father.

> 7Wherefore thou art no more a servant, but a son; and if a son, then an heir of God through Christ.

In other words, the Law, the great Law of Moses was just a baby-sitter until Christ came. The Law waited for Christ to come. It helped keep man in check and pointed the way to Christ.

Today we have housekeepers or babysitters who look after our children when we are yet to arrive at home or when we are away. Paul says we were under tutors and governors. Tutors? Governors? What did they teach us? They taught us to look to Christ. You find the Law and the prophets telling of the coming of the Messiah.

A virgin shall have a Son. His Name shall be called Immanuel. Out of you, Bethlehem, shall come He that shall be Governor in Israel.

Sacrifices and offerings, You would not, but a body you have prepared for me, I come to do Your will, O God. Thou art My Son, this day have I begotten Thee. The Sun of righteousness shall arise with healing in His wings.

My God, why hast thou forsaken me? You will not leave My soul in hell, not suffer Your Holy one to see corruption. The chastisement of our peace was upon Him, with His stripes we are healed.

These are all statements from the "Law and the Prophets", "tutoring us and governing" and showing us that the Christ would one day come, *in the fulness of time*, and accomplish Redemption.

The babysitter functioned "until the time appointed of the father", until the fulness of the time. Then God sent forth His Son.

Now, Paul says we are no more servants or children, because the Christ has come, and we have been redeemed. We are no more waiting. He is here.

Because ye are sons, God hath sent forth the Spirit of his Son into your hearts, crying, Abba, Father.

You are no more a servant, but a son. Instead of the bondage that's been in the past, we have been born again and He has given us the Holy Ghost.

In the letter to the Ephesians, Paul said we were sealed with the Holy Spirit as a "down-payment" till the day of redemption. The indwelling of the Spirit has replaced our need for the Law in obeying God. More than that, it means that Christ fulfilled the Law for us.

Days, Months, Times, Years

Paul's incredulity at the Galatians boils over here in Chapter 4.

> 10Ye observe days, and months, and times, and years.

> 11I am afraid of you, lest I have bestowed upon you labor in vain.

You observe days, months, times, years. That scares me.

How could you? I am afraid of you. Is my labor on you in vain? There are folks (Christians!) out there today who are obsessed with dates, times, years. Some of these people are blowing shofars, praying with so-called Jewish "prayer" shawls. They go to pray at the Wailing Wall in Jerusalem. They are returning to Judaism.

You observe days, months, times, years. I'm scared for you.
For Christians, days like Yom Kippur and Rosh Hashanah or the Sabbath have no special significance. If you are a believer in Judaism, it would be important to you. If you are into Judaism, that is OK, to practice what you believe in your religion. They are not Christian practices.

I have no issues with a Muslim going on a pilgrimage to Mecca. I have no issues with a Muslim praying 5 times a day. I don't have issues with a person practicing Judaism marking their "holy" days or praying at the Wailing Wall.

We don't worship the same God, anyhow.

Christianity worships the God, the Father of our Lord Jesus, Judaism and Islam do not. That may be hard for some folks to swallow.

I have seen TV shows, read magazine articles, where these Jewish days and feasts are lifted up by Christians. They say things like "Yom Kippur is the holiest day of the year". They ask Christians to send in an offering on this holiest day so that they can receive a special blessing from God.

They ask their viewers to take advantage of a 24-hour window because that blessing would not return for another year or another 50. This would be funny if it was not so sad. These are supposed New Testament believers!

You observe days, months, times, years. That is worrisome.
I'm referring to actual TV shows that I watched myself. This is not a second-hand account.

In 2017, I watched one of those in which the head of the Christian network asked viewers to send in offerings on Yom Kippur because there was, according to him, a special blessing they would receive if they sent them on that day. The receiving of the offering was to end at a particular hour in Israel.

When the hour rolled by, these people rolled out a box he called the "Ark of the Covenant", which according to the man, was built to the exact dimensions of the one Moses was told to build in the Old Testament.

He told the people that all their prayer requests and offerings were going to be put in this Ark, and then they were going to pray.

The Ark of the Covenant! That is what you want to go back to? You want to go back to the Law of Moses?

If you still need the Ark, what was the need for Christ? If you still need the Ark or the Law, what was the point for Christ's sacrifice for us? The Ark, the Law of Moses are all about punishment, not grace. Can't you see that? Have you never read about the Law of Moses?

> **Hebrews 12**
> 18For you are not come to a mountain that might be touched, and a burning fire, and a whirlwind, and darkness, and storm,
>
> 19And the sound of a trumpet, and the voice of words, which they that heard excused themselves, that the word might not be spoken to them:

20For they did not endure that which was said: And if so much as a beast shall touch the mount, it shall be stoned.

21And so terrible was that which was seen, Moses said: I am frighted, and tremble.

This is a description of the introduction of the Law. Burning fire, whirlwind, darkness. The very people who were handed the Law were so scared, they couldn't bear to hear what was said. Moses himself was scared to "death."

Fear and punishment or the threat of them. You want to go back to that? Going back to the Feasts, the days, months, times, years that Paul is making reference to here is going back to fear and trembling.

You want to put yourself under the bondage of the Feasts, under the dread and threat of death and punishment that they had in the Old Testament? You want to put yourself under a reward system? Don't you know that you could never measure up or be good enough?

To say that you receive a blessing outside Christ because of a particular day on the calendar is to say that Christ died for nothing. It means you are fine under the Law and there was no need for Christ to have died. Do you see this? If you associate your blessing to a particular day, you have put yourself under the Law.

Going by the Law is a negation of faith. In Christ, is there a blessing attached to a particular day? Are we not blessed in Christ already?

You observe days, months, times, years. I am afraid of you.
Think about this, folks. Think about what this means. Is this what some of our friends think Christianity is? Is Christianity Judaism? Are we now going back to the Ark of the Covenant of the Old Testament? Has Christ not died? Has He not fulfilled the Law for us? Is the presence of God still in the Ark?

> **Colossians 2:16, 17**
> Let no man therefore judge you in meat, or in drink, or in respect of an **holyday, or of the new moon, or of the**

sabbath days: Which are a shadow of things to come; but the body *is* of Christ.

This version from the KJV can be blind to us. The NLT version brings it out better, I think.

> 16So don't let anyone condemn you for what you eat or drink, or for not celebrating certain **holy days or new moon ceremonies** or Sabbaths.

> 17**For these rules are only shadows of the reality yet to come. And Christ himself is that reality.**

It is obvious that Paul is taking a dig at Judaizers who insist on the observances and the keeping of the Law.

Paul in these two verses summarizes the Law, it's ceremonies and commandments, all of it.

For these rules are only shadows of the reality yet to come. The Law is the shadow, Christ Himself is that reality.

If Christ is here, if the reality is here, why are people going back to the Law? Why do people think the shadow is more important than the Body casting the shadow? Why would you need the shadow instead of the reality?

You observe days, months, times, years. I am afraid of you.
You are acting as if the Messiah has not come! You are acting like you still need a Messiah. You are acting like Christ has not met the Law's demands.

Your action shows that you have not accepted the sacrifice of Jesus. You are saying that Christ is not enough.

To say that we still need to keep or are still under the Law is to say that Jesus is not the Messiah!

Repeatedly in the Old Testament, God tries to illustrate and inform the people of what He was going to do. He pointed them to the Christ. He tried to create a desire and vision of the Messiah in their hearts. The Law, the feasts, the ordinances were a shadow of the reality.

> **I Corinthians 10:4**
> 1Moreover, brethren, I would not that ye should be ignorant, how that all our fathers were under the cloud, and all passed through the sea;
>
> 2And were all baptized unto Moses in the cloud and in the sea;
>
> 3And did all eat the same spiritual meat;
>
> 4And did all drink the same spiritual drink: for they drank of that **spiritual Rock that followed them: and that Rock was Christ.**

As early as the Crossing of the Red Sea, the allegories and parables of Christ were already with them, showing Him as the essence of God's dealing with them.

Christ is the reality. The reality is here now. The Passover, the passage through the Red Sea, giving of the Law at Sinai, the Tabernacle of Moses, the killing of the lamb, the scapegoat, the feasts of Trumpets, Tabernacles, and other observances or instructions like that in the Old Covenant pointed to Calvary. Abraham, Isaac, Sarah, Jacob, David, were, in a sense, figurations in the Plan.

I heard someone interpret "You observe days, months, times, years" to mean that Paul was referring to the idolatry and pagan practices that the new Christians of Galatia used to be part of before they became born again. In other words, this person was saying that the days, times and years that Paul was talking about was not a reference to Jewish practices and ordinances.

He was making a case for Christians to still practice the feasts, times and ordinances of the Old Testament. He believed in still observing things like Yom Kippur and the Feasts of Tabernacles, Passover, food laws, offerings etc.

Do you see how dishonest and disingenuous this argument is? Do you see that that is taking things out of context? In the context of the Book of Galatians it is obvious that Paul has been focusing on the Law of Moses, is it not?

Lusting after Egypt

Remember that the children of Israel wanted to go back to Egypt? As early as the **Exodus 16**, they had started to miss their life in Egypt. That is staggering if you consider that it was just in **Exodus 15**, that they escaped from Egypt.

In short, they started talking about returning to Egypt within a matter of hours of crossing the Red Sea! They would repeat that desire a number of times after this one.

> **Exodus 16:3**
> And the children of Israel said unto them, Would to God we had died by the hand of the LORD in the land of Egypt, when we sat by the flesh pots, *and* when we did eat bread to the full; for ye have brought us forth into this wilderness, to kill this whole assembly with hunger.

> **Numbers 14:2, 4**
> And all the children of Israel murmured against Moses and against Aaron: and the whole congregation said unto them, Would God that we had died in the land of Egypt! or would God we had died in this wilderness!
>
> 4And they said one to another, Let us make a captain, and let us return into Egypt.

Paul did not pick up on these instances to explain his point, but you see that this is not an unfair comparison. You can see that given the way Paul has described the differences between the Law and grace, you will see, that advocating for Christians to be under the Law is the same as the children of Israel wanting to go back to Egypt.

Paul said that anyone who seeks to be under the Law is under bondage and because Christ has redeemed us from the slavery of the Law.

Wanting to remain or go back to the Law for the Christian is the Israelite wanting to go back to Egypt. It is ridiculous, crazy and unbelievable.

Why would anyone want to be under the rules and bondage of the Law? Every action is scrutinized, every step is a potential sin, punishable by death. What is the freedom in the Law? What could possibly be the reason for anyone wanting to go back to living under a system that condemns you.

If you find it ridiculously unbelievable that the children of Israel ever wanted to go back to Egypt, then you should also be scandalized that any Christian should want to be under or advocate for the Law.

God gave them the Law, but they never fully obeyed or pleased Him. From Exodus to Malachi. The children of Israel would obey God, then backslide, obey, backslide, obey, then backslide again, the obey...and the cycle went on and on like that. It did not work.

They were taken captive into Babylon, the Temple, the great Temple of Solomon was totally destroyed – because they could not obey and please God under the Law.

The Temple was re-built after Babylon by the ministries of Nehemiah and Ezra. They put in a great effort to build that Temple! They repented and confessed their sins, and the King of Babylon let them go free from captivity back to Jerusalem.

Yet, by the time the Lord Jesus was born, they were back into captivity – of the Romans. The Temple was still there, but it had lost its spiritual significance. They had turned it into a den of thieves and robbers and moneychangers. That Temple was eventually destroyed in AD 70.

It is obvious that the Law was something the Israelites, and indeed any one could not live up to. It is obvious that it was not working. From Moses to Malachi, they just could not be doers of the Law. The story was one of failure. Moses called them, "children in whom there is no faith". **Deuteronomy 32:20.**

You hear the Lord "lament" about their condition in the whole of **Deuteronomy**. Chapter 5:

> 29O that there were such an heart in them, that they would fear me, and keep all my commandments always, that it might be well with them, and with their children for ever!

You hear his lament in the **Lamentations of Jeremiah**. You also hear in that book the frustration of the people themselves in not being able to do the Law. You hear them groan under the bondage and yoke of the Law. You can see from the prophets Nahum, Daniel, Malachi, Joel, Habakkuk, Micah that they have a desire to please God, but you also see that their efforts were a failure, and these prophets always ended up asking for forgiveness and mercy on behalf of the nation.

In short God is "lamenting", the people are lamenting, so to speak. He wants a heart in them to do His will, they just cannot under the Law. Listen to how Peter summarizes the Old Testament in **Acts 15**, talking about the Law of Moses and the New Covenant:

> 10Now therefore why tempt ye God, to put a yoke upon the neck of the disciples, which neither **our fathers nor we were able to bear**?

Here, Peter is calling the Law a **yoke**. What is yoke? A burden, a weight, a load. The fathers could not bear the load of the Law. The children too can't. The Old Covenant or the Law did not work.

And this is not just about the Jews. This is the condition of humanity. That is the point. It shows that man, Jew and Gentile was/is not able to attain righteousness by their own works and efforts.

It easy to condemn the Jews and those that provoked God in the Old Testament. This is about the failure of humanity to do right.

Two Women, Two Covenants

Now then, this brings us to the latter part of Paul's discourse in chapter 4 where he makes the most amazing of interpretations!

131

He is making his final arguments here, it seems. **Tell me, ye that desire to be under the law, do ye not hear the law?**

You notice that that is not really a question. Paul is actually telling them that they actually do not know what the Law is all about.

Paul is really telling them that those who want to be under the Law really have no idea what the Law says. He was not asking them a question. He was telling them.

You want to be under the Law?! You really want to be under the Law of Moses? You think the Law is on your side? Look, let me tell you, the Law is not on your side. The Law is actually against you.

Imagine that you have to argue a case in court, and you need to call a witness. You better call a witness that would be on your side and give testimony that will corroborate your story.

You surely don't want to call someone that will give testimony against you. In this case, the people who want to be under the Law are calling a witness that will help convict and condemn them, and they can't see that that is what they are doing.

All that the Law does is testify against you and confirm your status as miserable and wretched sinner. **Ye that desire to be under the law, do ye not hear the law?**

Let's read the next few verses from the NLT version.

> 22The Scriptures say that Abraham had two sons, one from his slave wife and one from his freeborn wife.
>
> 23The **son of the slave wife was born in a human attempt** to bring about the fulfillment of God's promise. But the **son of the freeborn wife was born as God's own fulfillment of his promise**.
>
> 24**These two women serve as an illustration of God's two covenants.** The first woman, Hagar, represents Mount Sinai where people received the law that enslaved them.

25And now **Jerusalem is just like Mount Sinai in Arabia, because she and her children live in slavery** to the law.

26But the other woman, Sarah, represents **the heavenly Jerusalem. She is the free woman, and she is our mother.**

28And you, dear brothers and sisters, are **children of the promise,** just like Isaac.

29But **you are now being persecuted by those who want you to keep the law, just as Ishmael,** the child born by human effort, persecuted Isaac, the child born by the power of the Spirit.

30But what do the Scriptures say about that? "**Get rid of the slave and her son,** for the son of the slave woman will not share the inheritance with the free woman's son."

31So, dear brothers and sisters, we are not children of the slave woman; we are children of the free woman.

I suspect that many folks will struggle with what Paul is saying here and the direction in which he is taking this conversation. Sarah and Hagar are an allegory, a figuration, an illustration he says, of the New and Old Testaments respectively.

Paul's position here maintains that much of God's dealing with the Abraham was, to us today, allegorical. Sarah and Hagar are a figuration, an allegory, a parable representing the Law and grace.

It means that Abraham himself is an allegory. Israel is an allegory. The Law is symbolic. The Promised Land is a parable, an illustration of a point. The tabernacle is a figuration. The Ark of the Covenant is an example of a spiritual thought or reality and goal.

So, Hagar represents the Law, that was given to the children of Israel on Mount Sinai: the 10 Commandments, the sacrifices, the feasts, etc.

Hagar represents the Law, the physical children of Abraham. She represents self-righteousness, the effort of the flesh, human endeavor and enterprise, and the uselessness of it all in the light of salvation and eternity.

Ishmael, Hagar's son, came from Abraham's own personal human effort at achieving God's promises. It failed miserably.

Figuratively speaking, Hagar and Ishmael represent the self-effort, self-striving, self-righteousness that all of humanity tries to do to be pleasing to God. Hagar is the Law of Moses. Hagar is Mount Sinai, where the Law was given.

Hagar is Israel – the natural Israel. Hagar is the bondage of the Old Testament, of the Torah.

Hagar is the false righteousness that comes from observing the Law of Moses. Paul calls her bondage.

Hagar is a reference to the Judaizers.

Not just that, **he says that the present physical Jerusalem is the embodiment of all the bondage that the Law represents**. In short, the Law is bondage. There is no freedom in the Law.

This is not really about the geographic Jerusalem. It is about what Jerusalem stands for and symbolizes. You find the Temple there. You find the sacrifices and observances there. You find the bondage of the Law there.

Sarah and Isaac, on the other hand, represent the New Covenant and the New Birth. They represent the irrevocable first covenant that God made with Abraham. Sarah represents the work and the supernatural provision of God through the Promise.

Sarah represents the Covenant of Faith made with Abraham. Sarah represents the righteousness of God without the Law. She represents freedom and liberty, the heavenly Jerusalem, the true city of the living God, the presence of God, peace with God.

"Heavenly Jerusalem", means the fulness of the will of God, the fulness of His presence, His dwelling, His Spirit.

Jerusalem

It seems that you can hardly hear the average American Evangelical utter a sentence without adding Jerusalem or Judaism or Israel to it. They have deceived and schooled themselves into believing that the present physical Israel or Jerusalem is the center of the God's universe and plans. They say Israel, the 1948 version, is "God's time-table for the end times".

If the physical, natural, unbelieving Israel is God's timetable, what is the Body of Christ? A non-entity? Something on the side? A mistake?

Some people have actually called the Body of Christ a "parenthesis" in the plan of God. If there is a parenthesis, it would be Israel! Israel was not, never was, the end goal. Israel was a parable on the road.

One particular person said on his television show that he would pray over people's prayer requests – *sitting in a boat in river Jordan, as if that has any power to it in itself.*

It is tragic that some folks think that their prayers would be answered because they prayed on a particular piece of real estate, after the Lord Jesus has done what He did for us.

God will hear you if you pray at the Wailing Wall, not because of it. He would hear you anywhere. He would hear you praying in a Buddhist temple if you pray with faith in the Name of Jesus. God will answer your pray if you prayed in the Muslim holy site in Mecca. That is what I am saying. There is no power praying in Israel or in any other place. It is your faith!

There is no more need to go and pray in the temple because you yourself have become the temple of God. **Galatians 2:22** says we have become the habitation of God through the Spirit. You are the temple! Of course, I could go to Jerusalem as a tourist, but that, for me, is where is starts and ends. Tourism.

The Christian focus is the new and heavenly Jerusalem.

> **Hebrews 12**
> 22But **ye are come unto mount Sion, and unto the city of the living God, the heavenly Jerusalem**, and to an innumerable company of angels,
>
> 23To the general assembly and church of the firstborn,

Hebrews 11:10, talking about Abraham:

> For he looked for a city which hath foundations, whose builder and maker *is* God.

Down the passage, we are told about the other faith heroes:

> 14For they that say such things declare plainly **that they seek a country**.
>
> 15And truly, if they had been mindful of that *country* from whence they came out, they might have had opportunity to have returned.
>
> 16**But now they desire a better *country*, that is, an heavenly**: wherefore God is not ashamed to be called their God: for **he hath prepared for them a city**.

The heroes of faith had a **heavenly** focus on their mind. It was not, was never physical. It was not natural.

They were not looking for a piece of real estate. *They looked for a city which hath foundations, whose builder and maker is God. They desired a better country, that is, an heavenly country.*

It was not Palestine. It was not Israel. It was the presence of God that they desired. It was righteousness they desired. It was the indwelling of the Holy Ghost they desired.

Something inside their spirits yearned upwards. They sought a country, a presence, an affirmation of the presence of God around them. A land. A country, a place, an existence, a time, a dispensation, the presence of God.

A city which hath foundations, whose builder and maker *is* God. Physical Israel and physical Jerusalem represented that God's presence **could** dwell among men. These men still knew that there was more to the presence of God than physicality. The New Testament confirms that God's presence is **now**, in fact, in us.

One more thing while we are on the subject of Israel and Jerusalem. Look at the text of the words God initially spoke to Abraham when He made the promises.

> **Genesis 12**
> 3And I will bless them that bless thee, and curse him that curseth thee: **and in thee shall all families of the earth be blessed.**
>
> **Genesis 17**
> 7**And I will establish my covenant between me and thee and thy seed after thee** in their generations for an everlasting covenant, to be a God unto thee, and to thy seed after thee.
>
> 8And I will give unto thee, and to thy seed after thee**, the land wherein thou art a stranger, all the land of Canaan, for an everlasting possession;** and I will be their God.

I will repeat some of the things I already said in preceding chapters.

All About Christ

Galatians 3:16 says that the promises were made to Abraham and to his seed. **The seed is Christ**, and the Seed came down the line, over centuries. Does it not follow that the land that God promised to Abraham's seed is not a piece of physical real estate?

If the Seed is Christ, and in Abraham's seed all the nations of the earth would be blessed, then the land of Canaan is a reference to all the earth that would become children of Abraham because of Jesus, the Seed.

If you belong to Christ, then you are Abraham's seed, and heirs according to the promise.

Then you are the fulfillment of the Promise that God made to Abraham. Know ye therefore that they which are of faith, the same are the children of Abraham.

Does it not make sense that the land of God's promise to Abraham is Christ when the world will hear the gospel of Jesus Christ?

And I will give unto thee, and to thy seed after thee all the land of Canaan. And Christ is the Seed. In thee shall all families of the earth be blessed.

It follows that the blessing is not physical. The land is not physical. The land is not Palestine. The land is not Jerusalem. You can see that the promises to Abraham was always about Christ.

The "land" was just figure of speech. The promise of the land in its true vitality and essence is spiritual, in Christ, as people from Lima, Peru to Cairo, Egypt, to Tel Aviv, Israel, to Seattle, Washington, to Osaka, Japan, to Ho Chi Minh City, Vietnam get born-again.

John 2
18Then answered the Jews and said unto him, What sign shewest thou unto us, seeing that thou doest these things?

19Jesus answered and said unto them, **Destroy this temple, and in three days I will raise it up**.

20Then said the Jews, Forty and six years was this temple in building, and wilt thou rear it up in three days?

21**But he spake of the temple of his body.**

You notice that the Lord Jesus was thinking and speaking spiritually, while the people He was talking to were thinking only naturally or carnally. They took Him literally. Spiritual blindness.

But He spoke of the temple of His body. What did He say? I will destroy the temple. But He spoke of the temple of His body.

138

I feel sorry for the Christians who are hung up on the natural Jerusalem "which now is" and its politics– all this in the light of the New Creation and New Covenant. It is sad that these people focus on these things when the Messiah is here.

These things are the doctrines of men. Israel was, used to be, God's chosen dwelling place. Not anymore.

The Body of Christ is the Israel today. The Body of Christ is comprised of born-again Jews, and born-again Papua New Guineans, born-again Canadians, born-again Costa Ricans, born-again Lebanese. There is no Jew. There is no Greek. There is only Christ. He has made of both Jew and Greek, one Body.

> **Colossians 2: 16, 17 (NLT)**
> 16So don't let anyone condemn you for what you eat or drink, or for not celebrating certain holy days or new moon ceremonies or Sabbaths.
>
> 17For these rules are only shadows of the reality yet to come. And Christ himself is that reality.

Christ himself is that reality.

Our focus is heavenly, the heavenly Jerusalem, not the earthly. We have already referred to **Galatians 3:26**

> 26But Jerusalem which is above is free, which is the mother of us all.

We, of the New Covenant, are children of the heavenly Jerusalem. We are children of Sarah, children of the promise.

We are the children not born by human effort. We are the children born supernaturally by the work of God Himself, just like Isaac was.

It took a supernatural work of God for Isaac to be born. In the Book of Romans, we are told that God "who quickens the dead" was the One who gave life to Sarah's womb for Isaac to be born. He was born by faith. We are the children born **by faith,** by the Spirit of God. We are the ones born by wholly trusting in God's faithfulness.

In concluding chapter 4, Paul tells us to "cast out the bond woman". We are the children of promise, like Isaac. We are not children of bondage. We are not children of the Law.

> **Galatians 4**
> 30But what do the Scriptures say about that? "**Get rid of the slave and her son**, for the son of the slave woman will not share the inheritance with the free woman's son."
>
> 31So, dear brothers and sisters, we are not children of the slave woman; we are children of the free woman. (NIV)

Cast it out of your life. It is the effort of the flesh, and there shall no flesh be justified in God's sight by the Law. Cast the Law, the Old Covenant out of your life.

Stop depending on your own efforts. Cast self-righteousness out of your life. Stop trying to earn a blessing or rightness with God. Let it go. Live by faith.

Get rid of works, the rules and laws of Moses. Lean on grace through faith. We are children of the free woman; we are children of faith. We are not children of the Law. We are not children of the Old Covenant.

Quit trying to follow rules of days, months, years, of not eating with Gentiles, of not touching "unclean" things, observing things in the Law of Moses as ways to please God.

Quit trying to win God's approval with what you wear or don't wear. Or through how you dress or don't dress. Or through whether you give your tithe or not. We can't do anything enough to earn it.

Do you see why it is sad and frankly ridiculous for Christians to keep saying that they want to be under the Law? Do you see why it was alarming to Paul? Jerusalem which is above is free.

Before leaving off Chapter 4, I want to you consider one more thing.

According to verse 24, Hagar and Ishmael on the one hand, and Sarah and Isaac on the other symbolize the *two covenants.*

They were allegories of parts of God's plan. If the four of them were allegories of some part of God's plan, it should follow that Abraham himself was an allegory of something in God's plan. Abraham was symbolic of faith.

Baby Sitter

In Bible days, the baby-sitter was usually one of the household slaves. He was given charge of his master's sons from the time they were about 6 or 7 until they were considered adults, at about 16 or 17 years of age. It was his job to teach the boys to obey and discipline them when they didn't.

It reminds me of a baby-sitter I had when I was a child. To a kid, that means you can get away with anything. You can have all the cookies you want…go to bed as late as you want, and don't have to clean up your toys. When my brother and sister and I were good, we got that kind of baby-sitter.

But when we were misbehaving, my parents always threatened us with a "mean" baby-sitter. Her name was Mrs. Redkay. Now, with a name like that, we were sure she was a secret KGB agent; We could have only two cookies, and they had to be eaten at the table. She made us pick up our toys and sent us to bed early, even though we weren't tired. I was sure she had a big stick somewhere to clobber us if we ever misbehaved.

That, my friends, is the law. It is a mean, strict baby-sitter, which threatens us with punishment every time we misbehave. But the good news is we believers are no longer under such a baby-sitter. We…in Christ are no longer under the law.

From SermonCentral

Chapter 5

There's a seemingly endless personal impasse that comes with being a new citizen in a country.

So, I have a proud Nigerian accent, but my kids have the Canadian. My kids like the snow, how could I? They would have pickles on their burgers, I just can't.

But I have come to love and thrive in Canada. I celebrate Canada Day proudly. I celebrate Thanksgiving. I like poutine, have tried skating and even seen a live hockey game!

Occasionally, though, a Yoruba word slips into my English conversations, and while I would still rather have jollof rice for lunch, I am now a Canuck. I think.

We live in that endless tensile stalemate between our spiritual realities and fleshly-carnal existence:

We are seated with Christ in heavenly places yet live in a fallen world. We are redeemed, but not "home" yet. Our spirits have been re-born, yet we deal with the flesh.

"But ye are not in the flesh, but in the Spirit. **Romans 8:9**
"Since we live in the Spirit, let us also walk in the Spirit." **Galatians 5:25**

Since you are now in Canada, live like you are in Canada. Live in your new country, in your new existence and reality. Live in the spirit. You are now spiritually alive.

Galatians Chapter 5

I t is important to start chapter 5 by reading it as a continuation of chapter 4. Paul just got through telling us that we are children of the free woman. We are children of the New Covenant. We are children of Jerusalem above, not the earthly one. We are not of the Law.

Hold on to Your Freedom

30Nevertheless what saith the scripture? Cast out the bondwoman and her son: for the son of the bondwoman shall not be heir with the son of the freewoman.

31So then, brethren, we are not children of the bondwoman, but of the free.

1Stand fast therefore in the liberty wherewith Christ hath made us free, and be not entangled again with the yoke of bondage.

2Behold, I Paul say unto you, that if ye be circumcised, Christ shall profit you nothing.

3For I testify again to every man that is circumcised, that he is a debtor to do the whole law.

4Christ is become of no effect unto you, whosoever of you are justified by the law; ye are fallen from grace.

5For we through the Spirit wait for the hope of righteousness by faith.

6For in Jesus Christ neither circumcision availeth anything, nor uncircumcision; but faith which worketh by love

Stand fast therefore because you are children of the free woman, not of bondage. You are children of the true covenant, not the Law. You are children of the reality, not the shadow.

144

We are now free. It is for freedom that Christ has set us free. Indeed. And whether some folks like it or not, Paul is calling the Law of Moses bondage – to the extent that man is unable to fulfil it.

Do not let yourself be burdened again by the yoke of slavery and bondage that is the Law. Verse 1 in some other translations:

> 1**It is for freedom that Christ has set us free**. Stand firm, then, and do not let yourselves be burdened again by a yoke of slavery. (NIV)

> 1So **Christ has truly set us free**. Now make sure that you stay free, and don't get tied up again in slavery to the law. (NLT)

To put yourself back under the Law is to put yourself under bondage. Why? Because you could never do the Law. You can never please God through the Law. It is impossible.

Christ has set you free from the Law, why would you want to go back? You are free! Free to love, serve God. Free from sin, from the Law. And if you want to be justified by the Law, Christ shall profit you nothing, and you would be falling from grace.

In the book of Romans, you will notice that Paul goes to great extents to tell us that there was nothing wrong with the Law itself. It just could not save man. It did keep man in check. What was the problem?

> **Romans 8:3**
> The law of Moses was unable to save us because of the weakness of our sinful nature. **So God did what the law could not do**. He sent his own Son in a body like the bodies we sinners have. And in that body God declared an end to sin's control over us by giving his Son as a sacrifice for our sins. (NLT)

The Law was rendered ineffective by the sinful nature in man. There was nothing wrong with the Law. The spiritually dead state that was man's nature was just what made it ineffective. That was what weakened the Law. Man was spiritually dead, and the Law was not going to be the tool to wake him from the dead.

7...*Is* the law sin? God forbid...

12Wherefore the law *is* holy, and the commandment holy, and just, and good.

14For we know that the law is spiritual: but I am carnal, sold under sin.

In a sense, the Law attempted to deal with a spiritual problem. **The law is spiritual.** Did you notice that? It aimed to deal with a problem that stemmed from the spirit of man. **But I am carnal**, a slave to sin. What this means is that sin was the spiritual nature and dominance of man. Sin had the rule, the grip of man's spirit.

The law is spiritual, I am a slave to sin. The Law was powerless to do it. God did what the Law could not do in Christ Jesus.

What could the Law not do? The Law could not give life to man's spirit that was dead, cut off from God. Man had to be re-created spiritually. That was the only way to do it. Man had to be born-again. Reborn. Recreated. Regenerated.

This is Paul's conclusions in **Romans 7:6**

But **now we are delivered from the law**, that being dead wherein we were held; that we should serve in newness of spirit, and not *in* the oldness of the letter.

Newness of spirit. That was the problem. The fallen human nature weakened the effectiveness of the Law.

And back to **Galatians 5.**

Falling from Grace

So now, you have to make a choice. Christ or the Law. You can't have both. Verse 2:

Listen! I, Paul, tell you this: If you are counting on circumcision to make you right with God, then Christ will be of no benefit to you. (NLT)

In verse 4, he even uses more serious language.

> For **if you are trying to make yourselves right with God by keeping the law, you have been cut off from Christ!** You have fallen away from God's grace. (NLT)

Cut off from Christ. Fallen from grace. Some friends of mine want to be justified by the fact that they give their tithe; by their women not wearing jewelry, by the fact that they dress a certain way, or do not dress a certain way.

Some folks go by something they chose to take out of the Old Testament. Don't put tattoos on your body. No blood transfusions. Let's go back to **chapter 3**. Something that Paul had said earlier on in that chapter bears repetition here and will help us greatly.

> 2This only would I learn of you, Received ye the Spirit by the works of the law, or **by the hearing of faith**?
>
> 3Are ye so foolish? having begun in the Spirit, are ye now made perfect by the flesh?
>
> 4Have ye suffered so many things in vain? if *it be* yet in vain.
>
> 5He therefore that **ministereth** to you the Spirit, and **worketh miracles** among you, *doeth he it* by the works of the law, or by **the hearing of faith?**

First, notice that he mentions the "hearing of faith" 2 times. Then, there are 2 classes he talks about about here, that are yet the same, if you read closely.

One, there is that position that holds that to be saved at all, you need to observe the Law, to be circumcised.

Two, there is that position where a person may already be a Christian but they are depending on performance and their own efforts to walk with God and receive from God.

The second class is where a lot of Christians today belong today. We say things like:

"God will release what is in His hands if you release what is in yours."

"God will bless you financially if you sow this seed of $100".

"If you fast for this many days, God will answer your prayer."

"You will miss heaven because you wear jewelry."

"You displease God because you dress in this way."

We expect to be blessed because we give our tithes. We expect to be healed because we fasted for 90 days. We think we receive blessings because we sowed a seed and are reaping 100-fold. We expect to "make" the rapture because we don't wear make-up.

He therefore that ministereth to you the Spirit, and worketh miracles among you, doeth he it by the works of the law, or by the hearing of faith?

What is Paul saying? He is implying that every other thing that we receive after we get born-again; we receive by faith. The working of miracles is by faith. The ministration of the Spirit is by faith.

The working of miracles is by fasting? It is not by performance of something, of anything. The working of miracles and everything else that we receive in Christ is only, totally only by the same way that we came to Christ: **by the hearing of faith, by the finished work of our Lord.** Anything other than that is falling from grace.

We hear preachers say things like, "Give $100 to Israel so God can bless you with the blessing of Abraham."

"Go will bless you if you sow $20 into this (or my) ministry."

"Take advantage of the anointing of the hour."

"God will increase you if you give a financial seed to your spiritual father."

"You must sow a seed into your man of God."

To say things like that is to say that we need to do and perform something before God can bless us. But the Bible insists that there is nothing we can do to deserve anything on our own. It insists that we are already blessed with every spiritual blessing in Christ Jesus. Cast out the bondwoman, the effort of the flesh to earn and deserve God's favor and blessing.

What did we do before God gave the Lord Jesus to die for us? Why do we now think we can give or do something, anything, for Him to bless us for the material, mundane things of this life?

We can't improve our behavior enough to deserve a blessing.

Some people almost boast about their tithing.

"I tithed so the devourer is rebuked for me."

"I tithe therefore the windows of heaven are opened to me. I tithe so God will now bless me."

That is the works of the Law. That is human effort. That is the bond-woman. That is ignoring and making light of the work of redemption.

The Bible says that Christ shall profit you nothing. If it is your tithing that rebukes the devourer for your sake, what did you then profit from the work of Christ?

If your tithing is what opens the windows of heaven to you, what then has Christ's death and resurrection brought you?

If it is your tithing that obtained all that for you, then you don't need Christ. Just keep tithing!

But know that the moment you stop tithing, your wrong (un)belief and fear and works will open the door for the enemy. And that won't be God punishing you. It's your own fear that would have done it.
I hope you see what I'm saying: You say the windows of heaven are opened BECAUSE I tithe.

You should be saying that the windows are open because of what Christ did for you. That is how to stay in freedom. You are trusting in the work of Christ, not in your tithing.

If your faith is your tithe, then just keep it up. The tithing is your defense against the devourer. Christ is not. Just know that the moment you don't do it, you should expect the devourer to come, because that has been your faith.

You have placed yourself under the bondage of "If I do this; this is what I get as reward. If I don't do this, then I get the repercussion or punishment."

The Bible says about the Law **Galatians 3:10**:

> For all who rely on the works of the law are under a curse, as it is written: "Cursed is everyone who does not continue to do everything written in the Book of the Law".

What that means is that the moment you fail to do what the Law says, if you're relying on your obedience of it, the curse that was meant to come on you will now come.

You have to keep doing it. *You cannot sustain it.* And I don't want you to get me wrong: While we give financially in churches and to the causes of the Body of Christ, that is not, will never be, the reason why we prosper or are blessed. If we prosper, and we should, it is not because we did this or did that. It is because grace and peace have been multiplied to us in Christ Jesus!

Am I saying people should stop tithing? I'm just saying that it is our faith in the finished work that is our defense, trust and confidence.

Absolutely not! Is it possible for the Lord to lead us into giving, even when it is not convenient? Emphatically yes.

But if it's your fasting, your giving to Israel, as some have said, that constitute your healing and blessings, what then is the point of the work of redemption?

If there are still things that you can do yourself to achieve something or obtain a blessing, why then do you need Christ? You evidently don't. In Christ Jesus, we have arrived. We are complete in Him.

Faith in the Finished Work

We prosper because of the "grace of our Lord Jesus Christ, that, though he was rich, yet for your sakes he became poor, that ye through his poverty might be rich." **II Corinthians 8:9**

That means we have faith in *His finished work*. That is why! That will always be why. There will not be any other reason. Anything else, other than this is falling from grace.

We will never deserve anything, that is what some of us have failed to realize. Yet, in Christ, we have received everything.

He therefore that ministers to you the Spirit, and worketh miracles among you, doeth he it by the works of the law, or by the hearing of faith?

By the hearing of faith. The hearing of faith. It is by faith. We continue to live a life of faith. We continue to prosper and triumph by faith. We live by the faith of the Son of God.

> **Romans 1:17**
> For in the gospel the righteousness of God is revealed--**a righteousness that is by faith from first to last**, just as it is written: "The righteous will live by faith." (NIV)
>
> This Good News tells us how God makes us right in his sight. **This is accomplished from start to finish by faith**. As the Scriptures say, "It is through faith that a righteous person has life." (NLT)

God's approval is revealed in this Good News. **This approval begins and ends with faith** as Scripture says, "The person who has God's approval will live by faith." (God's Word)

Faith from first to last. Accomplished from start to finish by faith. Paul goes to tells us to live out our lives like the free people that we are. Let's live like the new creations that we have become.

If we are not under the Law, what are we then to do? We follow the Holy Spirit. He leads us. We follow His leading and we please God. The leading of the Spirit means that we are not under the Law.

> 16*This* I say then, Walk in the Spirit, and ye shall not fulfil the lust of the flesh.

> 18**But if ye be led of the Spirit, ye are not under the law**.

We walk in the spirit, in the realities of our new spiritual life, of the new man in Christ Jesus. This is really talking about the human spirit. If you are a new man in Christ: live that out.

Romans 8 tells us pretty much the same things that these verses do.

> 2For the law of the Spirit of life in Christ Jesus hath made me free from the law of sin and death.

> 9But **ye are not in the flesh, but in the Spirit**, if so be that the Spirit of God dwell in you. Now if any man have not the Spirit of Christ, he is none of his.

> 12Therefore, brethren, we are debtors, not to the flesh, to live after the flesh.

> 14For as many as are led by the Spirit of God, they are the sons of God

You are not in the flesh, but in the spirit.

This is how we live. We are not in the flesh. We are in the spirit. We are debtors in that reality. We are led by the Spirit of God, and by doing so, we put to death the deeds of the flesh.

Let's conclude with what Paul concluded chapter 5 with.

> 24And they that are Christ's have crucified the flesh with the affections and lusts.
>
> **25If we live in the Spirit, let us also walk in the Spirit.**

They that are Christ's have crucified the flesh, and its lusts and affections. Wow. You notice that the "if" in verse 25 is not a question. It is a statement of fact. It is more in the spirit of "since". That verse should really read like this: *Since we live in the Spirit, let us also walk in the Spirit.*

Since. It is a fact that we live in the spirit, having been re-born by the Holy Ghost. Since that is true, we live with that reality and consciousness. This is walking in the spirit. It also means we walk by faith. Walking in the spirit, is really walking by faith: not being moved by the flesh, not being moved by our bodies, not being moved by what we hear or see or touch. It is responding and acting from our recreated born-again spirits.

Verse 18 says if we are led of the spirit, we will not fulfill the lusts of the flesh. If we respond form our spirits and let our new spiritual life and reality lead and dominate us, then we will not be giving space to the flesh.

Doing that means that issues like fornication, idolatry, witchcraft and the things that Paul called the "works of the flesh" are dealt with in our lives. By walking in faith. By walking in the spirit.

I know that Christians can have issues with the flesh, with habits, with sinful thoughts, with private sins. Whatever the sin, whatever the issue, the way we win over those things is becoming conscious of the fact that we are new creations in Christ. Realizing this, we walk in faith, in the reality of the new man.

Romans 6:14 says that sin does not have dominion over us. Realizing this fact, we walk in it by faith. We confront every sinful tendency of the flesh, every unwholesome thought, every wrong habit with this fact of God's Word.

We walk by faith. We refuse to be moved by our flesh. We refuse to be moved by how we feel or don't feel. We yield to who we are in the spirit. We yield to our spiritual realities.

Abraham's Tough Obedience

It seems that Abraham's life perfectly represented the person who is made right with God even in the New Testament. The New Man in Christ, as we have said, is not under the Law, just like Abraham was not under any Law.

The beauty of Abraham's relationship with Jehovah God lies in the righteousness that was bestowed upon him, and the spontaneous obedience that flowed out of Abraham.

Was Abraham perfect? Did Abraham make mistakes before and after God counted his faith for righteousness? God did not give Abraham any laws, did He? Did He give him any rules, sacrifices, feasts to keep him in check?

No laws, no rules. Was he not a sinner like the rest of humanity? No, Abraham was not given any rules or laws to live by. Now, it was in **Genesis 22**, that God had asked Abraham to do the most difficult thing imaginable. He asked Abraham to offer "thy son, thine only son Isaac who thou lovest" as a sacrifice. What an impossible ask, you would say.

For a man who had been barren most of his life losing his son would have been one thing but killing him with your own hands was another thing. The boy would be the *one* thing he couldn't give up. Anything else!

But what did Abraham do? The Bible says that Abraham *rose up early* the next morning to do what God asked. There is no record of

Abraham grumbling or complaining or cursing. He just rose up to obey God.

Notice that God did not threaten Abraham with the fear of repercussion or punishment. It was not a matter of, "If you will not obey my command of offering Isaac to me as a sacrifice, I will make you poor, I will afflict you with sickness and disease" as was the case with the Law.

At the same time there was no promise of a blessing or benefit. It was not, "If you obey this commandment to offer Isaac to me, I will bless you with riches and substances; I will lift you up above your enemies."

No promise of blessing, no threat of curse. Abraham did not fear repercussion because he knew he was already blessed. He was secure in his standing before God. He knew without the shadow of a doubt that he was righteous, and that God loved him unconditionally.
So, Abraham gladly, without fuss, obeyed God. He obeyed God in the most difficult ask imaginable.

Do you now see how this represents the difference between the life of faith and the life of works and the flesh?

The life of works is lived in fear and insecurity, of repercussion, of punishment, of failure, of never doing enough, of death.

In the New Testament, we obey God from the heart, by faith, secure in His unconditional love for us. There is no fear of being cursed, of being punished, of sickness or disease. We are already blessed beyond any curse. We are secure and rest in His work.

Like Abraham, we trust our Father. We might not see the whole picture, but we know He has a plan for us, for our lives. We trust Him from the heart. We obey Him by faith, not from Law, not by the Law, not by a set of rules and regulations.

You see, righteousness frees us to walk in holiness. It frees us to walk in obedience. The Law or rules and regulations only put us in bondage. This, Christian, eventually, you will see, is a love affair. The book of Hebrews has a commentary on Abraham's action of **Genesis 22**.

17By faith Abraham, when he was tried, offered up Isaac: and he that had received the promises offered up his only begotten *son*,

18Of whom it was said, That in Isaac shall thy seed be called:

19Accounting that God *was* able to raise *him* up, even from the dead; from whence also he received him in a figure.

By faith. He obeyed God by faith. Faith is the way we obey God. He offered up his son, believing that God was able to raise him up. Figuratively, he received him back from the dead.

We lay down, resting on nothing but the Promise. We step into the void carried on the wings faith.

Jeremiah 31
31Behold, the days come, saith the LORD, that I will make a new covenant with the house of Israel, and with the house of Judah:

32Not according to the covenant that I made with their fathers in the day *that* I took them by the hand to bring them out of the land of Egypt; which my covenant they brake, although I was an husband unto them, saith the LORD:

33But this *shall be* the covenant that I will make with the house of Israel; After those days, saith the LORD, **I will put my law in their inward parts, and write it in their hearts**; and will be their God, and they shall be my people.

This is the New Covenant. I will write my laws in their hearts, in their inward parts. They will obey me from the heart. They shall all know me. No, this is not the covenant of the Law, which they broke.

No More Rules

More than 28 years ago, before I married Sandy, I was a lousy cook. I could maybe cook hot dogs and beans (out of a can), and those didn't always turn out so well. That's because I was confined to a set of instructions called a "cookbook." It was a list of rules and regulations, a law, which could never make me into a good cook.

Then I married Sandy, and I had someone to lead me through the process of cooking a meal. She showed me everything I know about cooking. Now, I can roast a turkey, bake a cake, and even make a mean potato salad. Did you like that potato salad we had at the Bethel Builders picnic this last Monday? I made that!

I'm a pretty good cook, if I do say so myself. Why? Because I am no longer confined to a cookbook. I am under a better system. I have someone to lead me through the process.

Now, that's exactly what the Believer has in the Holy Spirit. We who know Christ are no longer confined to the law, a list of dos and don'ts. We're under a better system. We have the Holy Spirit to guide us through the process of living a holy life. All we have to do is listen to Him. All we have to do is follow His lead.

From SermonCentral

Chapter 6

You may have seen an episode of Extreme Makeover Home Edition. They are up there on YouTube. All wonderful stories of grace and unmerited favor.

Episode after episode, a family in dire need of financial or accommodation help is given the gift of a beautiful new house — the kind most people will ever see only in magazines. Communities would come together to support this one family, giving of their time and resources. The recipient family, emotional wrecks, always weep their eyes out, surprised by the magnanimous and unexpected gift.

There was only one thing for the recipient family to do: receive and accept the gracious gift of the new house. Could there be any other reaction?

And, after receiving the house, should they be able to boast and brag about their own goodness or prowess as homeowners?

They are given a gift. They could not afford it. They did nothing to get it, nothing to deserve it. It was their poverty and need that birthed the kindness of the gift.

God's grace in Christ Jesus is somewhat like this. Purely a gift.

Because God so loved the world. We can only receive it. We cannot boast about doing anything to deserve or merit it.

We boast only in the Cross.

Galatians Chapter 6

IT seems that Paul tries to end the epistle on a gentler, softer note. Chapter 6 begins with a bit of an indication that he's let off most of his steam. He's probably now hoping to make the folks relax.

1Brethren, if a man be overtaken in a fault, ye which are spiritual, restore such an one in the spirit of meekness; considering thyself, lest thou also be tempted.

2Bear ye one another's burdens, and so fulfil the law of Christ.

3For if a man think himself to be something, when he is nothing, he deceiveth himself.

4But let every man prove his own work, and then shall he have rejoicing in himself alone, and not in another.

5For every man shall bear his own burden.

It seems that he's talking about the men who brought in the false teachings from Judaism into the churches. It seems to me that he's saying, yes, they were wrong, yes, they got into this foolish slant, but if they repent and change their ways and beliefs, let's restore them with wisdom and humility. *Restore them in the spirit of meekness.*

Let's be humble even as we help our brothers who might not understand the gospel, the way we have. Let's not mock them. I think he is referring to the "fault" of bringing this doctrine to the church, not necessarily a fault as in being nasty or falling into sin the classic sense.

The word "fault" means a lapse from the truth, a deviation, an error, a "slip up." These folks had fallen into the error of requiring Christians to be circumcised and to follow the Law. This is why I'm convinced that Paul is trying to get the church to help and restore the folks that may be out of order doctrinally or otherwise.

Besides, that explanation fits the context and subject of the epistle. Now he enjoins us to be humble in correcting others, considering ourselves. I have seen many people try to correct others, with a lack of humility and meekness. I know folks who can be like that. Some laugh at the ignorance of other members of the Body of Christ.

Some just ignore and can't relate with other members of the Body of Christ because they probably don't understand everything they understand. If a brother or sister has been wrong, and we have an opportunity to correct and restore them, let's do it in love, not harshly, not arrogantly.

Bear ye one another's burdens, and so fulfill the law of Christ. If a man think himself to be something, when he is nothing, he deceives himself.

Stay humble. Then he says that all said and told, everyone is responsible for their own lives. Compare verses 2 and 5:

> 2Bear ye one another's burdens, and so fulfil the law of Christ.

> 5For every man shall bear his own burden.

What's he saying? There are times when we should, are required to help a brother or a sister – but ultimately you are really responsible for your own life. That is a truth we will do well not to ignore.

> 6Let him that is taught in the word communicate unto him that teacheth in all good things.
> 7Be not deceived; God is not mocked: for whatsoever a man soweth, that shall he also reap.

> 8For he that soweth to his flesh shall of the flesh reap corruption; but he that soweth to the Spirit shall of the Spirit reap life everlasting.

> 9And let us not be weary in well doing: for in due season we shall reap, if we faint not.

> 10As we have therefore opportunity, let us do good unto all *men*, especially unto them who are of the household of faith

Then he tells us to invest in our own spiritual growth. I don't think he was talking about money. Don't sow to the flesh, don't feed your fleshly desires. Invest in your spiritual growth and development. Spend time in the Word. Spend time in prayer. Spend time increasing your knowledge of God things. Exercise your spirit in the things of God. Sow to the spirit. Don't tire. Pay-day will come. You will reap spiritual development and growth.

From verse 11, he returns to the subject matter of his discourse, and he says, "Ye see how large a letter I have written unto you with mine own hand." I think he was smiling, finally, when he wrote that. It seems like he's relaxing a bit, having let off steam. I hear a chuckle in those words, I see a grin on his face. He's signing off. So here are the last few instructions, then.

Bragging Rights

In verse 13:

> 13For neither they themselves who are circumcised keep the law; but desire to have you circumcised, that they may glory in your flesh.

In verse 14, I think he makes one of the greatest statements or utterances of the entire Bible.

> 14But **God forbid that I should glory, save in the cross of our Lord Jesus Christ**, by whom the world is crucified unto me, and I unto the world.

> 14But **it's unthinkable that I could ever brag about anything except the cross of our Lord Jesus Christ**. By his cross my relationship to the world and its relationship to me have been crucified. (God's Word)

God forbid that I should glory in anything other than the Cross! I will not glory in anything I do, good or bad. *In fact, especially the good things.* I will not glory in my seed sowing, I will not glory in my sending money into a ministry, I will not glory in my tithe, I will not glory in fasting. I will glory in what Christ has done! I will not repose faith in anything other than the Cross.

I will glory only in the work of redemption in Christ. Some folks tend to find reasons to glory in things other than the Cross. I will brag only in what Christ has done.

I heard a preacher once say that the reason his church and ministry are prosperous is because they give to the nation of Israel! He implied that the way to be blessed is to give to the nation of Israel. Why? Because he believes that the Bible says, when God spoke to Abraham, that, "I will bless those that bless you, curse those that curse you."

But we know that that is not what that verse is really saying. That is bragging and boasting in a thing other than the Cross. Every blessing proceeds from the work of the Cross.

"I will bless those that bless you, curse those that curse you" today is a reference to the born-again child of God – the true Israel of God. **But it's unthinkable that I could ever brag about anything except the cross of our Lord Jesus Christ**.

Take one more look at verse 13:
> 13For neither they themselves who are circumcised keep the law; but desire to have you circumcised, that they may glory in your flesh.

Like I said before, today, we would call them Judaizers. They call themselves "Messianic Jews", "Hebrew Roots Movement", and talk about the "Jewish Jesus" or the "Hebraic roots of Christianity" etc. If you can't simply call yourself a "Christian", but use such appellations, you are glorying in the flesh. You are glorying in your Jewishness or "Hebrewness".

I'm not against pride in who you are. All I'm saying is that this buys me nothing as far as God's kingdom is concerned.

If you are Jewish, I hope you are proud of that heritage. But your heritage counts for nothing in the light of eternity and salvation. Faith in Christ Jesus is the only thing that does. You have no advantage whatsoever.

In Christ Jesus, there is no glory in this. What advantage has the Jew? None. **Romans 3.**

A lot of Christians who still want to hang on to Judaism like to quote the first verses of this chapter.

Recently, I was listening to someone defending the Judaizers. He spoke from **Romans 3:1**, saying that the Jew has an advantage over every other people on the earth. That's exactly what he said!

The dishonesty of some people in making religious points is unbelievable sometimes. This person quoted from just the first verse and did not bother to quote from the rest of the chapter, at the same time ignoring the context of the discourse.

This is what verse 1 says, and I want you to look at what the other verses from the same chapter say:

> 1**What advantage then hath the Jew**? or what profit *is there* of circumcision?

> 2**Much every way: chiefly, because that unto them were committed the oracles of God**

> 9Well then, **should we conclude that we Jews are better than others**? No, not at all, for we have already shown that all people, whether Jews or Gentiles, are under the power of sin. (NLT)

> 29*Is he* **the God of the Jews only?** *is he* **not also of the Gentiles? Yes, of the Gentiles also:**

> 30Seeing *it is* one God, which shall justify the **circumcision by faith, and uncircumcision through faith.**

> 31Do we then make void the law through faith? God forbid: yea, we establish the law.

The advantage the Jew has is just that the Law came through them. The Messiah came through that race. They have enjoyed the blessing of God throughout the ages, yes.

They were a conduit, the way that the Messiah was delivered to earth. But in terms of salvation and eternity, what advantage do they have? Nothing. None, not anymore. Not since the Messiah came and died for us.

There is no Jew. No New Zealander. No Angolan. No Tongan. No Botswanan. No Korean. No Iranian. No Fijian. No Chilean.

If you are born again, to keep insisting on your ethnic origin is to surreptitiously glory in the flesh. You are in Christ and a Christian or you are not! It's as simple as that.

You have not done God a service or a favor by accepting Christ as Savior. You have been rescued from bondage and spiritual death. The Jew has no advantage *whatsoever*. **Galatians 6:15** should put all and any argument to bed:

> 15It doesn't matter whether we have been circumcised or not. What counts is whether we have been transformed into a **new creation**. (NLT)

> 15Certainly, it doesn't matter whether a person is circumcised or not. Rather, what matters is being a **new creation**. (God's Word)

What matters is being a new creation. Have we become a new creation or not? That is what matters, that is what counts.

Another way to say this is what matters is "are you born again or are you not"? What matters is being born again. Being Jewish or Arab or Caucasian or Asian means nothing. Being Gentile means nothing. Are you born again?

John 3

> 3Jesus answered and said unto him, Verily, verily, I say unto thee, Except **a man be born again**, he cannot see the kingdom of God.

> 6That which is born of the flesh is flesh; and **that which is born of the Spirit is spirit**.

It means that our spirits needed to be re-created by the Holy Spirit and this happens when we get born again. It's a spiritual transaction. Paul says this is what must and needed to happen. Being Jewish is nothing. Being Pakistani is nothing. Being Zambian is nothing. All in the light of eternity. What matters is being a new creation. Something the Lord said in **John 4** is what some people latch on to in an apparent misinterpretation.

In **John 4**, the Lord was talking to the "woman at the well", when He said this:

> 22Ye worship ye know not what: we know what we worship: for **salvation is of the Jews.**

Salvation is of the Jews. I know some folks refer to this verse to say that God has a special provision of thing or the Jews. In extreme cases, they imply that the Jews do not need to accept Jesus as Lord and Savior, that they already enjoy the covenant blessings of God.

That would be fine only if you did not read the whole of what the Lord said. This is what He said before and after verse 22, in context:

> 21Jesus saith unto her, Woman, believe me, the hour cometh, when ye shall neither in this mountain, nor yet at Jerusalem, worship the Father.

> 22Ye worship ye know not what: we know what we worship: for **salvation is of the Jews.**

> 23But the hour cometh, and now is, when the true worshippers shall worship the Father in spirit and in truth: for the Father seeketh such to worship him.

24God *is* a Spirit: and they that worship him must worship *him* in spirit and in truth.

Yes, salvation came from the Jews. Yes, the Savior came from their tribe, but God's intention was always to bring the Christ through them. That *was* the case. Not anymore. The hour has now arrived when worship is no more in Jerusalem or in the temple or on a mountain.

Now, worship has nothing to do with location or Judaism. Now we worship God in the spirit and. We worship the Father unconfined by geography, anywhere all over the world.

Do you see how context matters when we read and study Scripture? I want to point out to you one more example of this.

In **Matthew 10**, the Lord sent out his disciples to go heal the sick and preach the gospel. See what He said, when He commissioned the 12.

5These twelve Jesus sent forth, and commanded them, saying, **Go not into the way of the Gentiles,** and into *any* city of the Samaritans enter ye not:

6But go rather to the lost sheep of the house of Israel.

The Lord told them to go only the children of Israel *only*. He specifically instructs them not to go to the Gentiles, or to the Samaritans?

The question we need to ask then, is, is that valid today? Is the Lord saying the same thing today? Why did He say that anyways? We know that the Lord said it only because the He had not died and the Old Testament was still I n force. Only the Jews enjoyed and were partakers of that covenant.

The New Covenant for which He would soon give His life was not yet in force. So, we know that what He said here is no more valid today. This is what He said later in **Matthew 28** and is what is valid today:

19Go ye therefore, and teach *all nations*...

167

And in **Acts 1:8**

> 8But ye shall receive power, after that the Holy Ghost is come
> upon you: and ye shall be *witnesses unto me both in Jerusalem, and in
> all Judaea, and in Samaria, and unto the uttermost part of the earth.*

He specifically mentions Samaria, then, the uttermost parts of the
earth. Salvation is no more of and for the Jews, glory to God!

Context matters! A good, calm heart will ponder and consider the
whole counsel of God's will in studying the Word.
In that sense it matters who was talking, with whom and when the
conversation took place.

What is the point of these examples? That no one, no tribe, is special
any longer. The Jew is no more special than the Gentile.

Returning to our study, back to Chapter 6 verse 16:

> 16And as many as walk according to this rule, peace *be* on
> them, and mercy, and upon the Israel of God.

> 16Peace and mercy will come to rest on all those who conform
> to this principle. They are the Israel of God. (God's Word)

As many as walk according to this rule. What rule? What principle?
What standard is Paul talking about?

The principle is in verse 15, of course:

The principle of what matters is being a new creation.

As many as follow this rule or principle of "circumcision or
uncircumcision mean nothing." The standard of, "What matters is a
new creation".

*Peace and mercy will come to rest on all those who conform to this principle. They
are the Israel of God.*

The Israel of God is the Body of Christ. The real Israel of God are those that follow this principle. These are the ones that glory in nothing but the Cross.

These are the Ones that God spoke to Abraham about: "In thee shall all nations be blessed". Paul is saying that the real spiritual Israel that God always had in mind is made up of those who have become new creations in Christ Jesus and repose no confidence in their genealogy or efforts.

The Church has not replaced Israel. The Church is the Israel of God. The true Israel of God is the Body of Christ and is made up of all who walk according to the standard and rule of faith of the New Creation in Christ.

The Israel of God is made up of born-again Jews, Nigerians, Guyanese, the Dutch, the Finnish, the Japanese, the Haitian, the Mexican, the Guinean, the English, the Indonesian, the Saudi Arabian, the Palestinian, the Egyptian!

We are made up of "all the families of the earth", of "every nation, kindred, tribe and tongue", just like God told Abraham, because we believe and know that in Christ Jesus, what matters is a new creation!

> **Galatians 3**
> 18For if the **inheritance** *be* **of the law,** *it is* **no more of promise**: but God gave *it* to Abraham by promise.

> **Romans 4**
> 14For if **they which are of the law** *be* **heirs, faith is made void,** and the promise made of none effect:

God gave it to Abraham by promise which implies that it is and has to be by faith. It is not by the Law; it is not by inheritance or by race or by genealogy.

If they which are of the Law, those who hold on to Moses are heirs, God's whole enterprise falls down.

If the inheritance is of the Law, it is no more of promise and faith is defeated. If the natural, DNA Jew get the inheritance, then, God has broken His Promise, His covenant and His Oath to Abraham. If they who work for their salvation are heirs, faith is defeated.

Romans 11:26 is where many derive their end-time theology from.

> 26And so **all Israel shall be saved**: as it is written, There shall come out of Sion the Deliverer, and shall turn away ungodliness from Jacob:

Does that mean EVERY ISRAELITE will be saved? Could that mean that **every Jew** will finally be saved even if they did not receive Jesus as Messiah?

It does not say, "All Israelites", or "All Jews". It says all Israel. Many people who have read **Romans 11** tend to think that somehow, suddenly, something will fall upon the Jews, and they will, out of the blues, accept Jesus as Christ.

Listen, folks, there is no difference between Greek and Jew. Scripture has concluded all under sin. There is no separate plan or covenant for the Jews. There is just one plan for the whole of humanity, and it is through the Lord Jesus. **Romans 3**.

> 9What then? are we better *than they*? No, in no wise: for we have before proved both Jews and Gentiles, that they are all under sin;

Jews have been getting born-again since the Lord was here, and that will continue to be the case, just as it is with other nations and tribes in the world.

If you have seen **Galatians 6:15 and 16**, it should not be difficult to see that the "Israel" in "all Israel shall be saved" is referring to the same Israel in "Israel of God."

> 15For in Christ Jesus neither circumcision availeth anything, nor uncircumcision, but a new creature.

170

16And as many as walk according to this rule, peace *be* on them, and mercy, and upon the Israel of God.

It is not the natural, DNA, physical Jew. It is those who have accepted the Lord Jesus as Lord and Savior and constitute the Body of Christ from all nations on the earth that are the Israel of God.

It is ridiculous for Christians to say things like, "Israel is God's time-table for the end times" or, "Israel is God's clock"; "God does everything through the nation of Israel".

Some have dared to call the Church a parenthesis in the plan of God, thus implying that the natural DNA seed or children of Abraham are the main focus of God. That would have been funny if it wasn't so sad.

Has God forsaken the DNA natural Jew? No, a thousand times no. Nor has He forsaken the rest of the world. The Jew just needs to get born again like every other person in the world.

There is no exception to the rule (actually to the Promise confirmed by the Oath and the Covenant) with them.

> 22This righteousness is given through faith in Jesus Christ to all who believe. There is no difference between Jew and Gentile,
>
> 23For all have sinned and fall short of the glory of God,

All have sinned and fallen short. Jew and Gentile. I have friends who quote a Rabbi here, a Rabbi there, especially when it comes to end time matters. You ask, "is this Rabbi a Christian? Is he born again?" They say no, he's not.

"I know he's not born again, but they have been studying the Old Testament for a long time. They have studied the Torah and the Talmud, and the stars."

A Rabbi that does not accept the Lord Jesus as Lord and Christ is as helpful to your Christianity as a Buddhist monk or Muslim Imam. A

171

Rabbi that does not accept the Lord Jesus as Lord and Christ is an unbeliever, plain and simple.

> He that hath the Son hath life; *and* he that hath not the Son of God hath not life. **I John 5:2**

What am I really saying? The Christian attitude and disposition toward Jews should be the same as Paul's in **Romans 9-11**. We should be concerned for their salvation.

We should be willing to urgently show them that this Jesus is the very Christ of Old Testament prophecies. The Christian's only obligation to the Jew is to let him see that the Messiah has come. It is not political; it is not geographic.

We pray for them just like the Apostle Paul did in **Romans 9**– that they will accept the righteousness of faith in Christ Jesus and not one of their own. It is our obligation to do this, just like it is our obligation to let the rest of the world, from New Delhi to Kosovo to Yakutia to San Jose to Yellowknife know that Jesus is Lord. Anything other than this would not be the gospel.

The Little Flower

A story is told about Fiorello LaGuardia, who, when he was mayor of New York City during the worst days of the Great Depression and all of WWII, was called by adoring New Yorkers 'the Little Flower' because he was only five feet four and always wore a carnation in his lapel.

He was a colorful character who used to ride the City fire trucks, raid speakeasies with the police department, take entire orphanages to baseball games, and whenever the New York papers were on strike, he would go on the radio and read the Sunday funnies to the kids.

One bitterly cold night in January of 1935, the mayor turned up at a night court that served the poorest ward of the city. He dismissed the judge for the evening and took over the bench himself. Within a few minutes, a tattered old woman was brought, charged with stealing a loaf of bread. She told him that her daughter's husband had deserted her, her daughter was sick, and her two grandchildren were starving.

But the shopkeeper, from whom the bread was stolen, refused to drop the charges. "It's a real bad neighborhood, your Honor," the man told the mayor. "She's got to be punished to teach other people around here a lesson."

LaGuardia sighed. He turned to the woman and said "I've got to punish you. The law makes no exceptions - ten dollars or ten days in jail." But even as he pronounced sentence, the mayor was already reaching into his pocket. He extracted a bill and tossed it into his sombrero saying:

"Here is the ten dollars fine which I now remit; and furthermore, I am going to fine everyone in this courtroom fifty cents for living in a town where a person has to steal bread so that her grandchildren can eat. 'Mr. Baliff, collect the fines and give them to the defendant.'"

So, the following day the New York City newspapers reported that $47.50 was turned over to a bewildered old lady who had stolen a loaf of bread to feed her starving grandchildren, fifty cents of that amount being contributed by the red-faced grocery store owner, while some seventy petty criminals, people with traffic violations, and New York City policemen, each of whom had just paid fifty cents for the privilege of doing so, gave the mayor a standing ovation.

From SermonCentral

Last Words

In Christ is the fulfillment of the Promise, Covenant and Oath that God made to Abraham.

Galatians 3
14That the blessing of Abraham might come on the Gentiles through Jesus Christ; that we might receive the promise of the Spirit through faith.

22But the scripture hath concluded all under sin, that the promise by faith of Jesus Christ might be given to them that believe.

This is the essence of Paul's message to these Galatian Christians. The Promise of the Christ, that the Old Testament saints and prophets saw and waited for is now the reality of the born again one.

It is to be greatly regretted that some folks misread Paul's message to be the exact opposite of all he meant it to be. I have listened to sermons titles something like "Paul's letter to the Galatians proves that we are still under the Law". How anyone can use Paul's words in this epistle to reinforce their position that circumcision and the Law are still relevant today in the physical sense is totally beyond me.

Paul himself may have given us the answer to this in one of his epistles to the Corinthians.

14But their minds were blinded: for until this day remaineth the same vail untaken away in the reading of the old testament; which *vail* is done away in Christ.

There is a veil over their minds. There is a potential blindness over the eyes of those who adhere to the Old Testament, when the Old Testament is not read with Christ as its focus. There is only one way to read Moses and the prophets, and that is in Christ.

The veil is done away in Christ.

15But even unto this day, when Moses is read, the vail is upon their heart.

16Nevertheless when it shall turn to the Lord, the vail shall be taken away.

We should read the Old Testament carefully. We should handle it with great care. If we fail to see Christ in the writings of Moses and the Prophets, we are not reading them right. They all point to Christ as their focus and goal. Those who miss Christ as the essence of the Old Testament are blinded.

Acts 10:43
To him give all the prophets witness, that through his name whosoever believeth in him shall receive remission of sins.

As for the epistle itself, I think there's a point to be made in the fact that Paul himself was a Jew. He was not just a Jew, he was a "super" Jew. He called himself a Hebrew of Hebrews. He was a well-educated Jewish scholar, a Pharisee. Yet, he is the one that the Lord has employed to teach us all these things.

If Paul had said the things he said in the epistle to the Galatians today, many Christians would have called him anti-Semitic, and you can understand why the Pharisees and Jews of his day hated him. They couldn't deal with his interpretation of the Old Testament in the light of Christ, being itself, the revelation of Christ.

Consider this also: If these letters had been written by someone like Titus, most people would have said, well, what does he know? How can he tell us this? Titus was Greek, not a Jew, and I think that most people, Jew or not would have said he does not qualify to comment on the Law and the commandments.

If Timothy had written these letters, many people would have said, pretty much the same thing. Timothy was a half Jew. His dad was a Gentile. People would have said, no, you don't qualify to comment on Judaism.

176

God has used Paul, a former Pharisee, a "perfect" observer of the Law, to write these things! He has chosen one who knows the Old Testament to write the heart of the New. No coincidence.

Paul has provided us with a clear understanding and explanation of the gospel without what would have been a Jewish bias.

If there was anybody who should be propagating the Jewishness of the Gospel and Christ, it should have been Paul. And Paul wanted and warned us to steer clear of it all.

Titus 1
14**Not giving heed to Jewish fables**, and commandments of men, that turn from the truth.

1 Timothy 1:4
3As I besought thee to abide still at Ephesus, when I went into Macedonia, that thou mightest charge some that they teach no other doctrine,

4**Neither give heed to fables and endless genealogies,** which minister questions, rather than godly edifying which is in faith: *so do.*

5Now the end of the commandment is charity out of a pure heart, and *of* a good conscience, and *of* faith unfeigned:

6From which some having swerved have turned aside unto vain jangling;

7**Desiring to be teachers of the law; understanding neither what they say, nor whereof they affirm**

Don't give heed to *Jewish fables.* Don't pay any attention to endless genealogies.

Don't give in to these Judaizers talking about the Law and past stories and fables. They are always talking about Jerusalem, the Temple. They romanticize the Torah, the Hebrew language, shofars, "prayer" shawls.

Paul called such talk *vain jangling*. Useless nonsense.

They talk about *"blood moons"*. They talk about the *"Shemitah"*. They talk about Gog and Magog, about eclipses and earthquakes and the destruction of countries.

Charge them not to preach any other doctrine but Christ! Charge them not to preach the Law, not to preach Moses, not to preach Israel or Jerusalem or *endless genealogies*. They have turn aside to vain jangling.

Don't let your focus be about the Old Testament and the Law. Fix your attention on things above, where Christ sits at God's right hand.

If we leave the doctrine of Christ, if we desire to be teachers of the Law as some of these folks are doing today, Paul says we would be *swerving and turning aside from the faith.*

They desire to the teachers of the Law, understanding neither what they say, nor whereof they affirm. Think about it.

They want to teach what the Law says. They want to force Christians to go back into the practices and observances of the Law and Moses. They preach the Torah, not Christ.

But Paul says, they don't what they are talking about. Why? Because they read the Old Testament and have failed to see Christ in them.

If you read the Old Testament Scriptures and don't see Christ in them, you have read them wrong. Your eyes are covered by the veil. He is the essence of the Scriptures – the power of God by which have been saved.

Revelation 19:10
For the essence of prophecy is to give a clear witness for Jesus. (NLT)

For the testimony of Jesus is the spirit of prophecy.

All many of them see is war. They see the Muslim nations destroyed by "God" and the nation of Israel winning the "war". They interpret Scripture purely in the light of their own political persuasions.

They really would not mind seeing all the Arab countries destroyed as long as Israel is OK.

We have not so learned Christ. He does not wish that any should perish but that all should come to repentance. God so loved the WORLD that He gave His only begotten Son, that WHOEVER believes in Him should not perish but should have life.

God does not love the Jew more than He loves the Muslim. He does not love the Christian more than He loves the Muslim. He just wants men to come to Him through Christ. He did not prefer David Ben-Gurion to Yasser Arafat.

He does not love Iraq or Iran less than He loves Israel. He does not love the Jew more that He loves the Palestinian.

You will see these Judaizers on Christian TV every day. They relegate Christ to nothing. They exalt and lift the Law and Moses. They negate faith and the Gospel and preach the works of the Law. Exactly what Paul cursed.

Listening to many of them, you wonder if they are truly Christians or not, because when they talk at their extreme, Christ just becomes a side issue, a by-word with them. The Cross to them is just another event in the Bible, like the crossing of the Red Sea, or the dedication of the temple. They don't see the Cross as the seminal moment in Scripture.

I have watched these folks many times, and many times after their programs are over, I'm left scratching my head, wondering if I heard the name of Jesus at all, wondering if the Gospel was preached at all.

They would spend about 90% of the time talking about Jerusalem, Israel, Judaism, blood moons or the *shemitah*. The remaining 10% they will spend advertising a trip or cruise to the "Holy" Land or a Pharisaic prayer shawl, or a plate or sculpture or painting of the Torah.

This happens repeatedly. They end up neglecting the Gospel, blinded by the veil of the Old Testament.

Paul's final submission in the letter to the Galatians is this:

> 17From henceforth let no man trouble me: for I bear in my body the marks of the Lord Jesus.

It is done! All striving has ceased! I am born again. I bear Christ on me. Let no man trouble me with the Law, with any need for the observing feasts, days, times, years.

The Christian is the truly circumcised one, because circumcision itself is a paradigm for the New Birth. It is, in its true essence and meaning, of the heart, in the spirit.

That should remind you of **Philippians 3:4.**

> We are the circumcision, which worship God in the spirit, and rejoice in Christ Jesus, and have no confidence in the flesh.

We worship God in the spirit and repose no faith in our own actions.

We trust in God's grace, promise and righteousness.

Amen.

We lay down, resting on nothing but the Promise. We step into the void carried on the wings of faith.

He who cannot fail has spoken to us and about us. He who by Himself swore has laid Himself on the line. Yea, we indeed have ceased from works for our actions are those borne of our faith and love.

Our actions indeed spring from our hearts of faith. On the Promise. On the Covenant. On the Oath. He who cannot fail has done it!

Glory to God!

Other book(s) by the Author:

Jesus My Righteousness

Available from **www.essencebookstore.com**
Available on **Amazon** and **Kobo**

You can subscribe to our monthly newsletter on our website:
www.newmanrealities.com

YouTube channel:
New Creation Life and Realities

Contact
taiwo.oyadiran@gmail.com

New Creation Life Ministries

www.ingramcontent.com/pod-product-compliance
Lightning Source LLC
LaVergne TN
LVHW091256080426
835510LV00007B/283